Where the Wild Things Were

Travels of a Conservationist

Stanley Johnson has been a conservationist for most of his life. A former Member of the European Parliament, he has been awarded the Greenpeace Prize for Outstanding Services to the Environment and the RSPCA Richard Martin award for services to animal welfare. He is an ambassador for the United Nations Environment Programme's Convention on Migratory Species and Chairman of the Gorilla Organization. He has written more than a dozen books on environmental subjects, a memoir and nine novels.

WHERE THE WILD THINGS WERE

TRAVELS OF A CONSERVATIONIST

Stanley Johnson

STACEY
INTERNATIONAL

Where the Wild Things Were
Travels of a Conservationist

Copyright © Stanley Johnson 2012

STACEY PUBLISHING LTD
128 Kensington Church Street
London W8 4BH
Tel: +44 (0)20 7221 7166; Fax: +44 (0)20 7792 9288
Email: info@stacey-international.co.uk
www.stacey-international.co.uk

ISBN: 978-1-906-768-87-4

CIP Data: A catalogue record for this book is available from the British Library

Printed and bound by CPI Group (UK) Ltd, Croydon, CR0 4YY

CONTENTS

Introduction

My maternal grandfather was the main source of support as far as my first travels were concerned. He put £40 into my Post Office savings account before he died, in 1956, and that money was still there two years later when I set out on my "gap year" journey across Europe, Asia Minor and South America. You could go a long way on £40 in those days.

Actually, it wasn't – strictly speaking – a "gap year"; more like a "gap nine months". I had stayed on an extra term at Sherborne for various reasons, including playing rugger for the XV, and only got started on my travels in January 1959.

Being at boarding school (first prep, then public) since the age of eight, I had of course already acquired the letter-writing habit. Writing home was not an optional extra. It was compulsory. You didn't (and usually couldn't) ring your parents up, but you sent them a weekly letter and in turn hoped and expected to hear back from them. At prep school at least, the letter-writing exercise was properly invigilated and you had to hand your effort in for inspection before you could escape to more congenial activities. I don't think the masters who looked over one's handiwork bothered too much about the content, unless it was plainly seditious, but they certainly minded about the length. Two sides was the minimum requirement. If you managed to run on to a third or even a fourth page, you had done well.

My mother kept all my letters home, as she kept those written by my brother and (two) sisters. After her death my younger sister, Birdie, found a great epistolary hoard, sorted the various missives and handed them back to the original senders. I started to read through some of my own adolescent efforts but quickly gave up. The banality was too excruciating. Molesworth himself could not have done better. "Dear Mummy and Daddy, my marks this week were 144. I came 1st. We beat Marlborough 12–6." That kind of thing.

I did much better when I started on those gap year journeys. Travel was obviously more inspiring than school. I wrote long letters to my parents and posted them wherever I could.

My first trip took me to Paris, Rome, Trieste, Athens and the Peloponnese and then on to Istanbul, Ankara and Izmir. I returned to England on the Orient Express, stayed on our farm on Exmoor a couple of weeks to help with lambing and then headed off again, this time for Brazil, Bolivia and Peru.

Those early letters, as contained in the large brown envelope my sister handed me, were immensely valuable when, more than fifty years later, I sat down to write my memoir *Stanley, I Presume* (published in 2009). One's memory of events, after a lapse of several decades, is not always reliable. Did I visit Tiryns before or after Mycenae? Did I take the train all the way from Cusco to Machu Picchu? Fortunately, I had the details to hand.

My gap year like all good things came to end. Days after arriving at Cardiff on a cargo ship which I had picked up (or rather which had picked me up) in the port of Vitoria, Brazil, I went up to Oxford for the first term of four stress-free years.

I found that travelling fitted in very well with the rhythms of life as an Oxford undergraduate. During two of the vacations I was employed as a travel courier (of questionable competence) and during my second Long Vacation spent the whole four months abroad, following Marco Polo's route to China on a motorcycle.

Once again I took extensive notes on that journey, some of which Tim Severin, who accompanied me, was kind enough to use in his excellent account of our journey across Europe and Asia, called *Tracking Marco Polo*.

As I made clear in my memoir, my life since then has had numerous twists and turns, as most lives do. I seem to have visited an inordinate number of far-flung places. Partly this has been the result of the nature of my work with various international organizations. Partly it has resulted from my love, nurtured on Exmoor, of wild places and wild animals. My father, a farmer for most of his life, probably preferred animals to people. I do not necessarily go as far as that. But I can certainly see where he was coming from.

Birdie, my afore-mentioned sister who has a discerning eye and quite a way with words herself, once told me that she regarded *Antarctica: The Last Great Wilderness* as one of my better books! If that is the case, I am sure it is because visiting Antarctica for the first time three decades ago was a tremendously invigorating and emotional experience. And I think that showed in the writing.

Many of the jobs I have had over the years have been involved with environmental issues. Some of them have been specifically concerned with nature protection. I was a Member of the European Parliament (MEP) between 1979 and 1984 and a Vice-Chairman of the Parliament's Environment Committee. I was closely involved in the successful efforts to introduce a ban on the import of seal products into the European Economic Community (as the European Union was then known) as well as other EU legislation relating to elephants, whales and the trade in endangered species. Later, after I had returned to the European Commission as an environmental adviser, I helped to draft the EU Directive on the protection of habitat and species, which led to the setting up of the nature-protection network known as NATURA 2000. The network now covers more than 17 per cent of the land area of the EU and a number of Marine Reserves have also been designated.

I left Brussels in 1990 to work for the Food and Agriculture Organization of the United Nations (FAO) in Rome in the hope that FAO would be able to sponsor a worldwide forest convention in time for the Earth Summit that was to be held in Rio de Janiero, Brazil, in June 1992. When that attempt failed (partly owing to implacable opposition from Malaysia), I spent a decade working as an environmental and animal welfare consultant. I was based in England but the assignments provided much scope for international travel and contact with nature and wildlife all over the world.

Towards the end of 2003, I decided that I would like to revisit the political career I had begun when I was elected as an MEP. This time, however, I decided I would try to become an MP rather than an MEP. After sitting an exam known as the Parliamentary Assessment Board organized by the Conservative Party to sort out the sheep from the goats, I was delighted to be allowed to join – at the advanced age of sixty-three! – the Party's official list of parliamentary hopefuls. In August 2004, just before my sixty-fourth birthday, I was even more delighted to be selected as the Conservative candidate for Teignbridge in Devon with a view to fighting the forthcoming General Election.

I much enjoyed my time as a prospective parliamentary candidate. Brief though it was (around nine months), I still managed to fit in a couple of long-haul trips on environmental themes: one to Darfur and another to the Brazilian Amazon. But my absences from the political fray were not prolonged and in any case I don't think they influenced the result in Teignbridge.

I am sure the electors of Newton Abbot and its surrounding towns and villages had seen quite enough of me by the time the General Election in May 2005 was called. David Cameron (now Prime Minister), my son Boris (now Mayor of London), and several members of the Shadow Cabinet very kindly came down to canvas for me but even their exertions were not enough to tip the scale against the Liberal Democrat incumbent.

Not all of my travels qualified for air miles. One of my most enjoyable trips as a parliamentary candidate was a four-day walk with all necessary gear along the Two Moors Way from Winsford, the Exmoor village where our farm is, to Widecombe-in-the-Moor, in the heart of the Teignbridge constituency. George Strickland, Winsford's carpenter, took time off to accompany me. Our object was to raise money for new ropes for the bell-ringers of both parishes. "Money for new rope" was the slogan. Once when I was stung in the mouth by a wasp (concealed in a blackberry), and was having difficulty breathing (by then we were in the middle of Dartmoor with no help at hand), George told me that there were two possible courses of action: "One, I can perform a tracheotomy with my penknife. Two, I can rip your tongue out!"

Having survived the Two Moors Walk, and having failed to enter Parliament in 2005, I had to find something else to do. One day my mobile telephone rang. It was Ian Katz, the deputy editor of the *Guardian*. Ian said he had been reading my election blog on the *Channel 4* website and wanted to know if I would like to be a weekly columnist for the *Guardian*.

I was only too delighted. Back in London, I sent in my first column describing how I had managed to lose the family's Jack Russell terrier, Harry, on Primrose Hill. The day it appeared, Katz left a message on my phone. Though I have no way of proving it now, having lost the phone and its stored messages long ago (where are the hackers when we need them?), I remember Ian saying that he regarded my first effort for the *Guardian* as a "perfect example of a good column. It just slipped into the slot without touching the sides."

With hindsight I can see that it was probably a good thing for all concerned that I failed to relaunch my political career because, free of the burdens of an MP's life, I have been able to concentrate on doing what I most like: namely, travelling and writing about the experience.

Of course I do not actually regard myself as a travel writer as such, though I am sure this is a high calling and that there are and have been some great practitioners of the art. I would like to think of myself as a writer who also happens to travel, quite often, to interesting places.

The material included in this book represents my personal selection of articles I have written over the last six or seven years. Some of the journeys described, for example my second trip to Antarctica in 2007, were quite long. Some of the articles are quite long too. Most of the pieces are about wildlife or wilderness or have the conservation of the environment as a main theme because that, after all, is what I have mainly been concentrating on. I suppose the high point (literally) of all this journeying came in April 2011 when I climbed Mount Kilimanjaro, the highest mountain in Africa, to celebrate having turned seventy and to raise money for the Gorilla Organization whose chairman I am.

There are some exceptions, of course, to the environmental and nature protection theme.

That first column for the *Guardian* is included under the heading "The *Guardian* ruined my political career!" It doesn't stray beyond London NW1 and, apart from the reference to losing our dog, does not mention animals or conservation. But I am proud of it anyway.

I have also included the account I wrote for the *Sunday Telegraph* of a visit I paid to the Glastonbury festival. Another non-animal piece is the article I wrote for the *Evening Standard*'s *ES Magazine* about the Angkor Wat monuments in Cambodia. Though there were plenty of animals (mythical and otherwise) depicted on the monuments, there were no actual living wild animals to write about at Angkor Wat, except for one nasty green snake which fell out of a tree onto my shoulders at Angkor Thom, then slithered to the ground.

Then there is the story of the trip I made to Kalfat in eastern Turkey, to discover whether there are any more blonde-haired Johnson relatives living in that remote village on the Anatolian plateau!

But on the whole this is a book, as the title implies, about wild animals (elephants, gorillas, tigers, desert antelopes, whales, sharks, albatrosses, etc.) and wild places (the Galápagos, Borneo, the Congo Basin, Antarctica, etc.). It is also about the people, like Dr Jane Goodall in Tanzania or Dr Hotlin Ompusunggu in Indonesia, who are trying to protect them. It is often an uphill struggle. If you look at the statistics, the loss of wildlife and biodiversity on a worldwide basis is staggering. And the situation is getting worse, not better.

I originally thought of calling the book *Have Pen, Will Travel* and that I am sure would have been a good workmanlike title. But then one day, when I was having a coffee with my publishers, Stacey International, in Kensington Church Street, inspiration struck. For almost fifty years, the late Maurice Sendak's book *Where the Wild Things Are* has been an inspiration to children all around the world. Surely there was a case, I argued, given all the pressures nature and wild animals were under, for calling the book, *pace* Maurice Sendak, *Where the Wild Things Were*!

I have been tremendously fortunate in the commissions I have had from editors on a wide variety of publications. My hearty thanks go to those who have been so ready to send me off on my recent travels and who have helped to present the material in a lively and accessible way.

I am particularly grateful to my publisher. In the early 1970s, Tom Stacey published my book *The Politics of the Environment*. And last year he masterminded the publication of the large-format volume I wrote with Robert Vagg called *Survival: Saving Endangered Migratory Species*.

Thanks, Tom, and all Stacey colleagues, for this renewed vote of confidence.

Last, but not least, I must thank my wife Jenny, who has had to put up with my increasingly long absences. I suspect it is the thought of home and the love and friendship he finds there, which – paradoxically – sustains the long-distance traveller in his sometime lonely orbit.

Will the time come when I tire of setting out for Heathrow and yet another intercontinental flight? I'm not sure. Even when you travel as much as I do, there are always places left to visit and wild animals yet to be seen. I have never (so far) seen a jaguar in the wild, nor a snow leopard, nor a polar bear for that matter, though last year I went to the Canadian Arctic. And there are whole phyla of the natural world that quite simply don't get a look in this book.

I would, for example, definitely like to see the monarch butterfly as it makes its extraordinary migration from Mexico and across the USA into Canada. And very recently I have read about a whole new range of weird species living on the ocean floor, deep in volcanic trenches. There is scope here, surely, for some new adventure.

Stanley Johnson
10 May 2012

1

Rumbles in the Jungle

The escort vehicle was waiting for us at the roundabout. The Toyota pick-up had backed up against a great mound of lava, a grim reminder of the time two years earlier when Goma, on the northern shore of Lake Kivu in eastern Congo, had nearly been overwhelmed by the eruption of Mt Nyiragongo.

The previous day, when we flew into town, we had seen how the molten flows had pushed their way – at 40mph – across the runway itself. The lava was still there, wave after wave of dark, now inert, rubble. Under the best of circumstances, pilots had to be bold to fly into Goma. Now they had to be super-bold because the runway had lost at least a third of its former length.

There were four armed guards in the back of the pick-up, AK47s bristling defiance. The route we would be taking that morning was still considered insecure. For years, the Interahamwe rebels had been using Kivu's forests as a base. Now the Rwandans had decided to take the fight to the opposition. Ten miles out of town, once you pass the remains of the refugee camp, you can see the Rwandan army dug in above the road – yet this is still officially Congolese territory.

We headed that morning for the Jomba patrol post in the Congo's National Park of the Virungas. Jomba lies in the easternmost part of the Congo, where three countries – Uganda, Rwanda and the Democratic Republic of the Congo (DRC) itself – meet.

When we got there after a three-hour drive on rough roads, the park ranger took us through the drill. "Don't eat food in front of the gorillas," he said. "Don't smoke. Don't use a flash. If you have to defecate, bury your droppings at least one foot deep. Remember, gorillas can catch diseases from man."

Tunnelling our way through vegetation so thick you wondered if you would ever come out the other side, we trekked at least two hours that morning before taking our first break. Trackers went ahead of us and armed guards followed. During the brief pause, I exchanged a few words with the ranger. Speaking in French, he told me that his name was Kivuya.

"In the past four years," he said, "four guards have died. On 4 January 1999, two guards who were following the Kwitonda gorilla family group were killed. On 6 August 2000, I myself escaped an Interahamwe attack at park headquarters. Two other colleagues were killed." He beckoned one of the other guides. "This is Sebirembo Bwoba. He also escaped."

As I shook hands with both men – it seemed the least I could do – Kivuya added: "We are proud to give our lives for the gorillas." Just at that moment, the radio he was carrying crackled into life. One of the trackers ahead of us was calling in. "This is Mike Papa."

"Come in, Mike Papa."

Moments later, we came across gorilla dung and some chewed bamboo sticks. "How recent are these traces?" I asked Kivuya.

The guide shook his head. "One or two days old."

Greg Cummings, the executive director of the Gorilla Organization (previously the Dian Fossey Gorilla Fund – UK), took an upbeat view. He is an upbeat kind of man, which explains why the fund went on working in the Congo during years of civil war while other NGOs (non-governmental organizations) pulled out or left only skeleton staff.

"Gorillas like to stay within about one or two square miles. We'll find them soon."

Four hours later, tired and muddy and with our water bottles long since exhausted, we staggered back into camp. The total number of gorillas seen was zero.

I ought to explain that the particular subspecies of gorilla that we had been hoping to see that day is known as the mountain gorilla. The latest count gives a world total of 680 mountain gorillas. Of that total, 300 are to be found in Uganda's Bwindi Impenetrable Forest and the remaining 380 in the Virungas, the population being split between Rwanda, Uganda and the DRC.

Next day, we tried again. Rather than revisit Jomba, we drove over bumpy unpaved tracks to the patrol post at Bukema, on the slopes of Mt Mikeno. As we bounced and swayed through the villages, hordes of children ran out after us, shouting: *"Padire! Padire!"* (*"Padire"* is a corruption of padre. Because most of the white men first seen in the region were priests, the term has come to be used generically for any fair-skinned visitor.)

Our second day's trekking was no more successful than the first and no less tiring. We trudged up and down and in and out. That there were gorillas present on the slopes of Mt Mikeno was not in doubt. The signs were plentiful and by now we had learned to recognize them. Once we came across a gorilla nest and the guide explained: "This is last night's nest. This is the path he took this morning."

But six hours of steady trekking through the forest brought us no closer to our goal. By 4pm, with two hours of daylight left, it was time to return to base. The park warden offered what comfort he could. "Too many elephants," he said. "They messed up the tracks."

There was indeed some consolation there, I thought. It was good to know that elephants still survived in the Congo's Virunga National Park, whatever might have happened to the gorillas. I'm not sure Andrew Crowley (the *Daily Telegraph* photographer) was convinced. He wanted that picture of the mountain gorilla.

"Remember when David Attenborough is sitting there with his back to the gorilla and suddenly the gorilla takes a run at him and knocks him over?" he said. "That's what we want to see!"

"Not with me in the frame," I replied.

Well, Andrew got his gorilla shots in the end, not in the Virungas, but in the Kahuzi-Biega National Park, which lies to the west of the Goma-Bukavu road. It wasn't a picture of a mountain gorilla. There are no mountain gorillas in Kahuzi-Biega. It – or rather, he – was a Grauer's (or Eastern Lowland) gorilla, an eighteen-year-old silverback known as Chimanuka.

By now, we had shifted our base of operations to Bukavu at the southern end of Lake Kivu. To get to Kahuzi-Biega, you drive along the west shore of the lake for about an hour, threading your way through crowds of women bearing goods of every kind on their heads. At one point, I saw a woman carrying no less than five thick mattresses.

We were being escorted that day by John Kahekwa, the director of the Pole-Pole Foundation (POPOF), a local NGO with which the Gorilla Organization works.

"Don't the men ever carry anything?" I asked him.

"Sometimes they carry the umbrella!"

We had set off from the park headquarters at Tsivanga at about 10am and spent the next two hours following a wildly gushing watercourse upstream, climbing steeply all the time. The trackers, as usual, were somewhere up there ahead of us and messages were passed regularly on the radio.

After a particularly strenuous uphill stretch, when it seemed that we were dragging ourselves up a vertical slope clutching at roots and branches, we heard a sudden stentorian roar as a full-grown male gorilla burst out of the undergrowth.

I knew what I was meant to do. The chief guide at Tsivanga, Robert Mulimbi, had briefed us. "If a gorilla charges, stand still," he said. "Lower your head. Look submissive." He looked pointedly at me. "Better wear a hat. If they see your fair hair, they may think you're another silverback."

Yes, I knew what to do all right. But when Chimanuka sprang from the bush in all his glory, I didn't stand my ground and lower my head. I jumped behind our pygmy tracker and held my breath.

This was a huge and magnificent animal. I had never seen anything like it before. We share 96 per cent of our DNA with gorillas. Man and gorilla may descend from a common ancestor.

Shock and awe. That's what you feel when you first see a gorilla in the wild.

Chimanuka must have charged us half a dozen times that morning. He seemed to enjoy it. The pattern went as follows: a charge would be followed by a period of chewing the cud. He would sit on his haunches, rolling his eyes and swiping the available vegetation with his long prehensile arms so as to grab any surrounding fruits or succulent stalks. After ten minutes or so, he would rise, turn away from us to show off his magnificent coat (it really is silver), before crashing off again through the undergrowth.

But he never went very far. It was almost as if he wanted us to catch up.

He seemed to wait for us. Perhaps that is what being "habituated" means. At all events, our team of guards and guides would take out their pangas and thwack away and, a few minutes later, we would have the benefit of a repeat performance.

Paradoxically, even though there are still more Grauer's gorillas in the world (and all of them in the DRC) than mountain gorillas, the threat to the Grauer's may be more acute.

Take the eastern, more mountainous part of the Kahuzi-Biega National Park, the part we were in that day. In 1996, there were 254 gorillas there. Four years later, the number had fallen to 130. Today, there are probably less than 100. The continued presence of armed rebels in the park has been a major factor in this.

Concerning the much larger Western part of Kahuzi-Biega, the situation is much more dire. There are certainly substantial contingents of armed rebels inside the park. Another factor is the presence of as many as 8,000 "artisanal" coltan miners, mainly poor people who have made their way into the park to work the alluvial deposits of coltan or to quarry the minerals from the rocks.

As far as the gorillas are concerned, the combination of the two has been lethal. Nobody knows for sure how many Grauer's gorillas are left there. At one time, there were more than 10,000 in the lowland part of Kahuzi-Biega. Now the figure may be less than 1,000.

The DRC's Ministry of Mines has passed a decree banning mining in national parks, but, realistically, desperately poor people who have the chance to make some money from mining (still not much more than a pittance) cannot easily be told to stop. The tantalum that can be extracted from the coltan ore is a key ingredient in capacitors for laptops and mobile phones and, obviously, the international demand is extremely heavy.

Starting from the assumption that it is simply not realistic to prevent coltan being mined at all, the Gorilla Organization is trying to ensure that any coltan mining that does take place should be outside the park.

One day, we went to visit some coltan mines beyond Kalehe, three hours by road from Bukavu. When at last we reached the village of Bushushu, we found ourselves negotiating with the village chief, Juvenal Rushishu. At first, he seemed less than delighted by our arrival.

"Today is market day," he said. "The mines are shut. And it's late."

It was indeed market day and getting on for 4pm, but in the end Juvenal relented and personally escorted us through the banana groves. We followed him up the hill behind the village. The slope was pitted with deep holes and digging was still going on. Most of the diggers were school-age children, "there could be as many as ten children to a hole", said Juvenal.

"Why aren't they at school?" I asked.

"School costs money," he said. "How can these people pay for school fees? At least the mines bring some income."

One of the reasons the Gorilla Organization is working in Bushushu is the belief that the best way to conserve wildlife is to improve the livelihoods of local people. The fund has started a micro-credit scheme with a £50,000 primer grant. Working through

POPOF, they have set up workshops where pygmy women use sewing machines to make clothes.

John Kahekwa explained the thinking behind the project. "We have three sewing centres, each one with eight machines," he said. "The sewing provides an income and it keeps people out of the forest." Although trappers do not expressly target them, their snares can catch gorillas and chimpanzees.

The fund also supports micro-credit schemes and funds small-scale agriculture and reforestation projects around the park, once again with the aim of removing pressure on the park's natural resources.

Perhaps the most ambitious exercise the Gorilla Organization is engaged in is an attempt to shift coltan mining outside the Kahuzi-Biega National Park altogether. In the past couple of years, it has organized meetings in Durban and Arusha. Government officials, NGOs, industrialists and miners have come together to discuss how to ensure that no more mining takes place in protected areas. They have had some astonishing successes. The German company HC Starck, for example, which is the biggest coltan purchaser, has agreed not to buy any coltan originating inside the park. But there is still a long way to go.

I flew on from the eastern Congo to Kinshasha to see Olivier Kamitatu, the charismatic president of the Congolese National Assembly, and other Congolese officials. Happily, my visit coincided with that of Samy Mankoto, who works for UNESCO and who is a former director of the DRC's wildlife agency.

Mankoto and I were delighted when Kamitatu signalled his full support for the United Nations Great Ape Survival Project Partnership (GRASP), sponsored jointly by UNEP, the UN environment agency, and UNESCO. GRASP aims to unite all twenty-three great ape "range states" – twenty-one in Africa (including, of course, the DRC) and two in South-East Asia – in a common enterprise. The governments of industrialized countries that wish to assist in great ape conservation programmes will be part of this common enterprise. (Britain, for example, has already provided substantial support to GRASP).

Kamitatu went even further. He told us that the DRC was ready to host an international conference on all great apes – gorilla, bonobo, chimpanzee and orangutan – next year. The aim of such a conference would be to adopt a global strategy for the conservation of great apes and to encourage the necessary funding to be made available for a range of conservation programmes and projects.

International meetings, of course, can never be a panacea. But they can help. And the DRC could indeed be a propitious place for such a meeting to be held. During the long years of civil war, almost all the DRC's national parks have suffered catastrophic declines in wildlife populations, including elephant and rhino, as well as gorilla, chimpanzee and bonobo. What has happened outside the parks is anyone's guess.

Calling a high-level intergovernmental meeting to address the situation may be precisely the spur the country needs. If, coincidentally, the armed bands rapidly disperse and the weapons which are now so widespread in the country are somehow gathered in or neutralized, then at least one threat to the DRC's wildlife – probably the most acute threat at the moment – will have been removed. There may then be more time, more energy and, one hopes, more resources – both national and international – to build a new future for the gorillas and for so much else.

First published in the *Daily Telegraph*, 5 June 2004

2

On the Road to Ruin

"I was in Taos, New Mexico, on business," Hylton Murray-Philipson told me, "when I first met Tashka Yawanawa."

"And who is he?"

"Tashka is the chief of the Yawanawa, a tribe of about 700 Brazilian Indians who live incredibly deep in the rainforest not far from the Peruvian border. He happened to be in Taos when I was there. We met and hit it off. We shared a spiritual drink called *uni*. At the end of it, Tashka sensed a special connection and invited me to visit the Yawanawa community. I responded by saying that I felt as if one half of me was asking the other half to come home."

When you look at Hylton Murray-Philipson, you see – on the surface – a successful middle-aged banker and fund manager. Eton, Oriel College, Oxford, Morgan Grenfell, wife and two children, home in London – that kind of thing. Beneath the surface, though, you find a raging idealist. Hylton is a man with a mission and that mission is to help save the Brazilian rainforest and the indigenous tribes who live there. He is working with an organization called Rainforest Concern. I met him through John Hemming, the former director of the Royal Geographical Society, and this, our first lunch, was the prelude to an exhilarating expedition into an incredibly remote, endangered world.

"The Yawanawa may be one of the smaller tribes," said Hylton, "but they are located in an absolutely vital area of Brazil."

He drew a rough map on our lunch menu. "There is a largely dirt road that runs from Rio Branco, the capital of the state of Acre, to Tarauaca, a small town about 300 miles west. That's not an all-weather highway. You can't run timber lorries along it. But once you widen and tarmac that road, it will be open season on the forest. The logging gangs will move in, the cattlemen will come behind them. A network of secondary roads will be created, penetrating deep into the forests. Even if the Yawanawa reserves survive, they will be surrounded on all sides by a biological desert as the forests are destroyed."

I was puzzled. Where the Yawanawa lived was the middle of nowhere. "Surely, you're still thousands of miles from an Atlantic port? Tarmacking the BR364 to Tarauaca isn't going to change that."

Hylton jabbed once more at the impromptu map. "The timber won't go to an Atlantic port. That's the wrong side of South America as far as the Asian market is concerned. Once you build that road beyond Tarauaca, all the way to the Peruvian border, you can connect up with the Peruvian highway network and the roads that lead across the Andes to the Pacific. The heart of the Brazilian rainforest will be sucked out through that funnel with a giant whoosh. Those Asian markets are crying out for timber. They've destroyed the forests on their doorstep – Indonesia, Borneo, Malaysia. The Amazon is their next target."

"And the Yawanawa get trashed in the process?"

Hylton nodded. "That's what we're trying to prevent."

So, less than five weeks later, I found myself gazing down at the BR364 from the cockpit of a small, single-engine air-taxi as we flew from Tarauaca to a rough airstrip, another 80 miles west in the direction of the Peruvian border. I could see that the earth-moving equipment – the bulldozers, the giant diggers – had already moved into position. Great red scars in the earth indicated the route the BR364 would take. The land had already been cleared at either side of the projected road. From the air, the felled trees looked like a collection of matchsticks. Cattle had already been moved into some of the clearings.

I was sitting in the co-pilot's seat, keeping my feet well away from the rudder bar and my hands off the steering column. "How far is the road going to go?" I shouted.

"All the way to Peru," the pilot shouted back.

The light craft bucked in the wind and the pilot concentrated on the matter at hand. Living and working in the far west of Brazil, Francisco has seen more jungle airstrips than he cares to remember. He is a fine example of the adage that, while there are bold pilots and old pilots, there are few – if any – old, bold pilots.

San Vincente was where we picked up the canoes. Tashka had come downriver to greet us. The Yawanawa chief has the build of a front-row rugby player, stocky and broad-shouldered, with thick, shiny black hair. Hylton and he greeted each other with bear hugs, like long-lost brothers.

We walked from the airstrip into the jungle, carrying our baggage on our shoulders. This included 20lbs of assorted marbles, provided by the House of Marbles in Bovey Tracey as a present for the Yawanawa children from the people of Devon. It's surprising how heavy 20lbs of marbles turned out to be.

I took a firm line on this one. "We're not going to lose our marbles now."

Tashka, it turned out, was waiting not just for Hylton and me, but for urgent medical help. Upstream, deep in Yawanawa territory, there had been an outbreak of an unidentified illness.

"Four children are dead, forty are sick," said Tashka. "The governor of Acre is sending help."

We had more or less finished stowing our gear in the two motor-powered canoes that we were going to take upriver when we heard the sound of another plane. Minutes later, after it had landed, a doctor – Paulo Robert – joined us at the side of the airstrip. Having brought with him several boxes of antibiotics and other drugs, he was all set to go to work. The only problem was that there seemed to be no transport to bring him upriver.

We were happy to oblige. After rearranging our baggage, our two canoes headed off into the forest. We heard the sound of the planes taking off. Heaven knew when they would be back. We were on our own.

River journeys in the upper reaches of the Amazon basin have their own rhythms and cadences. The helmsman stands at the back of the canoe watching the swirling water like a hawk. The river is full of floating trees and submerged logs. If you hit one, you can easily capsize. Or else, as the depth of the water changes from one second to the next, you can come to a shuddering halt on a sandbar. If that happens, you have to jump and try to manhandle the canoe over or around the obstacle, hoping that the piranhas and the alligators are looking the other way.

When we started out, it was sunny. If we had not benefited from the breeze created by our movement through the water, the heat could have been harsh, but as it was it was tolerable. The rain was more of a problem. This was no ordinary rain. We are talking about tropical downpours.

One such downpour occurred at dusk, after we had been on the river about five hours, and within seconds we were drenched to the skin. We had a tarpaulin on board, but that was quickly thrown over the boxes of medical supplies. Hylton and I, anticipating trouble, had each bought umbrellas in our stopover in Tarauaca, but the first gust of wind blew them inside out.

In view of the rain and the lack of visibility, Tashka decided it was time to call a halt that first day. We pulled in to shore and tied up.

Tashka pointed to the small group of wood and thatch dwellings that had been built high up on the riverbank, out of reach of rainy season floodwaters.

"These are my people." He sounded confident. "We can stay here."

"We don't have a reservation," said Hylton.

"This is a reservation, isn't it?" I said.

By the time we had slung our hammocks and mosquito nets in one of the huts, it was quite dark. We were all asleep by eight o'clock. There must have been ten of us altogether in the room, including our Yawanawa host family, who took our arrival in their stride. The worst part of that night was the mosquitoes. We thought we had fixed our nets correctly, but we were bitten mercilessly. Hylton and I will bear the scars for months to come.

By 5am the next day, we were back on the river and by noon we had reached the Yawanawa village of Mutum. This is the fiefdom of Tashka's father, Raimundo. Approaching his ninetieth birthday, Raimundo decided a year or two ago to hand over the chieftaincy to his son, Tashka, but in his own village he still called the shots.

The afternoon we spent in Mutum was in many ways quite magical. First, there was Raimundo himself. As we sat there in his house, eating bananas and fending off mosquitoes, the old man started reminiscing about his wives and children. He had had seven wives altogether, although never more than four at a time.

"I had forty-seven children by my first three wives," he said. "Fifteen sons survived."

"How many daughters?" we asked.

Raimundo didn't seem to know the answer to that question. He seemed disappointed when I told him I had only had two wives and six children.

"Does wife number two live in the same hut as wife number one?" asked Raimundo.

One of the projects Rainforest Concern has been involved with is a new village school. This has been built along traditional lines, with a conical roof and open sides. The idea is to make sure that children learn the vital aspects of Yawanawan culture. The myths and legends have been written down. In time, a book may be produced.

It is in this kind of area that the old have such an advantage. Hylton, whose Portuguese is much better than mine, served as an amanuensis as Raimundo sat us down in front of him, just like schoolchildren, and told us about Yawanawan creation myths and symbols, about how each plant, each animal has its own importance, its own story to tell and how all must be treated with respect.

At one point, he held up the carved figure of an owl. "The owl is not of this world. The owl hoots when someone is about to die," he said. "The owl asks: 'Who is going to die?' And the Yawanawas answer: 'Yes, it is true there is someone here who is about to pass over to the other side.'"

Raimundo looked at us as we hung on his words. "'Give me the name,' hoots the owl, 'and I will look after him for ever.'"

We arrived in Nova Esperança, the main settlement in the Yawanawa reserve, about three that afternoon. Hylton had work to do. He had to review the progress made with the projects being supported by Rainforest Concern and to plan new ones. One idea is to establish a world-class collection of plants, trees and shrubs.

Tashka explained the concept one evening. "The world owes so much to the tropical rainforest – the coffee bean, cures for cancer, Viagra! And yet all they do is cut it down." Tashka confirmed that they have catalogued more than 1,000 plants – what they look like, what they are used for, what success they have in treating which diseases.

"The first time we tried, we wrote all the information down on sheets of paper, but the rains came and washed most of it away," he said. "Now we want to build a computer database."

That's the extraordinary thing about Tashka Yawanawa. He looks forward as well as back. Like his father, Raimundo, he is deeply versed not just in the Yawanawa language, but in the Yawanawan traditional ways. He knows all the medicinal plants of the forest, where to find them, how to use them. He knows the life-sustaining skills of hunting and fishing that his people have practised for time immemorial.

Yet Tashka is also, in some ways, a complete techno freak. One of the most vivid recollections I have of our trip is of the Yawanawa chief sitting in his hut in front of his solar-powered computer (with connected satellite dish) clicking on to the internet to bring up this or that website, surrounded by his tribesmen.

Although over the past forty-five years I have visited Brazil almost a dozen times and have camped in the Amazon, I have never lived in a community of Amazonian Indians, sharing their food, their lodging and, dare I say it, their dreams. What are those dreams?

One night, with the mosquitoes biting, all the elders of the tribe came to a meeting. Those who lived in other settlements came to Nova Esperança in their own dugouts and moored them beneath the steep cliff, where the path winds up to the village.

The atmosphere was upbeat. The health crisis was over. Tashka went around the table and asked each of them how they saw the future. Most of the Yawanawas wanted to retain their strong links to the past and their strong sense of identity.

But they want improvements at the same time. They need some simple water-filtration systems, a few more domestic animals, the chance to sell modest quantities of some indigenous products, such as the fruit of the urucum tree, which is used in perfumes and toiletries, and the possibility of developing a market for their traditional tribal designs.

When it was his turn to speak, Raimundo summed it up for all of us.

In a practical as well as a symbolic way, he had handed over power to Tashka, but still the Yawanawas listened to him. Because we were sitting in almost total darkness, it was difficult to distinguish the faces of the speakers, but there was no mistaking Raimundo's authoritative voice.

There was one sentence in particular that I remember. "When the owl comes to hoot for me," said Raimundo, "I want to feel that I have done my best for my people."

On our last morning, we all took part in the Marbles Ceremony. This was something Hylton and I invented. It involved distributing the hundreds of brightly coloured marbles that we had brought from Devon to the Yawanawa children, who delightedly crowded around us. It is good to know that in this sense at least, Bovey Tracey, Devon, has been twinned with Nova Esperança, Brazil.

First published in the *Daily Telegraph*,
Saturday 4 December 2004

The *Guardian* Ruined my Political Career!

I owe a special debt to the *Guardian*. During the recent general election, when I was the Conservative candidate for Teignbridge, my campaign team was taking a well-earned break in the Ship Inn, Cockwood, on the Exe Estuary, when my mobile telephone rang.

"This is Simon Goodley of the *Guardian* Diary," a voice said.

I wasn't sure I had heard it correctly. "Do you mean the *Manchester Guardian*?"

A pause. "We haven't been called the *Manchester Guardian* for years."

"You were last time I read the paper, back in the sixties."

The *Guardian* diarist very quickly levelled the score by pointing out that a couple of typos in my campaign literature had recently come to his attention. "You've left out the 'd' in Teignbridge."

I decided that this was a telephone call whose intimate details others did not need to hear, so I went outside where the sun shone and the wildfowl pottered about on the mudflats. You wouldn't have thought that there was an election on.

"Are you sure there is a 'd' in Teignbridge?" I parried. "This is pretty rich coming from the Grauniad!"

Goodley had kept his best shot till last. "You also say that the Conservatives believe in 'more talk and less action'."

Now I'm not trying to argue that my failure to win back Teignbridge for the Conservatives was entirely due to the unhelpful column that the *Guardian* ran the next day. I suspect other factors played a part. For example, in my *Channel 4* News election blog, which appeared daily during the campaign, I stated that, if I was asked on the doorstep what I would do if I was elected, I would reply, "Not too much, I hope." MPs should resist the temptation to reach for the statute book at the slightest opportunity. They should pass fewer laws, while repealing many existing ones, particularly some of the more insane regulations dealing with health and safety.

A week before the election, however, my Liberal Democrat opponent took out full-page advertisements in the local press in which he not so subtly distorted my meaning. "Tory candidate says he won't do much if elected," ran the headline.

The safest thing, of course, would have been to say "blog off" to *Channel 4* News' kind invitation right from the start, rather than hand free penalty kicks to the other side. But, on balance, I'm glad I agreed.

The damage from the "not too much" episode was probably not fatal, whereas a strong UKIP intervention and a low Labour turnout probably were. I received 21,583 votes, but the other fellow did better. That's democracy.

And being a blogger was good fun. I learned how to send photos with my copy, including a rather fetching snapshot of Esther Rantzen, who arrived in Newton Abbot one day on ChildLine business.

After two bottles of Montepulciano d'Abruzzo, I thought I had persuaded her to support my campaign. Eventually she wrote a message for me on a paper napkin. "I am a floating voter and I have not yet decided which way to vote, but I always enjoy Stanley's company."

Well, a lot of water has passed under the bridge for us all since 5 May. The Conservatives are yet again in the throes of a leadership contest, one which is of more than academic interest. David Davis, the shadow home secretary, has set out his stall, and I must say that I find his vision of a low-tax, legislation-lite future with a strong emphasis on civil liberties attractive. The fact that he has had his nose broken a couple of times also appeals to me. As Kipling might have put it, a man who can break his nose when others are all about him are picking theirs could go far.

I would like to end this first column on a lighter note. The other day, as we were driving down Parkway in the direction of Camden Town, my wife, Jenny, said: "I think we should split up."

I knew it had been a bad day (our twelve-year-old Jack Russell terrier had gone awol), but I didn't know it had been that bad. I carefully put the car into neutral at the traffic lights. There was an ominous silence.

"Yes, I definitely think we should split up," Jenny continued. "Why don't you go to the print shop to get a 'missing dog' poster made, while I go to Marks and Spencer?" Phew!

First published in the *Guardian*, 26 May 2005

4

Duty and the Beast

I had a window seat on the De Havilland Dash-8 plane from Khartoum to El Fasher, the capital of North Darfur. For most of the long journey I stared down at the desert, taking in the total emptiness of the immense landscape. How on earth did people manage to live here under "normal" circumstances, let alone in a war zone at the end of six years of drought and failed harvests?

The Khartoum–El Fasher shuttle is run by the United Nations Humanitarian Air Services and was full of relief workers of one sort or another. The bearded young man sitting next to me said he worked for *Médecins Sans Frontières*.

"And you?" he asked.

"I'm with SPANA, the Society for the Protection of Animals Abroad. We're trying to save the donkeys in the refugee camps, among other things."

The young man stroked his beard. "Saving donkeys would not be high on my list of priorities under present circumstances."

I understood his point. In a week when the International Criminal Court announced an investigation into war crimes in Darfur, the humanitarian situation in western Sudan has once again become the focus of global attention.

An estimated 300,000 people have died in Darfur in recent years, 200,000 have fled the country and there are about 1.5 million displaced persons living alongside a "host" population of 600,000. The whole region has been racked for years by conflict: Arabs versus Africans, northerners versus southerners, nomads versus pastoralists, the government versus the Sudanese Liberation Army.

Was there a place amid such misery and strife for any concerns other than for human welfare?

The flight that morning was the milk run. We put down briefly at El Obeid, Nyala and Jenin, and at every stop aid workers either boarded or disembarked. We finally reached El Fasher at about 2pm.

My travelling companions were Jeremy Hulme, a craggy ex-Black Watch soldier and Orkney farmer who has been SPANA's chief executive for the past fourteen years, and Karen Jones, the charity's veterinarian. As we waited for our vehicle, I mentioned my chat with the man from MSF.

"I get that reaction all the time," Jeremy said. "Talk to the humanitarian community about donkeys and they mark you down as a people-hating bunny-hugger. Yet, out here, donkeys are truck and taxi, often the only non-human resource these people have. If the donkeys die, the people have neither the incentive nor the means to get back home again. That's the situation we are trying to avoid."

Later that day, we were able to see for ourselves how its efforts to save the donkeys are succeeding. Our first stop was a mud-brick compound half-a-mile outside Abu Showk refugee camp. With its Sudanese partners, and in cooperation with the UK-based charity Kids for Kids, SPANA had organized the collection of 60,000 bundles of hay, which were starting to tower over the compound's walls.

"A year ago," Jeremy said, "there were probably 10,000 to 12,000 donkeys in Abu Showk, all brought in by the refugees. Today there are maybe 1,400. The rest were simply allowed to starve to death. The aid effort was so focused on the people that their working animals were ignored. It's understandable that people come first, but pack animals and livestock should at least be on the radar. The donkeys that are here now need food to survive – 60,000 bundles of hay will keep them alive for a couple of months."

"And the cost?" I ask.

"Around £50,000 so far, but it is money well spent. By keeping the animals alive till the rains come, in July or August, we give them a chance of surviving in the longer term. In the lives of these people, it's hard to imagine anything more important than saving the animals. They carry the scarce water from waterholes and haul the firewood to cook the food provided by the aid agencies. And when the refugees finally go back to their homes, as everyone hopes they will, they will need these animals more than ever. You don't have to be a sentimentalist to see that."

As we watched, donkey-carts trundled in laden with bales of hay that were transferred to the stack. More than 70,000 people live in the camp (20,000 more than six months ago), in tents or under tarpaulins provided by international relief agencies such as Oxfam and Save the Children. The organization is impressive. There are latrines on every corner. "The facilities here are probably better than in the villages," Jeremy points out.

Some people suggest that the reason the number of refugees in Darfur has been growing so dramatically is that it is seen as a "soft option" compared with life in the semi-desert. I realized just how cynical this notion was when we sat down in a tent for a series of briefings with Abu Showk's community leaders, as well as the women SPANA has trained to care for the animals in the camp.

Little by little they began to recount the horrific attacks that had brought them here. One man talked of grenade attacks by Janjaweed militia – some believe they are encouraged by the government – and of explosions and machine-gun fire in the middle of the night. Another spoke of villagers running away in panic into the dark and the desert. These were not old tales. Many of the people were recent arrivals.

Organizations such as SPANA and Kids for Kids are working for that brighter day when the refugees can return to their villages. SPANA is funding the training of "paravets" (like paramedics), and in Darfur we attended the first training course. Fifteen students had been selected by the Darfur villagers themselves for training in basic animal care so that when they return to their lands they can help maintain healthy livestock herds.

The charity's vet, Karen, was in her element. Local farmers had brought in ailing animals to the impromptu clinic and she spent a happy morning peering down donkeys' throats and rasping roughened teeth. "You've got to watch out for donkey rabies," she warned when I ventured too close.

SPANA knows it must change some minds if it is to succeed. It has begun, for example, to press the British Government's Department for International Development (DfID) about the effectiveness of its recent £1 million grant to the UN Food and Agriculture Organization in Darfur, designed to provide veterinary support, feed and health care for donkeys and livestock. The Secretary of State for International Development, Hilary Benn, at least recognizes livestock as "key livelihood assets".

On our last day in Darfur, we travelled three hours across the desert to the town of Mellit. I have travelled in many parts of the world and seen people living in conditions of extreme poverty, but I have never seen anything like the unofficial refugee camp we found there.

As I crouched on the sand, talking to a group of refugees, a glassy eyed donkey expired before my eyes. Call it an asset; call it an old and trusted family friend – either way, the passing of that animal in the desert heat will mean, ultimately, even greater hardship for the family that is now going to have to manage without it.

First published in the *Daily Telegraph*, Saturday 11 June 2005

5

Looking After Apes in Paris

Around this time last year, I went trekking in the Virunga Mountains in the eastern part of the Democratic Republic of the Congo (DRC), formerly Zaire. I had never seen gorillas in the wild before and, since I am a trustee of the Dian Fossey Gorilla Fund (now renamed the Gorilla Organization), Greg Cummings and Jillian Miller, who run the European arm from a modest office near Chalk Farm, kindly suggested it was about time I broke my duck.

We drew a blank in the Congolese Virungas. After two successive days when we hacked our way for hours on end through dense undergrowth with no sign of gorillas except a couple of old nests, Greg admitted defeat.

"Basically," he explained, "there's so much unrest in this part of the country, so many armed bands fighting each other, that the mountain gorillas have probably moved over to the Rwandan side. We had better go looking for Grauer's instead."

With a heavily armed escort, we drove west into the DRC's Kahuzi-Biega National Park, where one day, after a long morning's climb, our efforts were finally rewarded.

The Grauer's gorillas in the forests of the eastern Congo, such as Kahuzi-Biega, are probably even more threatened than the mountain gorillas of the Virungas, whose numbers, thanks to intensive protection efforts, have now stabilized at around 650 and may even be increasing. War and civil disorder, mining and deforestation, as well as the bush-meat trade, have taken a tremendous toll on the Grauer's gorilla. Population figures are hard to pin down, but what is beyond doubt is that a species that once was plentiful, now numbers in the low thousands – a range of sources estimates them at between 2,700 and 5,400.

Even though it may not feature at the G8 meeting in Gleneagles this week, the fate of the great apes (not just gorilla, but chimpanzee, bonobo and orangutan) is not entirely absent from the international agenda. In September this year, the first intergovernmental conference wholly devoted to the conservation of the great apes will take place in Kinshasa under the sponsorship of the Democratic Republic of the Congo. All twenty-three countries with wild great ape populations (including, from outside Africa, Indonesia and Malaysia) are expected to attend. The EU Commission has provided substantial support. Among the individual EU member states, Britain has played a leading role, not only in supporting the intergovernmental meeting, but in helping the UN's first efforts in this field through the Great Ape Survival Project (Grasp), which has recently been launched by UNESCO and UNEP, the UN's environment agency.

The hope is that the Kinshasha meeting, which is expected to adopt a world declaration on the future of the great apes and a detailed programme of action, will generate a new sense of urgency in the fight to save the great apes. This is more than a moral and philosophical issue. If you save the apes, you help save the forests and the people – millions of them – whose livelihoods depend on those forests. Given the crucial role of the tropical rainforests for the conservation of biodiversity and as one of the great engines of the world's climate, you may even help save the world. After Live Aid, Live Ape!

Because I have to attend a pre-Kinshasa preparatory meeting at UNESCO in Paris this week, I am going to miss tonight's *Spectator* party. I am sure there will be no shortage of Johnsons. At the last count, I noted a dozen or so writing for the national press, not all of them related to me. Apart from Boris, those springing immediately to mind include Paul, Frank, Luke, Daniel, Rachel, Jo, Martin and Ulrika (*honoris causa*). Perhaps the *Spectator* can produce a special issue one day written entirely by contributors called Johnson.

First published in the *Guardian*, Thursday 7 July, 2005

6

Conservation Begins at Home

It is surprising how much havoc a kestrel can wreak. While I was in London last week, the bird flew down the chimney of our Exmoor farmhouse, located the room where I work and installed itself at my computer. My sister, who lives nearby, happened to peer through the window and released the poor creature, but when I arrived I had to spend half an hour with a damp cloth cleaning copious droppings from the keyboard. The bird also destroyed an Anglepoise lamp.

At this time of year, we have a lot of kestrels around the house. "There were four perched on a bench in the yard the other day," my sister told me, "waiting for the house martins."

I sensed from the glint in her eye that my sister didn't entirely approve of the way the kestrels pounced on the smaller birds.

"You have to see this in perspective," I told her. "The house martins have already flown thousands of miles from the heart of Africa. They've crossed the Sahara. They've survived Malta, where the locals shoot anything that moves. By the time they reach Exmoor, they know how to cope with a kestrel or two."

It's not just the bird-life – the kestrels, the buzzards, the owls, herons, woodpeckers, kingfishers, etc. – that makes the valley where we have had a farm for fifty-four years so remarkable; it's the animal life too. As I write this, I can see a herd of red deer on the hill opposite. The otters are coming back. There are voles and stoats and dormice, not to speak of foxes and badgers.

This time last year, I spent a marvellous day looking for butterflies on our high ground. A few weeks earlier, English Nature had written to say that it had reason to believe that our farm might harbour rare or endangered butterflies such as the high brown or dark green fritillary. In due course, a small team of experts arrived one fine morning, and after a cup of coffee in the yard we headed uphill.

"Basically, you need a good south-facing slope," Nigel Bourn of Butterfly Conservation explained. "The bracken mustn't be too thick, mind you. You need cattle to break it up a bit. The larvae of the high brown and the dark green fritillaries feed on the leaves of violets, which grow under the bracken. That's the only thing they eat. If the bracken's too thick, the violets don't thrive."

As we climbed that day (our land starts at 960ft above sea level and rises to around 1,200ft), the butterfly experts grew increasingly excited. They found tell tale bites in the violet leaves which could only have been caused by fritillary caterpillars. Suddenly, in a clearing among the ferns, we saw a butterfly, resting on a leaf with its wings spread.

"That's one of them!" Nigel exclaimed. "No question about it."

He unfolded his net, and stalked and swooped. Examination of the underside showed that the species in question was the dark green fritillary, rather than the high brown.

"Odds are you'll have both here," he said. Nigel photographed, then released the butterfly. "It's an ideal environment."

I've tracked Bengal tigers in the Sundarbans and gorillas in the Congo, but it's hard to beat the sheer thrill of discovering that one has, *chez soi*, one of the key species from Britain's very own endangered list.

We have also, I am glad to say, a tremendous quantity of bats. Different kinds of bats, big and small. They fly through the house at all hours, particularly at night.

As a child, I remember a Swiss au pair girl complaining at breakfast one morning that a bat had become entangled in her hair during the night. My mother gave her short shrift. She handed her a large aluminium utensil. "Put the saucepan on your head, Lottie, before you go to sleep."

In our house, animals came first. Conservation, like charity, began at home.

Years later, when I was in the European Commission's environment department, I drafted a directive about species and habitat protection. It wasn't easy to push it through the EU Council – there were eurosceptics even then – but we persevered. The United Kingdom, of course, already had its own system of nature protection, but the Europe-wide NATURA 2000 arrangements have enabled that system to be strengthened and expanded.

Looking back at my time in Brussels, I have come to the conclusion that working on that particular directive was probably the most useful thing I did, apart from learning how to say "More waffles, please" in Flemish.

First published in the *Guardian*, Thursday 21 July 2005

7

Conference in Kinshasa

The view from my room on the seventeenth floor of the Grand Hotel, Kinshasa, is superb. As I write, I can see Brazzaville across the wide grey sweep of the Congo River. There are some advantages in this proximity. In the past, for example, diplomats could keep a speedboat ready so that when things got too hot in Kinshasa, they could make a quick dash to the other side.

The Grand Hotel was known then as the Inter-Continental. Former president Mobutu backed its construction in the 1970s and his men didn't hesitate to avail themselves of the worldly facilities it offered.

Sometimes, things got nasty. The story goes that the manager of the hotel showed exemplary heroism in blocking the elevators to the guest floors one night when a party of Mobutu's henchmen arrived at the hotel, set on murder and mayhem. The fact that hotel guests nowadays are not quaking in fear of a sudden banging on the door shows how much things have changed since May 1997, when Mobutu was overthrown.

That doesn't mean that everything in this equatorial garden is lovely. Fifteen months ago, when I last visited the Democratic Republic of the Congo, we crossed the border from Rwanda. When we drove up a stretch of eastern Congo from Bukavu to Goma, we took armed guards with us and had to endure constant roadblocks. A few days after I left for Kinshasa in the west of the country, a shooting war broke out between rival factions in the east. These factions none the less still manage today to be part of the overarching coalition put in place following an agreement struck in Sun City in 2003 between the Kabila government and its main adversaries.

In Kinshasa, I was invited to meet the president of the National Assembly, Olivier Kamitatu. He took a sanguine view of the troubles. "The movement towards democracy is irreversible," he told me. "The elections will take place as planned."

That was in May 2005. Technically, the Sun City process is still on track because twelve months' grace has been allowed if "special circumstances" require more time to set up a constitution and elections. All of that extra time will surely be needed. Just registering the electorate in this vast land of 60 million inhabitants without an efficient transport system is a gigantic task. We are talking, moreover, about not just one, but a whole series of popular votes, beginning with a referendum on a new draft constitution and ending with the direct election of the president.

Forty or more years ago, the eyes of the world were on the Congo. Some of the most tense dramas of the Cold War were played out here. After decades of pariah status, the wheel has come full circle and the DRC has again moved centre stage.

The international meeting on saving the great apes, for example, which I am attending this week, is a small but significant step in the process of normalization. Twenty-one African and two Asian countries are represented. Donor nations, including Britain, represented by biodiversity minister Jim Knight, are also present and seem ready to sign up to a practical, funded programme of action.

If hosting this first intergovernmental conference on the conservation of the great apes is one way the DRC can show its willingness, and readiness, to rejoin the comity of nations, why should we complain?

Tomorrow, the president, Joseph Kabila, will attend the meeting. What is an honour for us may also be useful for him, given the wide publicity this conference has attracted across the nation. Kabila was twenty-six when he succeeded his assassinated father, Laurent, five years ago. To prevent him standing in the upcoming election, his political opponents tried to write a provision into the draft constitution restricting presidential candidates to people over forty. The attempt was unsuccessful, but the question of age clearly has a resonance here.

The other night, in the hotel bar, a Congolese friend asked me: "What about Cameroon?"

"What's special about Cameroon?" I asked. Cameroon has a delegate at the meeting who had, I considered, been making a useful contribution to proceedings.

"Isn't he too young to stand for leader of your Conservative Party?"

I finally realized what he was driving at. "Oh, you mean David Cameron – you're very well informed! No, of course he's not too young to stand. He's much older than President Kabila!"

First published in the *Guardian*, Thursday 8 September 2005

8

The Great Ape Scandal

One afternoon, a few weeks ago, I stood in a clearing in a forest in the heart of Kalimantan, the Indonesian part of Borneo. The equatorial sun shone through gaps in the tree canopy above us, creating a patchwork of light and dark on the forest floor. Our guide put a hand to his lips, warning us not to make a sound.

We waited three, four, five minutes, while a wild boar rooted around in the nearby brush and mosquitoes homed in unerringly on unprotected expanses of skin. Then we heard it: the low, haunting call of the male orangutan.

I gazed up into the trees, trying to see where the sound was coming from. The forest seemed dark, impenetrable. Suddenly, high up in the canopy, I saw the branches move and as the sun pierced the foliage I caught a glimpse of a distant red-gold shape, heading our way.

There was movement to the left and right as well, as other orangutans swung by. There must have been ten or twenty animals altogether, and for two hours that afternoon we were privileged to be able to watch them go about their extraordinary business.

Aside from humans, there are four types of great ape in the world: gorilla, chimpanzee, bonobo and orangutan. I have seen them all in their natural habitat. For my money, the orangutan, with its strength and subtlety, its luminous intelligence and, above all, its glorious russet beauty, must come at the top of the list.

How can it be, I asked myself, as I stood there in that forest clearing, that the human race, in its greed and vanity, is driving this magnificent creature to the edge of extinction? Once the number of orangutans in South East Asia could have been in the hundreds of thousands. Today, fewer than 60,000 orangutans remain in the wild, and these are found only on the islands of Borneo and Sumatra, where they are classified as "endangered" and "critically endangered". An estimated 5,000 of them are lost from the wild every year. You don't have to be a genius to work out that the orangutan could be extinct within the next twelve years.

The most shattering aspect of this story is that a finger of blame can be pointed unerringly at food manufacturers and supermarkets in Britain and the products that they make and sell, and that we buy. Let's be clear about this. The biggest single threat to the orangutan is the destruction of its forest habitat, and the most important reason for the destruction of the forest has been the spread of palm oil plantations in Borneo and Sumatra.

Palm oil is a nightmare for ethically aware shoppers who are trying to do their bit for the environment. It is often labelled as "vegetable oil", which makes it almost impossible to avoid. To make matters worse, it is everywhere: as many as one in ten products sold in Britain's supermarkets – including margarine, ice cream, pastry, chocolate, crisps and chips – contains palm oil. It is also found in beauty products such as mascara and body wash.

More worryingly, between 1995 and 2002 there was a 90 per cent increase in the use of palm oil in the European Union. The EU imported more than 3.8 million tonnes, accounting for 17 per cent of the global trade. Almost a quarter of that comes to the UK, which is the second biggest importer of palm oil in Europe after the Netherlands. At least 100 UK companies either import or buy palm oil. These include producers of cakes and pastry, such as Allied Bakeries; of sugar confectionery, such as Cadbury Schweppes and Nestlé; of snacks, crisps and chips, such as United Biscuits and Walkers Snack Foods. Most important of all are the UK supermarkets. These are the major end-users of palm oil, Tesco chief among them.

And where does all this palm oil come from? According to Friends of the Earth (FoE), 87 per cent of UK companies have no idea. Perhaps they should consider this: in 2004 Malaysia and Indonesia together accounted for 85 per cent of global palm oil production and 89 per cent of global exports.

No surprise, then, that locals call it a "wonder oil". It has now pipped soybean oil as the world's largest vegetable oil crop.

Environmentalists, however, are calling it "cruel oil". In the decade between 1992 and 2003, the orangutan habitat declined by more than 5.5 million hectares (21,000 square miles), while the palm oil plantations across Borneo and Sumatra increased by almost 4.7 million hectares (18,000 square miles).

There is a direct link between the two statistics. The expansion of palm oil plantations has been achieved to a large extent by converting primary forest.

It is not hard to understand why. Even though there is plenty of degraded land on which to plant trees, selling the timber from the forest that you have cleared to make way for a plantation can do wonders for the bottom line. Add to this the ever-increasing demand for biofuels. Ironically, palm oil is currently being hailed as an environmentally friendly alternative to fossil fuels because it can be mixed with diesel to produce a part-biofuel that does not require engines to be converted.

Last September, Malaysia announced a joint venture with private partners to build three plants that will make this new fuel for export to Europe. Western businesses and governments will rush to exploit this new, seemingly laudable demand for biofuel, and more forests in Sumatra and Borneo will be destroyed.

As Henry Thoreau once wrote: "We have found the enemy and he is us."

One of the reasons I went to Borneo was to gain a first-hand impression of the grave situation facing the orangutan. Ashley Leiman, director of the Orangutan Foundation, invited me to accompany her to Tanjung Puting, a national park that occupies 400,000 hectares (1,500 square miles) in Central Kalimantan. Tanjung Puting is widely considered to be one of the crown jewels of the Indonesian national park system and of major biological importance. It is host to twenty-nine species of mammals, seventeen species of reptiles and 220 species of birds. Most importantly, it is the home of one of the largest groupings of orangutans in the world, with a population of at least 5,000 animals.

"If we can't save the orangutans in Tanjung Puting," Ashley asked, "where can we save them?"

Tanjung Puting, technically speaking, is a lowland peat forest of a type that once covered much of southern Borneo. It may not have the vast overarching canopies of the Amazon or Congo, but the effect is still dramatic enough. On our journey upriver into the park, we twice saw groups of proboscis monkeys, high up in the trees overhanging the river. We saw kingfishers, hornbills, and Brahminy kite. We even saw a huge salt-water crocodile, 3 or 4 metres long, with jaws that looked as though they would make easy work of a Dayak dugout.

We arrived in Camp Leakey early in the afternoon. The place is aptly named. Apart from his own fame as a discoverer of Early Man, Professor Louis Leakey identified, trained and otherwise encouraged three extraordinary female primatologists.

Dr Jane Goodall rose to fame as a result of her studies of chimpanzees at Gombe in Tanzania. Dian Fossey's devotion to the mountain gorillas in central Africa is already the stuff of legend, not least because of *Gorillas in the Mist*. The third of the "Leakey girls", Professor Birui Galdikas, is no less remarkable. Although she was lecturing in Canada at the time of our visit, her spirit dominates Camp Leakey and, indeed, Tanjung Puting National Park as a whole.

Galdikas and her former husband, Rod Brindamour, arrived in Tanjung Puting in November 1971 with two small canoes carrying their possessions and provisions. They set up camp in a bend of the Sekonyer River to begin what has become one of the longest continuous mammalian studies in the world.

Galdikas also set up the Orangutan Foundation International, which, with its sister organizations such as the Orangutan Foundation in Britain, has supported the ongoing research on apes

When Chimanuka sprang from the bush in all his glory, I jumped behind our pygmy tracker and held my breath. *See* p.18.
Photo credit: Andrew Crowley

Shock and awe. That's what you feel when you first see a gorilla in the wild. *See* p.19. *Photo credit*: Andrew Crowley

Coltan mining in the eastern Congo. There could be as many as ten children to a hole. *See* p.20.

Photo credit: Andrew Crowley

Above left: Tashka Yawanawa and Hylton Murray-Philipson on the river near Nova Esperança, Acre, Brazil
Above right: Tashka Yawanawa, chief of the Yawanawa tribe, Acre, Brazil
See chapter 2. *Photo credit*: Hylton Murray-Philipson

Great red scars in the earth indicated the route the BR364 would take through the Amazon forest. *See* p.24.

On the campaign trail in Teignbridge with David Cameron. *See* chapter 3.
Photo credit: Richard Austin

A high brown fritillary. The larvae of the high brown and the dark green fritillaries feed on the violets, which grow under the bracken.
Photo credit: Butterfly Conservation

We passed lines of tankers carrying the processed palm oil from the refineries down to the coast. *See* p.49. *Photo credit*: David Birkin

Author with orangutan in Tangung Putin National Park in Central Kalimantan, Indonesia. *See* chapter 8. *Photo credit*: David Birkin

Fateh Singh, one of India's most revered "tiger wallahs", served for years as the director of Ranthambore National Park. *See* p.52.

Yes, there are still tigers around and, yes, they can still be seen. But how long will this state of affairs last? *See* p.57.

Iguanas, both the land and the marine variety, seem totally unperturbed by man's close scrutiny. *See* p.61.

Above left: Blue-footed booby in the Galápagos. *See* chapter 10.
Above right: Pinnacle rock, Isla Bartolomé, Galápagos. *See* chapter 10.

With a giant tortoise on Isabela Island, Galápagos. *See* chapter 10.

in Tanjung Puting for decades. There has been a practical side to this work too. The foundation has liaised closely with the Indonesian authorities to wage war on illegal logging, which, until a few years ago, was having a serious impact on the national park.

The foundation, with the aid of a grant from the United States Agency for International Development, has put in place no fewer than seventeen guard posts. We did not see them all during our time in Tanjung Puting – some of them are two or three days' march into the forest – but we saw enough to realize that this kind of action is crucial. If you can stop illegal logging, you can protect the habitat not only of the orangutan but of so much else besides.

On our last weekend in Kalimantan, we drove upcountry to try to assess the extent of the palm oil threat to Tanjung Puting itself. There were rumours of massive new oil plantations being planned, with proposals to grant concessions for five palm oil plantations, totalling 16,000 hectares, inside the park. In addition, as much as 20,000 hectares of land could be lost outside the park. It might not be officially protected, but it is vital orangutan habitat. Without it, Tanjung Puting will be totally isolated, with the sea on one side and a desert of palm oil on the other.

After heading north for two hours on bumpy, potholed, tarmac roads, we turned east towards the Seryan River. The tarmac soon petered out, to be replaced by rutted dirt tracks. You begin to understand the sheer scale of the palm oil industry when you see the immense area of land in central Kalimantan, where primary forest has already been converted into plantation. More than once we passed long convoys of trucks loaded with bags of palm oil nuts, as well as lines of tankers carrying the processed oil from the refineries down to the coast.

Our worst fears seemed to be confirmed when, just before sunset, we finally reached our destination, a remote guard post at the north-east corner of Tanjung Puting. It was clear that palm oil plantations had already made substantial incursions into the park, and markers indicated that further, still deeper, incursions were planned.

That night we spread our maps on the floor of the hut. Stephen Brend, the Orangutan Foundation's senior conservationist, explained the situation as he saw it: "The marker stakes are now within a kilometre of the guard post here at Pos Ulin. If they go ahead, there will be palm oil plantations right in the heart of the park, within less than 20 kilometres of Camp Leaky itself."

We all felt numb. The scale of the current incursions, as well as the projected further "conversions", which seemed to be almost a fait accompli, left us stunned. The "crown jewels" of Tanjung Puting were not just in jeopardy, they were being pillaged before our very eyes.

Is the situation for the rainforests of Borneo and Sumatra hopeless? To my mind, the answer is not hopeless, but certainly critical.

UK and EU consumers can play a key role in helping to avoid further disasters. In February 2005, Friends of the Earth wrote to ninety-six UK companies asking them to trace the source of all the palm oil in their products, to adopt minimum standards to ensure that it comes from non-destructive sources and to join the Roundtable on Sustainable Palm Oil (RSPO), a joint initiative set up by WWF and businesses to "promote the growth and use of sustainable palm oil".

Shamefully, only eighteen of these ninety-six companies responded to FoE, and none of these was able to prove that it could trace all of its palm oil back to non-destructive plantation sources.

By September 2005, only fifteen companies had joined RSPO. They include Cadbury Schweppes (Fruit & Nut, Crunchie etc.) Unilever (Flora) and Anglia (which supplies palm oil to Nairn's), as well as the Body Shop and the Co-op. Encouragingly for the initiative, the Boots Group and Asda Stores recently also applied for membership.

However, Tesco, Britain's largest and most successful supermarket chain, which sells hundreds of palm oil products, has yet to apply. A spokesman told the *Daily Telegraph*: "Tesco is committed to sourcing palm oil in a responsible and sustainable way. We're engaging on the issue and have arranged a meeting with other retailers, through the British Retail Consortium, to consider the evidence and the progress made by the Roundtable on Sustainable Palm Oil."

While the big retailers "consider the evidence", we the consumers have to be ready to insist on a means of labelling that shows us whether products contain palm oil. We also have to put in place an accreditation system that allows products to be certified as "forest or orangutan friendly" because they come from non-destructive plantations.

And what's more, we have to be ready to boycott or stop investing in companies that refuse to join RSPO.

FoE suggests that we write to our MPs to urge an amendment to the Company Law Reform Bill to ensure that supermarket directors take greater environmental and social responsibility for the products they sell.

The British government can also help, by putting pressure on Malaysia and Indonesia. So can the EU. But at present the most effective weapon is consumer power: you and me in the supermarket aisles.

First published in the *Daily Telegraph*,
Saturday 21 January 2006

9

Hunting Down the Hunter: A Dying Breed

In Ranthambhore, one of India's premier tiger reserves in the heart of Rajasthan, the sense of gloom this week has been almost palpable. Fateh Singh Rathore looks despondent when you ask him how many tigers are left in the park. "In 2004, the official count of tigers in Ranthambhore was forty-seven, last year was twenty-six. Of the twenty-one lost at least eighteen tigers went 'missing'."

Fateh Singh, one of India's most revered "tiger wallahs", served for years as the director of Ranthambhore. Now retired from official duties, he heads a local NGO called Tiger Watch.

In his office on the outskirts of the park, he puts a disc in the computer and eighteen tiger "mugshots" appear on the screen. Beneath each picture is a stark caption, indicating the method of death. "Shot by poachers", it says under one, "poisoned" and "snared" under others.

"It gets worse," he continues. "In March last year, the Prime Minister, Manmohan Singh, set up a tiger task force in response to the epidemic of poaching which was wiping out our tigers. In May he flew into Ranthambhore with his helicopters. And what has happened since?" Singh pauses dramatically before pulling up another image. "Since the Prime Minister's visit, we have lost another seven. There could be fewer than twenty tigers left in Ranthambhore today."

The only reason the police belatedly took action against the poachers, apparently, is because Fateh Singh and his people presented them with the evidence. "We forced the police to act," Singh says. "In four or five months we caught thirty-five people.

One man confessed he had killed more than thirty tigers in two years. Charges were finally brought and convictions obtained. A number of poachers, including the ringleaders, are now in custody. But won't others step into their shoes as long as there is a demand for tiger skins?"

At this point, and perhaps for the first time that day, Fateh Singh's mood seems to lighten. The seizure of the poachers' mobile phone records had indicated a Tibetan connection. Demand for tiger skins by newly rich consumers in Tibet seemed to be one of the factors leading to the recent increase in tiger killing. Clicking the mouse again, he showed me pictures of young Tibetans parading in their traditional gowns or *chubas* lined with tiger skins, as well as leopard, otter and fox fur.

"That young man's father," Fateh Singh pointed to one of the pictures, "probably gave him the tiger-skin *chuba* as a graduation present. Close down that market and we will strike a major blow against the poachers."

Indian NGOs campaigning to save the tiger have enlisted the help of the Dalai Lama himself. As thousands of Tibetans streamed into India for the Kalachakra, one of the most important festivals of the Tibetan Buddhist calendar, the Dalai Lama made a personal appeal to his followers. Ashok Kumar, a founder and director of the Wildlife Trust of India, described the event. "It was a tremendously moving occasion. The Dalai Lama was completely passionate. He said he remembered the time when wildlife abounded on the whole Tibetan plateau and that he was ashamed of the recent photographs showing Tibetans wearing robes made out of tiger skins. Wearing animal skins and furs was, he said, against Buddhism."

The Dalai Lama made his comments in Delhi on 6 April, 2005. Since then reports, including film footage, have been coming in of piles of tiger and other skins being burned in Tibet. There has apparently been an impact on the price as well, with a drop in the "normal" price of a skin (around US$60,000 or £34,000).

Belinda Wright, founder and director of the Wildlife Society of India, is equally convinced the Dalai Lama's intervention has been crucial. However, even if the market for skins disappeared, the market for tiger bones could be more important than ever. On average, a tiger's skeleton weighs around 10–12kg (22–26lbs). With a kilo of tiger bone fetching up to $2,000 on the black market for use in traditional medicine, the incentive to poach was even greater. "And it's not just the Chinese who live in China who are the source of this demand," Wright told me. "There is increasing evidence that overseas Chinese, including those living in Britain, are buying products containing tiger bone in their search for alternative medicine. It won't say so on the label, but that is the reality."

Last month Willem Wijnsteckers, head of the Convention on International Trade in Endangered Species (CITES), wrote to the Indian Prime Minister to express concern about the slowness with which India seemed to be implementing anti-poaching measures and in clamping down on the illegal trade.

However PK Sen, a former director of Project Tiger (the government of Indira Gandhi's response to the first "tiger crisis" in the early 1970s), feels such appeals are largely ineffective. "The real problem," he explained, "is that the government is in denial. When the total disappearance of tigers from Sariska National Park in Rajasthan was first reported last year, the government's response was to say, 'the tigers have gone on holiday in Bhutan!'" He is strongly sceptical of official census figures, arguing that few national park officials wish to be recorded as having presided over a fall, rather than a rise, in the number of tigers in their area. PK Sen today works for WWF India. His deputy there, Ranjit Talwar, a retired brigadier, believes that when the current tiger census is completed later this year, even the official figures will show that India's tiger population could have fallen to as low as 1,200.

Maneka Gandhi, the widow of Sanjay Gandhi, who is an MP and former environment minister, said the true figure could be even lower. "If there are 500 tigers left in India, I'd be surprised.

They are even skinning the tigers in Indian zoos." She believes the Indian government should be "flexing its diplomatic muscle to force China to clamp down ruthlessly on the Tibetan market".

So how is the government to be persuaded to move out of denial mode into action mode? In August last year, the tiger task force established by the Indian Prime Minister reported on the state of the country's existing tiger population and ways in which it could be nurtured and increased. Its recommendations included the setting up of a wildlife crime bureau, strengthening the criminal provisions of wildlife protection legislation, and proposals to help local people enjoy more of the benefits that tiger tourism can bring.

So far, however, the government has shown little sign of giving the report the attention it deserves. Dr Ullas Karanth, based in Bangalore and technical director of the Wildlife Conservation Society's tiger programme, believes that the problem resides to a large extent in the mindset of those at the top.

"Between 1970 and 1990, there was a determined effort by the Indian government to save the tiger. But over time the protective mission has crumbled. The machinery for protection has gradually disintegrated as well as the political commitment both at the federal and state level. The priority of successive prime ministers has been good economic management, the dash for growth. Okay, someone may nag them at a cocktail party and they'll do something. But it's gesture politics. There is a lack of commitment."

Dr Karanth takes the poaching issues very seriously. But even more important, from his point of view, is the disappearance of the tiger's prey-base, through hunting or through the encroachment of human populations. The tiger task force had made some important recommendations about reducing human-tiger conflict but it would take major political will and resources to implement them. "You have to work at every level, not just with central government but at state and local level, in the courts, in the villages."

Dr Karanth is critical of the failure to counter the impression that the national parks and tiger reserves are "gardens for rich people" to play in. "Even the largest so-called 'ecotourist' operators have not put an effort into ensuring that the benefits reach the local people."

Shekar Dattatri, one of India's leading wildlife film-makers, based in Chenai (Madras), shares this point of view. "Unfortunately, almost all the money goes to enrich businessmen who live elsewhere. Almost no money goes either to the parks or to the people who protect the parks. The tourist industry in India will milk the parks to the very last tiger and then it will shift its attention elsewhere."

If it is true that the wrong kind of tourism can harm rather than help the tiger, not least by contributing to local antagonisms and resentment, there are now determined efforts under way to improve this state of affairs. Abhishek Behl, a young tourism and conservation graduate from Kent University, serves as the Indian director of Travel Operators for Tigers (Toft), a UK-based campaign currently grouping twenty-two tour operators, which aims to help India establish a more responsible and sustainable future for wildlife tourism. The idea is to use travel operators' purchasing power to advocate better tourism practices and help local communities.

Balendu Singh, a hotel owner in Ranthambhore and the local Toft representative, said he believed the future lay in "responsible tourism" that ensured local people and local produce were used to the maximum extent possible and that adverse impacts on the environment were kept to a minimum.

In Madhya Pradesh's Bandhavgarh National Park and Tiger Reserve, I spent four days with Dhruv Singh, a remarkable young man who has built an ashram-like retreat deep in the jungle where guests have the opportunity to contribute materially to the nearby village's prosperity and way of life. "We have to give something back to the villagers," he said. "I don't yet know what we will charge the guests who come here but it will be nothing like the prices at the top-end hotels. Every guest will have a chance to work, or contribute to, the local village."

Of course, responsible tourism, even if it can be made to work, can never be more than part of the solution. As Dr Ullas Karanth pointed out to me, the pressure on tiger habitat remains. When I first came to India in 1961, the human population was around 400 million. Today it is 1,200 million. On previous visits, I have been struck by the emphasis placed by the government on birth control and family planning. In the economic boom, with its double-digit growth-rates, population policy seems to be taking a back seat.

That makes it all the more important for the authorities – local and national – to achieve a successful coexistence between human beings and tigers. Of course, such measures, particularly where relocation of human populations is involved, may be expensive and unpopular. As ever, the vital ingredient seems to be the presence or absence of political will.

India's tiger population recovered from catastrophe in 1972 when the government set up Project Tiger. It survived a second crisis in the early 1990s, largely caused by the growing international demand for tiger skins and bones. Today, the country is in the throes of a third crisis, where renewed poaching pressures have been exacerbated by the destruction of habitat. Yes, there are still tigers around and, yes, they can still be seen. During my eight days in Ranthambhore and Bandhavgargh, I was lucky enough to see eight tigers altogether, some more than once.

But how long will this state of affairs last? It would be good to come back to India, say, ten years from now and to be able to report that the Indian tiger, miraculously, has once again bounced back from the brink.

First published in the *Independent*, Wednesday 12 April 2006

10

Tread Softly Among the Iguanas

If you measure the significance of a topic by how much media attention it receives, I would guess that in 2006 climate change came close to ousting the Iraq war as the number one issue. And as the new year stretches ahead of us I am sure that the future of the planet – in particular the seemingly unstoppable rise in greenhouse gas emissions – will dominate our press and television.

The event that truly triggered the rising wave of concern with global warming in this country was the publication, in October 2005, of the Stern Report on Climate Change. Sir Nicholas Stern, a former World Bank chief economist, pointed out that climate change could shrink global economies by 20 per cent; world temperatures were likely to rise by 2°C by 2050, or sooner, and up to 200 million people could become refugees through flooding or drought.

Stern the name, stern the message.

Because I have spent most of my professional life working on environmental issues, the headline that really caught my eye from the report was the one which read: "A temperature rise of only 2°C would threaten up to 40 per cent of species with extinction."

My thoughts turned immediately to that miraculous, iconic group of islands that I had been visiting while Mr Stern put the finishing touches to his document: the Galápagos Archipelago, 600 miles into the Pacific off the coast of Ecuador. The extraordinary wildlife of these islands, I learned while I was there, had already proved vulnerable to the effects of El Niño, that sudden and dramatic climatic perturbation of the ocean-atmosphere system that is affecting the tropical Pacific with increasing frequency. What would happen if the force and direction of the ocean currents changed as a result of global warming? Would the marine and bird-life of the Galápagos survive if the Humboldt Current ceased to deliver its vast load of nutrients?

How ironic that the place that has become so deeply associated in the public mind with the very notion of biodiversity could, as a result of man-made climatic change, turn into a biological desert.

As with most visitors to the Enchanted Islands – Las Islas Encantadas – my love affair with the Galápagos began as soon as I stepped off the aircraft on to the tarmac at Baltra Island. The Americans first built this airstrip during the Second World War to protect the Panama Canal; now it can handle jets – you can fly there from Ecuador's capital, Quito, in less than two hours. As we walked down to the little jetty to board the dinghy that would transfer us to our sixteen-berth, three-masted schooner, we had to climb over half a dozen sea lions that had hauled themselves out of the sea to sunbathe on the path. That was just the start and it got better every day.

So often, when you travel, you find yourself disappointed. The scenery, the wildlife, even the people don't come up to your expectations. This is simply not true with the Galápagos.

The extraordinary thing is that, more than 170 years after Darwin's visit, you can see with your own eyes exactly what the great scientist saw. All thirteen species of Darwin's finches are still found on the islands, each occupying their different evolutionary niche. The giant tortoises on the island of Santa Cruz still differ, as Darwin noted, from those on the island of Isabela.

Or take the remarkable geology of the archipelago, where volcanic hotspots erupt through the always-moving tectonic plate to produce the conveyor belt effect, with the older islands moving east and eventually sinking beneath the waves while in the west new islands are constantly being created.

Even if you have seen television programmes on the Galápagos, nothing prepares you for the reality.

Towards the end of my ten-day visit, I was walking with a guide on Espanola, one of the oldest islands of the archipelago. We were following a cliff-top path that wound its way between nesting blue-footed boobies and Nazca boobies, past some rocky promontories, towards a headland where we could see scores of waved albatross, a species endemic to the Galápagos. Some of the albatross were nesting; some were in the air, still others were engaged in a strange courtship ritual involving much nodding of heads and stretching of vast wings.

I was so absorbed in the distant scene that I failed to notice the ground immediately ahead.

"Don't step on the iguanas!" the guide called out as he saw me about to place my feet on a thick mat of red-black marine reptiles that had spread themselves across the path.

When you find yourself about to stumble over a marine iguana warming itself in the morning sun before it heads out to sea and a breakfast of seaweed, you have to pinch yourself and ask: "Can this be true?"

Then there were Darwin's beloved giant tortoises. We observed them on Santa Cruz Island on a wet and windy morning. Several hundred of them live in a vast forest reserve, where they are difficult to see. Happily, a score or more had emerged from the trees to graze on a nearby farmer's field, so we were able to watch them for an hour.

"Approach them from behind," the guide instructed. "That way you won't upset them."

Once, when I came too close, a tortoise gave a low whooshing hiss, like lift doors closing, but on the whole they seemed quite content to ignore us.

Another image I have is of the blue-footed booby diving for food. When you are snorkelling, you will often hear a loud smack as a booby hits the water, beak outstretched, airbags extended, at 40mph.

Sometimes the bird splashes down just inches away from you and you wonder whether you are about to become a freak accident statistic: "Snorkeller speared by diving booby!"

Seconds later, you might see the bird rise into the air with a fish in its bill. Apparently, diving birds such as boobies can even go blind in the end, as a result of the effect of their repeated high-speed collisions with the surface of the ocean. This is indeed the survival of the fittest.

Perhaps my most magical memory was when I peered down through my snorkel mask one day and in the blue depths below saw a huge turtle passing almost directly beneath me. It was a Pacific green turtle, doing a gentle breaststroke, with front and rear flippers moving in unison. I felt humbled in so many ways. Here was an animal that has existed since the age of the dinosaurs, certainly long before human beings made their appearance on the earth. And it is still around today.

One morning, when we were standing on deck, we had a grandstand view of turtles mating about fifty yards off the starboard bow. What surprised me, in the stillness of near-dawn, was the noise the turtles made – a strange bellowing sound. Other turtles swam around and even joined in the fun, offering – as far as one could tell – support and encouragement.

I had the same kind of thrill when seeing a shark at close quarters. I was snorkelling around the rim of a submerged volcano off Floreanna Island when a 5ft whitetip reef shark swam right in front of my face. Like the turtle, it was a creature from another age.

Visitors to the Galápagos never fail to comment on the placidity, the lack of fear of human beings, shown by the wildlife there. Darwin virtually plucked his finches off the boughs of trees. The same lack of alarm at human presence goes for other bird-life. If you were so minded, and if your guide wasn't vigilant, you could probably walk right up to a waved albatross on its nest and it wouldn't bat an eyelid. Iguanas, both the land and the marine variety, seem totally unperturbed by man's close scrutiny.

This state of harmony between man and nature didn't always exist. Vast depredations of Galápagos wildlife occurred in previous centuries. Tortoises were captured in their thousands by passing ships. The surrounding oceans were virtually emptied of whales. It is only really since 1959 when the Galápagos was established as a national park and, subsequently, as a World Heritage Site, that a proper framework has been created for safeguarding this paradise.

Can the good times last? Or will we once again see trouble in paradise? My own view is that this is a critical time for the future of the islands. The Galápagos National Park authorities, with the support of the Charles Darwin Foundation based in Santa Cruz, seem at the moment to have the situation under control.

One important initiative to remove feral goats from the islands (they had been chomping their way through the islands' vegetation and depriving the tortoises of their food source) has been spectacularly successful. A team of New Zealand sharpshooters working with park wardens from helicopters and using "Judas" goats has succeeded in eliminating 95 per cent of the invaders. Other threats, such as the harvesting of sea cucumbers for the Asian market, seem to have been more than adequately dealt with.

But there is one menace that, in the short term, looms larger than any other, including climate change, and that is an uncontrolled expansion of tourism. The Galápagos is the victim of its own fame, its own extraordinary and unique qualities. Already some 500 passenger cruise-ships are offering the Galápagos as a destination of choice in their brochures.

Nor is the problem confined to people on boats. It might not yet be a backpacker's dream but if you walk down Puerto Ayora's main street, with its sales boutiques offering "Galápagos Adventure Tours", you can see the potential for disaster. An explosion of short-stay visitors, including those on one-day-trips and two- or three-day mini-trips, might overwhelm the capacity of the authorities to manage and regulate.

Even if the authorities had the knowledge and the means to control mass-tourism, will they have the political will to do so?

In the Galápagos, as everywhere else, money talks. In recent years the islands have seen a high rate of immigration from the mainland and as many as 30,000 people now live there. Most of these are involved in the tourist industry. Pressures to increase the number of tourists permitted to visit the islands (about 120,000) are already being felt and many fear they will become irresistible.

We visited the Galápagos during the final throes of the Ecuadorian national election campaign. We were in the Santa Cruz capital, Puerto Ayora, for the eve-of-poll rallies. Pick-up trucks, garlanded with slogans, hooted up and down the streets and boats sounded their horns in the marina. I saw many signs calling, among other things, for jobs, better sewerage, and support for local fishermen. I didn't hear anyone on the islands calling for the power and authority of the national park to be strengthened and expanded. Or, if they did, I missed it. Yet, without strong political backing at every level, I doubt whether the Galápagos miracle can long survive.

What is increasingly clear, of course, in the light of the publication of the Stern Report, as well as other research, is that the fight to save the Galápagos has to be waged globally – with an international treaty to reduce CO_2 emissions going far beyond the Kyoto Protocol – as well as locally.

That wider battle, I hope we may now safely say, is at last firmly engaged in this country in the mind of both public and politicians. Whether the necessary actions will actually be taken is another story. Let's hope the giant tortoises of the Galápagos are still around, a hundred years or more from now, to give their verdict.

First published in the *Financial Times*, Saturday 6 January 2007

11

Niger Wildlife: In Search of the Addax

Tesker is the last village of any size in eastern Niger – that vast arid landlocked country in the heart of Africa – before the Sahel turns into the Sahara. With our small convoy of vehicles we had stopped at the local gendarmerie to pay our respects and to fill up with water. We also had a chance to pin down some of the facts about the recent massacre of Niger's wildlife.

Rumours of the massacre had been flying around for weeks. They had reached Niger's capital, Niamey, 600 miles to the west, before filtering out into the wider world. There were various versions of the story but the gist of it was that Saif al-Islam, son of Libya's President Gaddafi, had – it was claimed – recently flown into the Niger desert on a hunting expedition. The plane had landed at a desert airstrip. There had been a helicopter, too, and around seventy 4x4 vehicles. They had brought in bowsers with fuel and water and the party was, of course, armed to the teeth with Kalashnikovs.

Sometimes they hunted by day, setting their falcons on the great bustards that still roamed the plains or blazing away with their guns. Sometimes, they went out at night, using the headlights of their vehicles to immobilize the wildlife – desert antelopes or Barbary sheep from the Termit Massif.

What was worse, so the rumours went, this high-level Libyan visitation wasn't just a one-off. The Libyans had been seen in the area several times in recent months. They had even, it seemed, built a hunting lodge in the middle of the desert, a permanent structure whose presence indicated that they would return again and again as long as there was wildlife left to kill.

So as the gendarmes checked our passports and wrote down the details in a fly-blown ledger, we asked some gently probing questions.

Had any of them actually seen the Libyan hunting parties in operation? No, it didn't seem that they had, though they had definitely observed the massive convoys of vehicles passing through the village. Had they actually seen the Gaddafi hunting lodge? No, but they saw no reason why we should not go and look for it.

Piero Ravá, a fifty-eight-year-old Italian who has been leading expeditions into the desert for the past thirty years and was in charge of our trip, was up for it.

"Vous voulez voir la maison du Gaddafi? On y va!"

Ravá is an energetic, ebullient fellow. He is not a man to be ground down by adversity. Two or three years back he was driving his Range Rover through the Niger desert when the vehicle was blown up by a landmine, a relic of an earlier internecine conflict. His passengers were all killed, but Ravá miraculously survived, though with several broken ribs. Within weeks, he was back behind the steering wheel, leading as always from the front.

So we left Tesker, heading almost due north into the desert. John Newby, director of the Sahara Conservation Fund and a man who has spent a lifetime trying to save the fauna of the Sahara, rode in the lead vehicle with Ravá, keeping a close eye on the GPS. With so many years of desert experience between them, Ravá and Newby could probably navigate in the desert even without the GPS, but they would be the first to admit that the new technology has made life easier.

Between them, Ravá and Newby had a pretty good idea of the route to take. About two hours after leaving Tesker, our convoy breasted a high wide sand dune to look down into a saucer-shaped valley below.

Half a mile away we saw a most extraordinary sight. A house, complete with doors, windows and sloping shingled roof, had been built in the middle of the desert. Thirty yards from the front door, another pillared and roofed construction provided an outdoor dining room. Large empty packing cases, some with Libyan addresses stamped on them, were strewn around.

It wasn't so much the size of the place that amazed us. In terms of square footage, the hunting lodge was not specially large. What amazed us was that it was there at all.

Newby scouted around and came back with the desiccated skins of half a dozen Dorcas gazelles. Roseline Beudels and Arnaud Greth, both representing the United Nations Environment Programme Convention for Migratory Species (CMS), cast further afield and discovered a rubbish pit where other Dorcas gazelle relics – skulls and skin – had been thrown. There were also body parts from several bustards.

We had lunch in the Gaddafi gazebo. By then, two Toubou had arrived on horseback. They were obviously paid to guard the villa and they kept a watchful eye on us. They needn't have bothered. We were not in a boisterous mood.

"Basically," said Newby, munching gloomily on a bean salad that Ravá's loyal team of Tuaregs had manufactured seemingly out of nowhere, "the wildlife of the desert is in free fall and the root cause is hunting. Uncontrolled illegal unregulated hunting. With the 4x4s you can go virtually anywhere in the desert. You've got fuel tanks that hold 200 litres or more. You bring your own water, so that's not a limiting factor. In fact, the only limiting factor is how much wildlife a man can shoot before his holiday is up."

Just a few years back, we would have seen hundreds if not thousands of gazelle in this area west of the Termit Massif and north of Tesker. That day, we glimpsed only a handful. And it was clear that those which still survived lived in mortal terror. The moment they saw our vehicle, even half a mile away, they galloped off in a panic showing us a clean pair of heels.

If the spiralling excesses of hunting and the attendant massacres of Sahelo-Saharan wildlife shocked most of the members of our party, they also served to confirm the determination of the CMS team to do something about it.

I should explain that the CMS mission to the eastern deserts of Niger had been planned well before the rumours of the Libyan massacres arrived in Europe. When I first met Roseline Beudels in Paris in September 2006, she told me why the CMS had decided to make Niger one of its priority targets.

Environmentalists over the past decade or so have, she explained, tended to concentrate on what they term "biodiversity hotspots", such as tropical rainforests with their extraordinary concentrations of fauna and flora. But the mandate of the CMS was to look after endangered migratory species wherever they were to be found, not just in the biological hotspots. And desert biodiversity, although less abundant in terms of number of species, is unique and most remarkable in terms of adaptation to extreme conditions.

Beudels told me about the CMS's project to prevent the Sahelo-Saharan antelopes from sliding into extinction. Six species altogether were covered by the CMS strategy: the scimitar-horned oryx, the addax, the slender-horned gazelle, Cuvier's gazelle, the Dama gazelle and the Dorcas gazelle. The status of all these species, which had once been widespread throughout Saharan Africa, was now threatened or vulnerable. The scimitar-horned oryx had disappeared from the wild.

The CMS was closely involved in a project to reintroduce the addax in the wild in Tunisia, building on a captive herd that already existed in that country. As far as protecting the addax *in situ* was concerned, Niger was a key country since it was thought to contain the last viable population of wild addax. Between 100 and 200 animals had in recent years been observed in the area around the Termit Massif and in the contiguous great desert erg known as Tin Toumma.

"The CMS," Beudels told me, "is determined to try to help Niger save the last wild addaxes. We want to set up a protected area around the Termit Massif and in Tin Toumma."

Six weeks later I joined the CMS team in Niamey, Niger's dusty capital. Niger is one of the world's poorest countries. Each year the United Nations publishes a table called the Human Development Index. This is a comparative measure of life expectancy, literacy, education and standards of living for countries. Norway is top of the list. Niger – in 177th place – is at the very bottom, the lowest of the low.

It may at first sight seem perverse, in a country where human beings confront starvation on a daily basis, to talk about Niger's wildlife, but in reality protecting Niger's unique biological heritage is probably just as important in terms of basic socio-economic development as many of the other projects currently being undertaken.

The evening of my arrival in Niamey, Beudels, Greth and I met Ali Harouna, the Director of Niger's Department for the Protection of Wildlife. Harouna kindly drove out to see us at our hotel, outside the city centre.

While I fended off the mosquitoes, Harouna spoke of the need to involve the local people of the proposals to make Termit-Tin Toumma a protected area were the project to stand any chance of success.

"The process of consultation may take a long time. In the end we will need a Presidential decree." He pointed out that, if you added a Termit-Tin Toumma protected area to the existing protected areas in Niger, then almost 10 per cent of the country would be covered.

The key thing, of course, was not just to create another "paper park", but to have a system of protection that really worked on the ground.

The CMS team was able to confirm that the EU was likely to donate a substantial grant – more than €1.5m – to the Termit-Tin Toumma project, which was in addition to substantial funds already provided by the French government's Global Environment Facility. Harouna recognized that this was very good news. With the scimitar-horned oryx already extinct in the wild, saving the last viable population of addax would be a tremendous coup for Niger.

The following Monday, in Zinder, a dusty town near the border with Chad which we reached after a 600-mile drive through the Sahel, the CMS team and the Niger Environment Ministry together inaugurated the *Atelier de Lancement du Projet Antilopes Sahelo Sahariennes*. Tribal chiefs and group leaders had already spent days travelling into town from the outlying areas. Now they had a chance to hear what the CMS proposed and to make their own comments.

For two days I sat at the back, looking over rows of turbaned heads, as one presentation followed another. The Tuaregs, the Toubou, the Hausa – all had their point of view and didn't hesitate to put it across. With prayer breaks as well as meal breaks to be taken, the whole event had a rather stately rhythm to it but, by the end, it looked as though the main objective had been secured.

Of course, the details still had to be sorted out: how big would the protected area be; how would a ban on hunting actually be enforced; how did you square Niger's evident determination to have a world-class protected area in Termit-Tin Toumma with the bizarre fact that some hunting concessions were still being granted; could there be teams of "eco-guards"; what benefits would accrue to the local population? All these were important issues, but it seemed that at least the basic principles had been agreed.

I am sure the fact that relatively large sums of money are going to be available to the project made a difference in the minds of the audience, but I believe there is more to it than that. I remember listening one morning to one of the tribal chiefs and being struck by the passion with which he spoke. He talked about how as a child he had grown up with wildlife. He had been to a nomad school and the gazelles would sometimes wander right up to the open-air classroom in the desert.

"*La faune – c'est notre patrimoine!*" he exclaimed. The applause from the other tribal leaders gathered there seemed both heartfelt and spontaneous.

After the workshop was over we left Zinder for Tesker and the visit to the "*maison du Gaddafi*" I have already described. We then spent two days exploring the Termit Massif.

The Termit Massif is a most unusual geographical and biological feature. Extending almost 80 miles (128km) north to south and in parts more than 8 miles (12km) wide, the rocky cliffs seem to rise hundreds of feet almost vertically from the desert floor. Here, if you are lucky, you will see Barbary sheep moving from crag to crag, desert tortoises, desert foxes and Dorcas gazelles. If you are very lucky, you might see a leopard or a Dama gazelle.

Of course, I was hoping desperately to see the rarest item of all, the addax, even if that meant driving on east from Termit into the vast Tin Toumma desert erg. That addaxes had been seen there in the past was not in doubt but the last sightings had been more than a year ago.

On our last evening at the Massif, we pored over the satellite maps. Greth remembered precisely where he had seen addaxes – nine altogether – three years earlier. He placed a finger on the chart. Newby measured off the distance.

"Fifty kilometres more or less due east," Newby said. "Let's go for it!"

Piero Ravá is never one to duck a challenge. There is nothing he likes more than heading off into the unknown.

Next day our convoy moved on into the heat of the desert. We drove for several hours that day along a transect, our vehicles rising and falling with the sand dunes. After 50km, we turned 90 degrees south for 10km, before returning on a track parallel to our original one.

Newby read out the coordinates from the GPS. "12 degrees 12 minutes east, 16 degrees 12 minutes north." I'd like to be able to record that at precisely that moment we had our first sighting of a herd of addax, munching away on the unforgiving though still somehow nutritious desert grasses. But we had no such luck. The truth is that we were looking for a handful of animals in an area the size of Switzerland and it would have been almost a miracle if we had located them in such a short space of time.

The temperature in the desert dropped to 8°C that night and I was grateful for the shelter of my one-man tent. I lay with the flap open looking up at the stars.

Did it matter, I wondered, that we hadn't actually seen an addax? Surely not. It was enough to know that somewhere in that vast desert, they are still there. And if the CMS project for a Termit-Tin Toumma Protected Area comes to fruition, as I have every reason to hope it will, there is a chance that the world's last remaining population of wild addax will not only survive but prosper well into the future.

This will be good for the addax. And it will be a triumph for Niger as well.

First published in the *Independent*, Saturday 6 January 2007

12

Antarctica: The Last Great Wilderness

There is nothing cuddly about a leopard seal. I was standing on a rock in an ice-strewn bay on Cuverville Island, just west of the Arctowski Peninsula, enjoying some of the finest scenery the Antarctic has to offer, when the seal surfaced – like a submarine – less than ten yards away. It was a vast animal, ten or eleven feet long, with a huge head and a snake-like body. When it lifted its head from the water to gaze balefully at me, I could see on its throat and belly the spots from which it derives its name.

Cuverville Island is home to a colony of gentoo penguins, one of the seven species of penguin found in the Antarctic. Gentoos are not particularly large – around 30–32in and 12–13lbs – but what they lack in size, they make up for in numbers. There are several hundred thousand gentoos in Antarctica and quite a high proportion of that total seemed to be gathered that afternoon on that rocky beach.

It would be wrong to say that the penguins were totally undisturbed by the leopard seal's presence in the inshore waters where they were getting on with their daily business. They squawkingly registered its arrival, beating a hasty retreat from the water's edge.

The seal waited patiently, hull-down in the water with its nostrils just above the surface. When, a few minutes later, a gentoo decided to make a rash dash for the open sea, the leopard seal pounced. It grabbed the penguin in its mouth, like a gun dog retrieving a bird, and swam out with it into deeper water.

There then ensued one of the most extraordinary spectacles I have ever witnessed. The seal appeared to play cat-and-mouse with the traumatized bird, releasing it two or three times, then pouncing on it again before it could escape. Once the seal tired of this game, it settled down to the more serious task of preparing its meal. This involved thrashing the penguin from side to side in the water with such violence that the head eventually became detached from the body and the poor bird was, literally, turned inside out, so that it could be more conveniently eaten.

Nowadays, of course, we have all seen films in which animals – lions, leopards, cheetahs or whatever – seize and devour their prey. We know that nature is red in tooth and claw. But I have to say that this particular scene of a leopard seal catching and then eating its lunch on a brilliant sunny Antarctic day will stay with me for a long time.

It wasn't the first time I had seen a leopard seal. At the beginning of 1984 I was lucky enough to be invited by the British Antarctic Survey (BAS) to join its research and supply vessel, the *John Biscoe*, on a six-week trip to Antarctica. On that occasion, we left Punta Arenas in Tierra del Fuego, Chile's most southerly port, and crossed the dreaded Drake Passage below Cape Horn, to visit BAS bases on the Antarctic Peninsula, as well as the South Orkney Islands, South Georgia and the Falklands.

We saw plenty of leopard seals on that occasion. I remember the briefing I was given the first time I set out in a Zodiac inflatable on a ship-to-shore trip. "If you come across a leopard seal, give it a wide berth," the first mate warned as I climbed down the rope ladder into the rubber boat. "Their teeth can easily puncture an inflatable. You won't last long in the freezing water. A couple of minutes, I'd say. Maximum, five."

Leopard seals, of course, were just one element in the vast array of Antarctic wildlife that I saw on that trip. As the *John Biscoe* left South Georgia on the last leg of our voyage (we were heading for Rio de Janeiro), we passed tiny Willis Island, home to no fewer than 6 million penguin. The sight and sound of a penguin rookery on that scale has to be seen to be believed.

I wrote at the time: "When the elephant seals and the fur seals mass alongside those penguins on the beaches; when the albatross and petrels and blue-eyed shags beat their way across the icy waves; when you glimpse at close quarters – as I did one manky morning in the Lemaire Channel – the blurred shape of a humpback whale, you can quite easily believe you are in paradise, and a very special paradise at that."

Almost a quarter of a century later, and after a second visit to Antarctica, do I still feel as I did when I penned those words? Has Antarctica changed over the past few decades? What are the prospects for the future?

The first thing to say is that the sheer beauty and majesty of the Antarctic has in no way been diminished by the passage of time. The wildlife, the scenery, remain utterly spectacular. The ice-covered cliffs rise almost vertically from the water. The glaciers swoop down to the sea. If the weather is fine, the clarity of the light is unbelievable. Yes, it can be cold, and you need to take your balaclava and thermal underwear with you, but in the summer, at least when the sun is out, the temperature doesn't drop too far below zero and the air can be almost balmy.

Twenty-five years ago, one of the issues that preoccupied environmentalists was the fear that Antarctica would be opened for exploitation. In a foreword that he very kindly provided for a book I wrote called *Antarctica: The Last Great Wilderness*, the late Sir Peter Scott (son of the great Antarctic explorer, Robert Falcon Scott) wrote: "Another serious threat to Antarctica is the prospect of its oil and minerals being exploited. The Antarctic Treaty Consultative Parties are holding a series of meetings to discuss how, rather than whether, this should happen. They acknowledge that the risks of catastrophic pollution from oil spill, blow-outs and the increased human occupation of the few ice-free areas (which are also the most important areas for wildlife) are very real but they seem to regard them as acceptable if the world can be given perhaps another four or five years' supply of oil ... Will our children and grandchildren ever forgive us if we allow our short-sighted greed to despoil the beauty and the teeming wildlife of the last great wilderness on earth?"

It was a close-run thing. A treaty on the exploitation of Antarctic minerals was actually signed by governments in 1988. Happily, it was never ratified. Men such as Sir Peter Scott acted as pathfinders and spokesmen for an NGO community increasingly determined to make its voice heard against such madness. In 1991, the Antarctic Treaty's Protocol on Environmental Protection came into force, including an indefinite ban on mining and minerals exploitation.

If the adoption of the Antarctic environmental-protection protocol was a tremendous victory for conservation, it's hard to be so optimistic where the marine (as opposed to the mineral) resources of Antarctica are concerned.

Twenty-three years ago, I walked around the site of an old Norwegian whaling station in the South Orkneys. A piece of whalebone had been fastened to one of the huts with the following inscription: "Antarctic whale catches South Orkneys and South Shetland 1911–1930 – Right: 38; Blue: 61,336; Fin: 48,023; Sei: 1,796; Humpback: 6,742; Sperm: 184."

That brief record, as cold and factual as a tombstone, brought home to me as nothing else could the sheer scale of these Antarctic whaling operations in their heyday: 61,336 blue whales! The total is unimaginable. The blue whale is the largest animal that has ever lived on earth. If you go to the National Museum of Natural History in Washington DC, you can see a complete skeleton suspended in a room the size of an aircraft hangar, yet now the species is virtually extinct, since its population is at such low levels that recovery seems impossible.

The South Orkneys was just one whaling station of many. On the *John Biscoe*, I also visited South Georgia where the beaches were knee-deep in discarded whalebones from the factories of Grytviken and Stromness. And on my most recent trip on board *Antarctic Dream*, we stopped at Whaler's Bay on Deception Island where you can still see the huge rusting boilers and tanks that held the processed oil, as well as the flensing boats and water barges half-buried in the black volcanic sand.

The horrendous truth is that industrial whaling in Antarctic waters probably accounted for one and a half million whales, bringing most Antarctic whale species to the point of collapse. Recently, there have been signs that some populations are beginning to recover. On that recent visit to the Antarctic aboard the *Antarctic Dream*, we were fortunate to be able to see humpback whales on several occasions. On our last day in Antarctic waters, a group of humpbacks gave us a grandstand view of their feeding technique.

The captain ordered the engines to be shut down. We gathered round the taffrail at the stern of the ship while Rodrigo, the resident biologist, explained: "The whales circle the krill, trapping them inside a cylinder of air bubbles, like a net. Then they dive under the air-bubble cylinder and rise to the surface in an upward spiral with their mouth open, gulping great quantities of water and filtering the krill through the baleen-plates."

We must have stopped in a particularly productive stretch of ocean. For more than thirty minutes, the humpbacks circled, plunged and rose again to the surface, blowing and spraying. If you leant over the rail and looked closely, you could almost count the barnacles.

"Each whale," Rodrigo said, "may be carrying up to half a ton of them."

Ironically, that very day we learnt via the ship's radio of the confrontation then taking place further south in the Ross Sea between the environmental activists aboard the *Sea Shepherd* and Japanese whaling vessels determined to catch their self-allocated "quota" of 1,000 minke whales on the pretext of so-called "scientific" research.

As far as the Antarctic's marine resources are concerned, it is not just the whales that are under considerable threat. Commercial fishing is also taking its toll, particularly on the bird-life of the region.

In 1984, when the *John Biscoe* left the Magellan Straits and turned south for Antarctica, I remember being struck by the number of albatross that followed the ship. However sick you felt as you crossed the Drake Passage, one of the roughest seas on earth, you could – like the Ancient Mariner – take comfort from the presence of these majestic birds. Sometimes they would skim the water, with their long narrow wings, at wave-top level. Sometimes, they would rise high into the air, swinging in a wide arc far out to sea, before returning to follow in the wake of the ship.

After a while, and with the aid of a decent pair of binoculars, I learnt to distinguish the wandering albatross from the black-browed or grey-headed variety.

Petrels, too, were in abundant supply. Giant petrels, Cape petrels, storm petrels and half a dozen other types of petrel – the sky seemed full of them. There was, as it were, no petrel shortage.

Today, I am not so sure that is the case. When the *Antarctic Dream* left Ushuaia and headed south, I had the distinct impression that there were far fewer sea birds around than there had been on my earlier trip. Of course, there were birds in the air, including the great albatrosses that had so thrilled me in the past. But the numbers, surely, weren't the same.

Since I returned to England, I've had a chance to look at some of the mortality figures as far as albatrosses and petrels are concerned. Estimates made by organizations such as BirdLife International indicate that as many as 68,000 albatrosses a year, as well as 11,000 giant petrels and up to 178,000 smaller petrels may lose their lives as a result of commercial fishing techniques, notably long-lining. The birds dive for the bait on the long-lines as the lines are laid out. They are then dragged under and drowned.

Efforts are being made – under the Convention for the Conservation of Antarctic Marine Living Resources (CCAMLR) and the Convention on Migratory Species (CMS), to name just two – to address this problem, for example by prohibiting long-lining in daylight hours and by taking measures to ensure that the baited hooks sink faster. But there is still a long way to go. Even if you pass laws and regulations, how easy will it be to enforce them in the immensity of the Southern Ocean?

In 1984, when I first went to Antarctica, there was virtually no organized tourism apart from a couple of vessels, such as the *Lindblad Explorer*, making occasional visits. How things have changed. My second visit to Antarctica last month was actually on a tourist ship. The *Antarctic Dream* was built in Holland in 1957, incorporated into the Chilean Navy in 1959, rebuilt completely in 2004–5 and refurbished as an Antarctic expedition cruise ship. In its new configuration, there are thirty-eight double cabins located on four decks.

The *Antarctic Dream* is by no means unique. Today, Antarctica is witnessing a veritable explosion of tourists, with up to forty ships operating in Antarctic waters, mainly around the Peninsula, as well as – for those who have time for a more extended visit – South Georgia and the Falklands.

Towards the end of my recent voyage, the *Antarctic Dream* called in at Port Lockroy, on Goudier Island, near the tip of the Antarctic Peninsula. The base at Port Lockroy – designated a Historic Site and Monument under the Antarctic Treaty – was built in 1944 to house a secret British Second World War mission codenamed Operation Tabarin. It was subsequently taken over by BAS for ionospheric research.

A few weeks before the *Antarctic Dream* arrived, Princess Anne had visited the site as patron of the United Kingdom's Antarctic Heritage Trust, a splendid organization whose mission is to protect and restore Britain's Antarctic heritage.

If anyone is in a position to have an informed view on the issue of Antarctic tourism, it must be Rick Atkinson, who serves as the trust's project leader at Port Lockroy.

Atkinson spends four months of the year at Port Lockroy in conditions that exactly replicate those experienced by the wartime base. His team operates a post office, which each year handles over 40,000 items of mail, as well as running a souvenir shop and environmental monitoring programme.

"Most days" he told me, as we sat inside the bunkroom in the original prefabricated hut first brought down to Antarctica in 1944, "we have two or three cruise ships. Tourist numbers here have risen from 11,000 last year to 15,000 this year."

Taking Antarctic tourism as a whole, Atkinson believes that there could be well over 30,000 visitors to the region each year and that some overall limit should be set under the Antarctic Treaty.

"Last year the United States voted against limiting the number. Because you need consensus, the proposal was blocked. An alternative approach would be to require every tourist operator to demonstrate they have a system in place for dealing with an emergency. That would soon sort out the sheep from the goats."

Atkinson tells me that the issue of environmental accidents and emergencies in Antarctica is by no means academic. He is not convinced that all the ships operating in Antarctic are adequately ice-strengthened. Only a few weeks before we had met, a large tourist ship had run aground off Deception Island and it was only a matter of good fortune that the 300 passengers and crew could be rescued by a sister ship that happened to be in the area.

As to the impact of tourists on Antarctic wildlife, Atkinson is less emphatic. The monitoring programme at Port Lockroy has found no significant impact by tourists on the 800 pairs of gentoo penguins.

"Of course, tourists have an impact. They are all visiting a relatively small number of sites. And they don't always keep to the rules, staying away from the penguins, not stepping on moss and lichens and so on. But the direct impact of tourism in Antarctica is minor compared with the global impact – the air-travel undertaken by the tourists to come here, the clothes they buy, the fuel consumed by the cruise ships and so on. The biggest problem for Antarctica is going to be global warming. Compared to that, all other issues pale into insignificance."

I had plenty of time to reflect on Atkinson's words on the long haul back to Ushuaia. I had brought with me a copy of the latest report of the Intergovernmental Panel on Climate Change (IPCC) and I was now able to study it in detail.

Based on deep ice-core samples taken in Antarctica itself, the IPCC report linked, with great precision, historic atmospheric carbon dioxide levels with global increases in temperature. Future temperature increases, and associated sea level rise, were projected under a series of different scenarios.

Losses from the ice sheets of Greenland and Antarctica had very likely contributed to sea level rise between 1993 and 2003 and would, under all the projections, continue to do so in the future. The report further indicated ominously, "Global average sea level in the last interglacial period (about 125,000 years ago) was likely four to six metres higher than during the 20th century, mainly due to the retreat of polar ice."

Four to six metres! It wouldn't just be goodbye to the Maldives. It would be goodbye Piccadilly, farewell Leicester Square.

I took the report up to the ship's bar where the barman, Manuel, served me a very drinkable pisco sour. I spread the document out on the polished wood in front of me. At that moment a majestic iceberg with a strange and wonderful bluish tinge floated past the wide plate glass windows of the *Antarctic Dream*'s observation deck. What an amazing, utterly stunning place Antarctica was, I thought. How incredibly lucky I had been to visit it not once, but twice in my lifetime. And what a tragedy it would be if it just melted away into thin air. Currently, the Antarctic Peninsula was registering the highest temperature changes in the world, over three times the global average. Did we really want to live in a world without icebergs?

It suddenly occurred to me, as I flipped through the grim IPCC report, that maybe the authors had missed a trick.

"Ask not, Manuel," I said to the barman, echoing President Kennedy's inaugural address, "what Antarctica is doing for us. Ask rather what we can do for Antarctica. We may have flown a long way to get here, but when we go home, surely we can all of us join more determinedly than ever in the battle against global warming, knowing that we will be helping to save Antarctica as well? Isn't that so?"

"*Si, señor,*" he said, refilling my glass.

First published in the *Independent Magazine*,
Saturday 24 March 2007

13

Saving the Leatherback Turtle

Patrolling a two-mile-long windswept beach, hour after hour in pouring rain while the Pacific surf pounds relentlessly, swamping your already sodden limbs, may not be everyone's idea of fun. During the week I spent on Playa Grande with the Earthwatch team, in Costa Rica's remote Guanacaste Province, we must have walked 10 or 12 miles a night. We would start our patrol three hours before high tide and continue until three hours after, returning at daybreak – footsore and soaked to the skin – in time to catch a few hours' sleep. But when you're helping to save the endangered leatherback turtle you don't really think about the discomfort.

On the expedition I joined last October were four Earthwatch volunteers, all totally committed. Rick, twenty-six, from Brazil, and Adrian, thirty-six, from the UK, both work for a bank; Nick, twenty-three, works for the Ocean Institute in California; and Catherine, thirty-one, is a marine biologist from Texas. They had all taken time off from their high-powered jobs to help the turtles and, from conversations we had over breakfasts in the local eatery after a hard night on the beach, I knew they didn't regret it. For the past twenty-five years, men and women from all over the world have been volunteering to take part in this amazing endeavour.

They have been out there, year in, year out, pacing the sands throughout the entire six-month nesting season of the leatherback turtle, and – believe me – if they weren't there, the plight of this mighty animal would be even more precarious than it is.

The harsh truth is that, in the Pacific Ocean at least, the leatherback turtle is critically endangered. Its nesting beaches, all around the Pacific Rim, have been turned into seaside resorts. If a female leatherback does manage to reach the shore to lay her eggs, she may be hacked to pieces by waiting gangs, or her eggs, once laid, may be ruthlessly plundered. Industrial fishing, particularly long-lining, has further contributed to the tragic decline in leatherback numbers.

Playa Grande offers the last best hope of saving the species from extinction in the Pacific. Miraculously, the big-time developers have not yet got their claws into this part of the Costa Rican coastline. The bright lights from hotels and housing developments, so off-putting to the nesting turtle, do not shine here. Not yet, anyway. The local authorities have now declared Playa Grande and two neighbouring beaches a marine National Park, called Las Baulas.

The Earthwatch team at Playa Grande research station doesn't just protect the turtles and their nests; they run a hatchery, too. If, during the course of their beach patrols, the volunteers find a leatherback laying eggs below the high-tide mark, they will carefully collect them and move them to the hatchery for safety. A leatherback at Las Baulas lays sixty-five eggs per clutch, seven clutches a season and nests every three to four years. "Every egg protected, every hatchling saved, increases the chances of a turtle surviving to maturity," project leader Bibi tells me.

A quarter of a century ago, there were around 90,000 mating female leatherbacks to be found in the Pacific. Today, there are fewer than 5,000. Witnessing this giant creature – which weighs almost a tonne – emerging at dead of night from the rolling Pacific sea surge, hauling itself up onto the beach to lay its eggs, before heading back to the ocean, is one of the most stirring spectacles you are ever likely to experience. There is something primeval, elemental, about it.

Long after I had returned to England after my time patrolling Playa Grande every night, the roar of the ocean echoed in my ears. I could still see the phosphorescent foam of the waves, hear the howl of the wind. It took days for my shoes, soaked to the soles every night with salt water, to recover.

First published in *Harper's Bazaar*, April 2007

14

Reinventing the Whale

"I can promise you the trip of a lifetime." It was my first evening on board *Searcher* and the speaker was the vessel's captain, Art Taylor, a rugged fifty-year-old Californian. Four times a year for the last fifteen years, Art has been taking a maximum of twenty-four passengers on board his 95ft vessel on twelve-day whale-watching and nature tours around Mexico's Baja peninsula, at 800 miles one of the longest and narrowest in the world.

During that first briefing session, Art ran through the essentials. The accommodation would be comfortable – with air-conditioned cabins. The food would be plentiful, the crew skilled and knowledgeable. For those of us who wanted to see a desert environment, Baja California was *sans pareil*. On half a dozen occasions, we would be landing from skiffs on the mainland or on one of the islands and we would have a chance to hike through the wilderness, keeping a wary eye out for rattlesnakes, scorpions, tarantulas, centipedes and sandflies.

As for those of us who wanted above all to observe marine wildlife, we would, Art hoped, return home satisfied.

He ticked off the species we would be most likely to encounter – seals and sea lions, dolphins, pelicans, ospreys, humpback whales …

"You may even get to see a blue whale," he said. "We usually do on these trips."

I have to admit, when I heard that last claim I was incredulous. As far as I knew, the blue whale, the largest creature ever to exist on the planet, was effectively extinct, its population driven to such low levels by decades of commercial whaling that it could never recover.

Was Art joking, I wondered?

Five days later, we had just finished lunch in the salon when we heard the captain's voice over the loudspeaker.

"Blue whale on the surface. Two hundred yards at one o'clock."

As I rushed to the bow, I heard a great swooshing noise. In the water just in front of the boat, I saw an immense blue-grey shape. The column of spray must have reached 30 or 40 feet into the air, rising straight up like some gigantic geyser.

We stayed with that blue whale for three-quarters of an hour that afternoon. It spouted two or three times more as it moved slowly through the water ahead of us. Rob Nowajchik, *Searcher*'s resident marine mammal expert and on-board lecturer, told us what was happening: "After three or four spouts, he'll be getting ready to dive."

I could see that the leviathan now seemed to be hunching its enormous back. The head was already under the surface and the dorsal fin had appeared.

"He's going to fluke!" Rob said.

A blue whale fluking at a distance of not much more than 100 yards is one of the most awe-inspiring sights I have ever witnessed. Ahead of us, the water boiled and churned and then, suddenly, we found ourselves once more looking at an empty ocean.

There is luck in this, of course. But there is also judgment. Experienced whale-watchers look for the whale's footprints, unnaturally smooth and glassy patches of water caused by the upward pressure of the flukes on the water column. With clear seas and an animal the size of the blue whale, you can actually see the outline underwater long before it rises to the surface.

Still, as *Searcher* continued south, rounding the Cabo San Lucas and entering the Sea of Cortez, I found myself wondering whether that one sighting of a blue whale had been an accident. Seeing one specimen, however splendid, didn't mean that the species as a whole had been clawed back from extinction.

The Sea of Cortez, otherwise known as the Gulf of California, runs up on the inland side of the Baja California peninsula. Biologically, it is one of the richest bodies of water on the planet, supporting 900 species of marine vertebrates and 2,000 invertebrates. *Searcher* steamed north among some of the many islands that, collectively, have been designated a world heritage site. Around 4pm on Sunday 1 April, we were off the northern end of San José Island when we had a blue-whale experience that made that first afternoon's sighting seem like nothing more than the hors d'oeuvre. We found ourselves in the presence, not just of one blue whale but as many as twenty.

At one point, a whale actually swam right under the boat. Its head emerged one side of the vessel while passengers were still leaning over the rail on the other side watching the tail.

"Must be a juvenile," Rob said, standing next to me. "It's not big enough for an adult."

I found myself uttering a quiet prayer of thanks. Here at least, I thought, in Mexico's Sea of Cortez, the blue whale must be breeding. If the species could bounce back here, maybe it could bounce back in other parts of the world as well.

During our time on the Sea of Cortez, we didn't just see blue whales. We saw humpbacks and sperm whales as well as fin and Bryde's whales. The whole enchilada.

And the two days we spent with the grey whales in their lagoon breeding grounds on Baja's Pacific coast were, for many of those on board, as memorable as that magical afternoon we spent with the blue whales in the Sea of Cortez.

On our way south from San Diego, *Searcher* had encountered at various times at least ten grey whales, heading north on their annual journey from the lagoons of Baja where they mate and breed, to their feeding grounds in the Bering Sea, 6,000 miles to the north off the coast of Alaska.

This is one of the world's most spectacular migrations. The grey whale may not be as large as the blue whale (around 40 or 50ft in length as opposed to 100ft), but it is nonetheless one of the great denizens of the deep. Hunted virtually to extinction in the 19th and 20th century, the grey whale has made an extraordinary recovery, and the population is now around 18,000.

Around 10am one morning, after waiting for the tide to rise, *Searcher* crossed the sandbar that separates San Ignacio lagoon from the open sea. Here each year, the grey whales come to calve, the warm waters of the lagoon providing an ideal nursery for their young who, as it were, find their feet here before accompanying their mothers on the long journey north.

Almost as soon as we had entered the lagoon, we could see whales spouting around us. The funnel of spray as a grey whale "blows" does not rise as high into the air as that of a blue whale, but it is still a dramatic sight. And the closer you get to them, the more remarkable these whales appear.

For a species that has absolutely no reason not to fear and loathe the human race, the grey whale seems remarkably forgiving. Indeed, one of the remarkable features of whale watching in San Ignacio lagoon is that quite often this seems to be a two-way process. You can be out on the lagoon with a local boatman in one of the licensed pangas when a grey whale, often with her calf, will push alongside the boat. They will raise their huge heads right over the side of the panga and you can find yourself, literally, eyeballing a fifty-tonne monster, which could, if it so decided, send your frail craft to the bottom of the sea with one flick of its enormous tail.

I held out my hand to one animal as it approached us and felt the strange rubbery texture of the hide.

There seems to be no evidence that the whales object to this close contact and plenty of reason to suppose the opposite.

Our Mexican boatman that morning told us how a few years earlier, Mexico's then President Zedillo came to the lagoon with his wife and family. This was a crucial moment. The Japanese giant Mitsubishi was pressing very hard for permission to open a huge salt factory on the lagoon that could have threatened the very survival of the grey whale.

"The President and his wife and kids, they come out in my boat," Ernesto told us. "The President's wife, she kissed the whale right on its head that day. I saw it. I was there. So the President, when he saw his wife kissing the whale, he said 'Right. No more salt factory. We keep the lagoon just for the whales.' And he announced the end of the salt project that very day!"

This was not some apocryphal story. The Mitsubishi threat had been a real one. With an $80 million investment, the company hoped to generate annual revenues of $85 million. President Zedillo's intervention came in the nick of time. He left office the next day.

Whatever Mexico may have lost in terms of direct investment as a result of his brave decision, it has – I am sure – more than made up through the income generated by whale-watching in Baja.

But the story doesn't end there. The international ban on commercial whaling, which has been in force since the mid-'80s, is coming under increasing pressure. The battle between pro-whaling and anti-whaling nations was joined again in May this year in Alaska, when the International Whaling Commission held its annual meeting.

The Mexican government, proud of all that it has achieved in Baja, once more took the lead among nations determined to keep the ban in place. As a result, moves to end the moratorium on commercial whaling were defeated. As the importance of whale-watching as an alternative to whale catching is now increasingly being recognized, we must hope that those countries which still ignore or subvert the ban – such as Japan and Norway – will finally realize that killing whales has no economic, moral or environmental justification.

Looking back at those twelve days on board *Searcher* off the coast of Baja California, I can't help thinking that Art Taylor's talk of a "trip of a lifetime" was amply justified. Eco-tourism is a term much misused. But in this particular case, I think we all of us felt that we were somehow helping to strike a blow that might in the long run – perhaps the very long run – restore the whales to their rightful place in the ocean.

First published in the *Guardian*, Saturday 28 July 2007

15

International Protection for World's Sharks

Sharks have had a bad press ever since *Jaws*, if not before.

The great white shark which cleared the beaches of Amity Island, Massachusetts, one long hot summer thirty-eight years ago, has taken on an almost Freudian significance, like Moby Dick, the great white whale.

The sight of a fin in the water, any fin, has people stampeding for the safety of the shore.

From a conservationist point of view, it's hard to underestimate the damage done by just one no-doubt well-intentioned film director (Steven Spielberg) based on the work of just one no-doubt well-intentioned novelist (Peter Benchley).

You can talk about the need to save pandas, polar bears, elephants, turtles, even great crested newts, without losing your audience. Try to tell people that the threat to the world's sharks is one of the most important wildlife issues confronting us today and the odds are they will, at the very least, look at you as though you need your head examined.

And yet, in reality, sharks are under attack as never before. They are being targeted by fisheries all over the world.

Their fins are cut off while they are still alive, then they are thrown back into the ocean to suffer a slow painful death by drowning. You don't have to travel to China to find shark-fin soup on the menu. Try Soho in London. Try Greenwich Village in New York. Try just about anywhere.

The statistics are horrifying. According to the United Nations Food and Agriculture Organization (FAO), global shark catch reached 880,000 tonnes in 2003, an increase of 17 per cent on the level recorded just a decade earlier. And the odds are that these figures are substantial underestimates since they do not include discards.

The reality is that worldwide fisheries directed deliberately at sharks, together with the death and destruction of sharks as a result of by-catch (you're aiming to catch tuna, but you catch a shark instead or as well), has resulted in a situation where, today, almost 50 per cent of the world's migratory shark species are classified as "critically endangered", "endangered" or "vulnerable", with almost 30 per cent being classified as "near threatened".

The fishing fleets of around twenty nations account for 80 per cent of the world's shark catch.

Taking the period 1990–2004, the top scorer was Indonesia with 12.3 per cent of the world's catch, followed by India (9.1 per cent), Taiwan (6.3 per cent), Pakistan (5.8 per cent), and Spain (5.7 per cent). The United States comes in seventh with 4.6 per cent and France eleventh at 2.9 per cent. The UK features in the list at thirteenth, as does Portugal (sixteenth).

Indeed, since fisheries is a competence of the European Union as such, rather than the individual EU nations, we have to recognize the harsh fact that the EU as a whole has been one of the principal agents of worldwide shark destruction. Our fleets have been out there in international and well as European waters and sharks in the Atlantic, Pacific and Indian Oceans have paid the price.

Admittedly, there have over recent years been some cosmetic approaches to address the problem. The UN General Assembly has called for a shark-finning ban, and some fishing nations, and at least one of the regional fisheries management organizations (RFMOs), have responded. But you have to look at the small print. This is an Alice-in-Wonderland world. A shark-finning ban is not the same as a ban on shark finning. Complex calculations relating to the weight of fins and landed carcass means that in practice fins can still be removed from living sharks and that finning bans in any case cannot be seen as an effective tool to control shark mortality.

As far as the latter point is concerned, the FAO adopted in 1999 an international plan of action on sharks, but that seems to have been honoured more in the breach than the observance.

For three species of shark – namely the great white (of *Jaws* fame), the basking shark and the whale shark – the situation is improving because they have been listed both by the Convention on International Trade in Endangered Species of Fauna and Flora (CITES) as well as by the Convention on Migratory Species (CMS). This is progress but it does not go nearly far enough – ironically, however spectacular these three species listed so far may be, they are not as seriously threatened as, for example, the daggernose or angel shark which are both listed as "critically endangered".

Conservationists have been arguing for years that what is needed now is real, as opposed to cosmetic, bans on finning, together with moves by the fishing nations and the RFMOs to ban completely the taking of the most seriously threatened shark species, together with the setting of strict catch limits for less-threatened but still vulnerable species.

At last, that call seems to have been heeded. Earlier this month (11–13 December 2007), the government of the Seychelles hosted a meeting of more than forty governments, together with representatives of fisheries bodies and non-governmental organizations. Those present agreed that the time had come, finally, to put in place an international mechanism to protect the world's sharks. Such a mechanism would specify not only the species of shark to be included but also the measures to be taken.

Participants pledged to have an agreement in place by the end of 2008, but the meeting was unable to agree at this stage whether the instrument would be legally binding. Would it, like the sharks themselves, really have teeth in other words?

My own view is that CMS decisions on sharks should be binding in law and enforceable in practice. Of course, the detailed application of the agreement should be left to the competent authorities at national level, working as necessary through the regional fisheries organizations. But at least a clear framework for conservation and management would have been set.

Sharks have been around for 400 million years, longer than most other species, a fact that makes the prospect of their imminent extinction particularly poignant. Maybe, after the Seychelles meeting, things are at last looking up.

First published on the *Daily Telegraph*'s Earth website,
28 December 2007

16

Nature's Chance Meeting

An hour after midnight on 11 June 1770, Captain Cook's ship, the *Endeavour,* struck the coral reef off the shore of what is now called Tropical North Queensland. As the ship came off the reef, a large piece of coral broke away, plugging the hole and stopping an inrush of water – which would have sunk the vessel – and giving the crew time to plug the hole. For three days, gale force winds prevented the vessel from putting in to shelter. Cook gloomily named the nearby headland Cape Tribulation. "Here," he wrote, "began all our troubles."

Today, Cape Tribulation has shaken off its troubled image. If the Daintree National Park, home to one of the world's oldest tropical rainforests, is the crowning glory of Tropical North Queensland, I would say the stretch of coast running north from the Daintree River up past Cape Tribulation is the jewel in that crown. How many other places are there where the rainforest comes right down to the coral reef? At Cape Tribulation, two World Heritage sites – the Daintree Rainforest and Great Barrier Reef – converge and the result is little short of miraculous.

From Cape Tribulation's beach of blazing white coral sand with its clusters of mangrove trees, you can wade into the warm azure sea, lie on your back in the water and look up at the thickly forested hills rising up to the plateau.

In the 1980s, the Queensland government planned to drive a highway through the Daintree from Cairns to Cooktown, only to be frustrated by determined environmentalists who blockaded the track. As a result, the road now stops at the south side of the

Daintree River. There is no bridge. If you want to drive north through the forest along the coast, you have to put your vehicle on a homely little ferry.

From the nature lover's point of view, the Daintree forest and coast offers almost everything you can possibly want. One morning, my wife Jenny and I took an escorted tour in a flat-bottomed boat along the lower reaches of the Daintree River. We must have counted a dozen huge crocodiles sunning themselves on the bank. Our guide knew several of them by name.

"That's fat Albert," he said as a giant crocodile pulled itself out of the water and on to the sand. "Five metres long. Weighs over a tonne. Biggest croc I've seen here was almost 9 metres long, weighed over 2 tonnes, probably 120 years old."

There have been no incidents, as far as I know, of crocodiles attacking one of the tourist boats but our guide warns us to watch out anyway. "Don't trail your hands in the water," he tells us. "If you fall in, you won't even have time to get wet."

One morning, an Aboriginal guide agreed to take us into the heart of the rainforest. Harold Wawubuja was part of the Kuku Yalanji tribal group, who have lived in the Daintree forest for 50,000 or even 100,000 years.

We followed a well-worn trail up into the hills behind the Daintree Eco Lodge where you can have a herbal massage to the accompaniment of piped Aboriginal music. Wawubuja's one ambition, he told us, was to try to ensure that the traditions of his people, and their knowledge of how to live in harmony with the forest, did not die out. Though many of the young Kuku Yalanji were employed at local tourist centres or hotels, he tried to bring them together in tribal or family gatherings at weekends or in the evenings.

As we rested beside a gigantic "strangler" fig tree, he taught us the benefit of traditional remedies. "Say you're on the beach," he said, "and you get stung by a stinger [jellyfish]. Best thing is: you get a wild potato vine, peel off the bark and mush it all up. Then apply it to the skin, leave it to cool for an hour, then peel it off."

Later, he stopped to grind up some pebbles to make an ochre powder and painted a highly stylized cassowary bird for us on a nearby rock.

It was almost as good as seeing the real thing. Before Captain Cook renamed the place, the aboriginal people called Cape Tribulation Kurranji, meaning cassowary, after the flightless bird. In Australia, around 1,000 cassowaries survive and about sixty are to be found in the Daintree.

We failed to spy the giant bird during subsequent walks through the forest in the Mossman Gorge. I think that, if we had actually seen a cassowary, our cup would truly have been full. Not having seen one on that occasion, we certainly have good reason to plan a return trip to the Daintree.

As a matter of fact, there are probably a hundred good reasons to return to this extraordinary part of the world. If you tire of the rainforest, you can head for the Great Barrier Reef. Years ago, I used to worry that a plague of starfish was destroying all the coral in one of the world's most famous ecosystems. But as we cruised out to the reef one morning on *Poseidon*, a specially built catamaran, it was reassuring to know that the starfish problem had proved to be cyclical rather than chronic.

"Global warming is a much bigger threat to the coral," our guide told us as we sorted out snorkels and flippers for the first plunge of the day. "Remember, we're dealing with the largest live-animal structures in the world." He told us that a difference of 2°C could affect coral growth. "If projected temperature rises occur, that could be the end of the Great Barrier Reef as we know it."

Of course, when you're out there on the reef, face down in the water, it's hard to believe that this extraordinary undersea world, full of the most startling shapes and colours – 1,500 species of fish and 400 species of coral – could one day disappear.

Will the politicians, the decision-makers, be up to the challenges posed by climate change? Long-distance travellers, such as myself, must take some responsibility. But I was heartened to see that not long after we returned from Australia, Kevin Rudd, the new Prime Minister, agreed to ratify the Kyoto Protocol on climate change at the end of last year. It is, of course, too soon to say that the threat to the Great Barrier Reef has disappeared. But this latest news is certainly a step – an important step – in the right direction.

First published in the *Financial Times*, 26 January 2008

17

Forty Years on from Tet:
How the US Won Vietnam

For the last few days they have been putting the flags and bunting up in the streets of Hanoi and Ho Chi Minh City in preparation for the nationwide celebrations that will mark the Lunar New Year or Tet. Forty years ago, on the night of 30–31 January 1968, the Liberation Army, as it is now known here, launched its famous Tet Offensive with a series of coordinated surprise attacks on a wide range of targets south of the 17th parallel. In and around Saigon, mortars pounded the US airbase at Tan Son Nhut, as well as the US embassy, the Presidential Palace, the General Staff Headquarters of the South Vietnamese Army and the Navy Command.

In the United States, the Tet Offensive had a devastating impact on public opinion. President Lyndon Johnson might have proclaimed: "We cannot be defeated by force of arms. We will stand in Vietnam." But at the end of April 1968, he announced – in a televised addressed to the nation – that he would not run again for President. Robert McNamara, Secretary of State for Defense and one of the principal architects of the war, left to run the World Bank. The 1968 Tet Offensive marked the beginning of the end of American efforts to "win" the war in Vietnam. After that, the only way out lay at the negotiating table.

I first visited the now reunified Vietnam in 1991 when I toured the country as a guest of the Vietnam National Women's Revolutionary Committee. Hanoi then was still a delightful backwater. You could buy a meal from a street vendor for twenty American cents. The bicycle was the principal, often the only,

Camels drinking at a bore-hole, Sahara Desert, Niger. *See* chapter 11.
Photo credit: John Newby

Cuverville Island is home to a colony of gentoo penguins, one of the seven species of penguin found in the Antarctic. *See* p.72.

Enjoying some of the finest scenery the Antarctic has to offer. *See* p.72.

The leopard seal waited patiently, hull down in the water, with its nostrils just above the surface. *See* p.72.

It grabbed the penguin in its mouth, like a gun dog retrieving a bird, and swam out with it into deeper water. *See* p.72.

The critically-endangered blue whale, diving in the Sea of Cortez, Baja California, Mexico. *See* chapter 14.

Grey whale, San Ignacio lagoon, Baja California, Mexico. "I held out my hand to one animal as it approached us and felt the strange rubbery texture of the hide." *See* p.86.

Whale-shark off the Maldives. *See* chapter 15.
Photo credit: Melody Sky

Above left: About 1,000 cassowaries survive in Australia and about sixty are to be found in the Daintree rainforest. *See* p.94. *Above right*: One morning, an Aboriginal guide agreed to take us into the heart of the rainforest. *See* p.93.

Vietnamese schoolchildren visiting the Reunification Palace, Ho Chi Minh City, Vietnam. *See* chapter 17.

My son Max, emerging from a tunnel at Cu Chi, outside Ho Chi Minh City. *See* p.96.

With Jenny and Max, Angkor Wat, Cambodia. *See* chapter 19.

Wild dogs, southern Africa's most endangered carnivore, hunting in Botswana's Tuli Block. *See* chapter 23. *Photo credit*: Jim Buckby

Giraffe, Northern Tuli Game Reserve, Botswana. *See* chapter 23.
Photo credit: Jim Buckby

Elephant, coming down to water in Northern Tuli Game Reserve, Botswana. *See* chapter 23.

mode of transport. Decent places to stay were few and far between. The Metropolitan Hotel, one of the loveliest relics of the French colonial era, had survived the bombing but it needed a substantial upgrade. The "Hanoi Hilton", a sinister square building in the middle of town, was the place where the American POWs were held.

Back then, even in the economically more vibrant south, the trauma of the war was never very far away. On that first visit, I flew from Hanoi to Ho Chi Minh City (the new name for Saigon) to learn about the efforts the government was making in the field of health and family planning. One afternoon some senior female cadres (the Party was very much in control) took me to visit a clinic in a village in the Mekong Delta, an area where so much of the fighting had taken place. I spent a long afternoon meeting village leaders and hearing about the various programmes on offer. From time to time, groups of schoolchildren would appear to chant revolutionary slogans.

For me, the most poignant moment occurred as we drove in a battered jeep back into HCMC. My official host, a woman of about forty, sitting beside me in the back of the vehicle, suddenly burst into song. The interpreter explained: "Mrs Nguyen is singing about how when Ho Chi Minh died the nation's heart burst with grief and all the birds fell from the branches of the trees."

We were driving along a narrow country lane at the time, weaving our way between buffalo carts and peasants on bicycles. Moments later, we crossed a rickety wooden bridge and I could see the water below. The interpreter went on to tell me: "During the war, Mrs Nguyen was one of the leaders of the guerrillas in this area."

I had a sudden vision of a younger, possibly slimmer, black-pyjama-clad Mrs Nguyen breathing under water through a rice-straw beneath the very bridge we had just crossed, and hoping against hope that some American GI wasn't going to throw a grenade into the river just for the hell of it.

Returning to Vietnam after an absence of seventeen years, I am struck by how much has changed. Of course, the symbols are still there. Ho Chi Minh is still the Revered Leader. In Hanoi last week I waited in line to pay my respects to Ho's embalmed body at the Ho Chi Minh mausoleum. (They had to fly Ho's corpse to Moscow for three months but, as far as I could tell, the Russians made a good job of it.) I queued again to visit the simple one-storey house where Ho Chi Minh lived until he died – in 1969 – with victory in sight if not yet achieved. Unless there is a Vietnamese Jung Chang (author of *Wild Swans* and Mao's biographer) out there somewhere, I doubt if we shall ever see the metaphorical defenestration of "Uncle Ho".

The Glorious Revolution is still remembered. "Say not the struggle naught availeth!" That could well be the motto of the Vietnamese nation. They fought the Japanese, the French, the Americans, even the Chinese. Vietnam's increasingly frequented tourist trail includes some must-see war-related sites.

Take, for example, the Cu Chi tunnel complex, an hour or so outside HCMC. At the height of the Vietnam war, there were 240km of underground passages where complete divisions of the Liberation Army holed up to fight. Today, if you are thin enough, you can wriggle down through a trapdoor to follow a section of a tunnel. My guide explained: "Sometimes, the guerrillas would have to stay underground three months at a time. The B52s dropped approximately three kilograms of bombs for each square metre of land at Cu Chi. They took the powder from the unexploded bombs and made it into anti-tank mines."

If you want a double dose of propaganda, go to the War Relics Museum in HCMC where you can see a collection of captured American weaponry, including tanks and planes, as well as the so-called "Tiger Cages" where America's South Vietnamese Allies (the "puppet-regime" of Diem and Thieu) kept its unfortunate prisoners.

And yet, with the passage of time, even potent symbols can lose their force. The Vietnamese Communist Party may still hold its regular congresses, producing National Plans and other exhortatory documents. The leadership may talk about their commitment to a "socialist market economy" but one can't help feeling that this is so much window-dressing. Like it or not, the world has moved on and Vietnam has moved with it.

The reality is that Vietnam today is one of the rising economic stars of Asia. A year ago it joined the World Trade Organization. Its growth rate may not equal that of China, its giant neighbour to the north, but at over 8 per cent a year for the last several years, its achievements in material terms at least are extraordinary.

In Hanoi today, bicycles have largely been replaced by motorcycles and the rush hour extends throughout the day. In Ho Chi Minh City, there seem to be almost as many cars now as there were once motorcycles, such has been the increase in affluence. There are over 100 Kentucky Fried Chicken establishments in HCMC alone and, unless bird flu intervenes dramatically, there will soon be more. Childhood obesity has become a national health problem. When I flew in from Laos, people told me not to bother to change money on arrival as the US dollar was universally accepted. At the end of 2006, foreign investment exceeded $3 billion, and the government had sold $750 million in bonds on the international market.

Did America, bizarrely, somehow manage to win the Vietnam war after all?

First published in the *Spectator*, Wednesday 30 January 2008

18

International Whaling Agreement is Needed

The current confrontation between Australia and Japan over Japan's whale-hunting activities in the seas surrounding Antarctica, which has been playing out almost nightly on our television screens, must have left many viewers totally perplexed.

In June 1972 I marched through the streets of Stockholm on a balmy summer evening with thousands of other delegates and observers attending the first ever world environment conference held under the auspices of the United Nations.

We were following a giant inflatable whale and, as we made our way through the streets of the Old Town, we chanted: "Save the whale! Save the whale!"

The conference's decision a few days later to call for a moratorium on commercial whaling was regarded as one of the first great triumphs of the international environmental movement.

Over decades of ruthless exploitation, many great whale species had been brought to the brink of extinction. In some cases 500 or fewer individuals were left from populations that might once have been numbered in the hundreds of thousands.

The moratorium on commercial whaling, agreed by the International Whaling Commission (IWC) in 1982 following the lead of the United Nations' Stockholm Conference (it entered into force in 1986), was seen by many as the last best chance to save these iconic denizens of the deep.

Since the moratorium is still in force today, and since the IWC – to make assurance doubly sure – subsequently agreed that the Indian Ocean as well as the Southern Ocean should be whale sanctuaries, the average punter might well wonder what on earth is going on down there in those chilly southern waters. Why are the Japanese there at all?

As far as the Australians are concerned, the issue seems to be clear-cut. Australia sees herself as one of the natural guardians of the southern oceans and has actually passed legislation designed to reinforce environmental protection in Antarctica, including anti-whaling measures.

Australia's new environment minister, Peter Garrett, a former pop singer, has been protesting vigorously against Japan's "illegal activities". Australia's new premier, Kevin Rudd, who gained much kudos recently from his decision to ratify (belatedly) the Kyoto Protocol on climate change, now finds himself under mounting pressure at home to send out patrol vessels from the Australian navy to see off the intruders.

Australia-Japanese relationships are, to put it mildly, under severe strain. The problem is: the Japanese don't quite see things in the same light.

I had the good fortune to attend the Pew Whale Symposium, which took place in Tokyo itself at the end of last month. Organized by the Pew Charitable Trusts, the meeting brought together around 100 participants of different nationalities.

One of the most striking features of the two-day event was the measured and confident way in which the high-level "official" Japanese participants argued that their current whaling activities were not "illegal" in international law since they are considered to be undertaken under the rubric of "scientific whaling" (where IWC rules allow states to act unilaterally in setting the number and type of animals killed for "scientific purposes").

They further argued that the catch limits they set were "sustainable". On the issue of cruelty, they maintained that much progress had been made, including reducing "time to death".

Predictably, many if not most of the other participants in the meeting rejected the Japanese rationale. South American speakers, for example, keen to establish their own whale sanctuary, questioned the whole basis of the system whereby Japan could allocate itself unilaterally its own quota of "scientific" whales. Where would it end, they asked?

The current confrontation in the Southern Ocean arises mainly from the fact that over 1,000 whales a year are now the subject of "scientific" quotas established by Japan and, to a much lesser degree, Iceland. Norway, too, is still a whaling nation.

Unlike Japan, which used the "scientific" loophole, Norway has simply filed an objection to the moratorium as such, thereby maintaining its right to continue commercial whaling, the net result being that for the 2006–7 season, according to IWC data, no less than 1,826 whales in total were reported as being caught.

As a participant in the Tokyo meeting, I had a strong sense that one of the reasons for the current row in the Southern Ocean was the growing feeling on the non-whaling side that it was no longer possible to turn a blind eye to the increasing number of whales being caught outside international control.

Of course, it takes two to escalate but it is hard not to see the rise in the vehemence of the anti-whaling movement as being caused by deliberate provocation by the whaling nations.

In Japan's case at least, one feels a smidgeon of sympathy. In 1945, a defeated starving nation was urged by America's pro-consul, General Douglas MacArthur, to go out to sea and catch whales to eat since everything else had been destroyed.

Though whale-meat, apparently, is nowadays difficult to shift in Japanese markets, consumer tastes having changed, Japanese officials at the Pew Whale Symposium argued that as a matter of principle they should not have to forswear the use of this particular marine resource.

Nevertheless, it is hard not to feel that the Japanese have pushed their luck too far. By steadily upping the number of whales they self-allocate, by going after (or threatening to go after) other whale species clearly more endangered than the minke (e.g. fin, sperm, humpback, sei and Bryde's), they have made it virtually impossible for the status quo to be maintained.

Where do we go from here? Will we see "whale wars" in the Southern Ocean? Or will a new, more permanent deal be struck?

Next month [March 6–8, 2008] in the unlikely setting of the Renaissance London Hotel, Heathrow Airport, the IWC is holding a special session to try to see a way out of the present impasse. Delegates from whaling and non-whaling nations, as well as their supporters, will have the report of the Pew meeting in front of them.

Though there were no agreed conclusions from the Tokyo symposium, in his closing remarks the Chairman, Tuiloma Neroni Slade, a former judge at the International Criminal Court, suggested one possible way forward.

A future deal over whaling could involve the whaling nations agreeing to abide by the international regime (i.e. no unilaterally-set quotas or so-called "scientific" permits). On the other hand, the anti-whaling nations would have to accept what proponents of whaling call the "sustainable utilization of whale stocks".

Such an arrangement would of course imply the lifting of the moratorium. It would probably be bitterly opposed by all those who believe the only "sustainable utilization" of whales should be through non-consumptive, non-lethal means, such as the increasingly popular whale-watching.

Yet, from the whales' perspective at least, a new deal along these lines might have something to commend it. Closing down the unilateral "loopholes" and setting strict international catch limits based on internationally agreed scientific assessment of whale stocks could actually result in fewer, not more, whales being caught. It might also include the enforcement of internationally acceptable humane methods as far as the capture and killing of whales is concerned.

If progress cannot be made at London airport, discussion of the future of whales and whaling will continue at the next meeting of the IWC, to be held in Santiago, Chile, in June this year. Such is the current turbulence, it may even have to be taken to a higher level, such as the United Nations General Assembly or a special Diplomatic Conference.

While enduring solutions are being sought, one can only hope that the whaling nations as a gesture of goodwill will accept the moratorium, in practice if not in law. To paraphrase Emperor Hirohito's famous remarks at the end of the War, continued escalation of the issue will not necessarily turn out to be to their advantage.

First published on the *Daily Telegraph*'s Earth website,
12 February 2008

19

Temples of Delight

If any place on earth deserves the description "the mother of all temples", it must be Angkor Wat, Cambodia. Built on a gigantic scale in the first half of the 12th century, in the reign of Suryavarman II, it is the grandest and most sublime of the great Khmer monuments. I first visited Angkor Wat ten years ago and I shall never forget the sheer excitement as, alone except for my guide, I climbed up the vast pyramidic structure from level to level until, reaching the central shrine high above the plain as the sun set over the surrounding forest, I found myself quite literally at the centre of the world.

I say "quite literally" because when Angkor Wat was built, and for centuries thereafter, it was seen as the microcosm of the Hindu universe. The 570ft-wide moat that I had just crossed represented the mythical oceans surrounding the earth; the galleries I had climbed through represented the mountain ranges. The central shrine, glowing gold in the sunset, was a solid image-rich metaphor for Mount Meru, the house of gods.

Ten years ago, Siem Reap, the nearby town that is the jumping-off place for a visit to the Angkor archaeological complex, was a low-key place with the whiff of a frontier town. Today, it has been totally transformed. The permanent population has risen to an astonishing 100,000 plus and there are some two million overseas visitors each year, benefiting from the new airport. Whereas on my last visit, backpackers were much in evidence, hanging out in some fairly downmarket hostelries, now four- and five-star hotels are springing up all over the place and new restaurants provide the best Khmer cuisine.

Does all this rapid development mean that somehow the magic of Angkor has been affected?

On the whole, I would say "No". Admittedly, you can no longer climb up to the very top of Mount Meru. The steep steps to the summit are now barred, no doubt for "health and safety" reasons, given the pressure of tourists at peak season. And I couldn't help feeling that some of the developments over the last ten years have been at the expense of surrounding jungle.

But there is still plenty of forest to be seen. Every visitor to Angkor has a favourite temple or temples. For some, it will be the majestic Angkor Wat itself, or the sublime and magical Bayon, built about a century later. My personal selection is still Ta Prohm, a 12th-century temple of flowers, narrow corridors and courtyards, where huge trees grow out from the very stones of the buildings and, at times, threaten to overwhelm them. On my previous visit, I wandered off into the forest near Ta Prohm and was taken by surprise, to say the least, when a large green snake fell from an overhead branch and slithered down my neck and shoulders to the ground. Nowadays, the encroaching jungle seems to have been brought under control, but as a place of mystery and enchantment, Ta Prohm can hardly be beaten.

One of the loveliest temples in the Angkor area is Banteay Srei, about 15 miles north-east of Siem Reap. Ten years ago, my guide drove me there with some reluctance, pointing out the danger of unexploded mines and the fact that remnants of Khmer Rouge forces were still reported to be hiding out in the vicinity. Although, in the event, we encountered no hostile elements, the road was rough and the journey long.

Today, a good metalled surface brings you in forty minutes to this perfect jewel in the crown of Khmer art. Banteay Srei is on a much smaller scale that most of the other temples. Almost every inch of the pink sandstone surface is exquisitely carved. If you are into Hindu mythology and want to see the most intricate depiction of Shiva and his wife Uma riding the bull Nandi, look at the pediment at the southern end of the "long gallery".

Visiting Banteay Srei gives you a chance to observe not just the beauty of the land, but something of the life of the people, too. When you stop to take a photograph, you will be surrounded by children offering to sell you picture postcards. Why they aren't in school, you wonder? Well, the answer is that in Cambodia, one of the poorest countries in the world, there is still no compulsory state education. It makes you realize how far there is still to go before the new tourist-generated wealth reaches down to the people whose far-distant ancestors by a combination of sweat and genius created Angkor's miracles.

First published in *ES Magazine*,
Friday 14 March 2008

20

Hope for Africa's Endangered Wild Dogs

After the Ethiopian wolf, the African wild dog (*Lycaon pictus*) is the second most endangered carnivore in the whole of Africa.

There are probably not more than three to five thousand wild dogs left throughout the continent.

Only six countries – Tanzania, Botswana, Zambia, Zimbabwe, Kenya and South Africa – are thought to have viable populations of more than 100 wild dogs.

At present, within South Africa, the only viable wild dog population is to be found in the Kruger National Park.

That could be about to change.

Wild dog packs have now been introduced into several smaller South African reserves such as Pilanesberg National Park, Hluluwe Imfolozi Park, Marakele National Park, Madikwe Game Reserve, Kkuzi Game Reserve, Tswalu Kalahari Reserve and – last but not least – the Venetia Limpopo Nature Reserve.

Together with a small group of colleagues from England, I was lucky enough to be able to spend three days and nights in the Venetia Limpopo Nature Reserve, near South Africa's border with Botswana and Zimbabwe, during the first part of April.

Our main objective was to observe at close quarters the efforts being made to re-establish a viable wild dog population in the reserve.

The Venetia Limpopo Nature Reserve is in many ways a uniquely interesting environment for a conservation exercise of this kind. It extends over some 35,000 hectares.

The land was originally bought by De Beers to safeguard the

route of a water pipeline from the Limpopo River to their diamond mine at Venetia, now the largest in South Africa.

Once that objective was secured, De Beers imaginatively decided to dedicate the area to nature conservation. The wild dog scheme is a tripartite initiative between De Beers Ecology Division, Land Rover (as a commercial sponsor) and the Endangered Wildlife Trust (EWT), a wildlife charity based in Johannesburg.

Wendy Collinson, a volunteer research assistant for the EWT's Carnivore Conservation Group, outlined the project to us as soon as we arrived after a five-hour drive north from Johannesburg.

(Venetia lies just south of the confluence of the Limpopo and Shashe rivers, where the frontiers of Botswana, Zimbabwe and South Africa come together.)

"Eight years ago there were no wild dogs on Venetia. The project began when first four males and subsequently five females were brought in from outside. Initially they were held in a *boma*, (enclosure) but on 8 January 2002, the dogs were fitted with radio collars and all the animals were released into the wild."

Wendy explained that wild dogs are "crepuscular".

"They move first thing in the morning and last thing at night. They can travel 10 to 15 kilometres on each activity session. They can run at 50 kilometres an hour or more for distances of 3 to 5 kilometres. They can corner their prey, such as kudu, in the steep riverbanks or chase it into a fence. If there are pups in the den, the adults will return after a successful hunt and regurgitate their food."

Putting a radio-collar on a wild dog doesn't necessarily mean you're going to find it as soon as your Toyota Land Cruiser heads into the mopane veld.

Yes, your radio antenna should pick up the signal if you're within range and it's not blocked by some inconvenient *kopje* (rocky outcrop) but you still have to get within striking distance.

The first evening we went out from camp (actually a well-appointed De Beers lodge complete with swimming pool and staff), we soon picked up a signal.

Wendy stood up in the back of the vehicle, holding up the antenna and calling out directions. "I'm getting two bars at two clock. Now three bars straight ahead."

In many ways, it's like a parlour game. You get hotter, you get colder. If the dogs are on the move, you can find yourself suddenly having to swing through a 90-degree turn or even reverse direction altogether.

Above all there are the *dongas* to contend with. *Dongas*, deep erosion-caused ditches, can prove quite impassable even to rugged Toyota Land Cruisers.

You can be getting a strong radio signal from, say, 200 metres dead ahead but with a *donga* in the way, it might just as well be the other side of the moon.

You can't get out and track the dogs on foot. "Quite apart from the risk of running into a lion," Wendy explained, "you'll spook the dogs."

That first evening as we hunted the hunters we found ourselves totally "*donga*'d out". Our vehicle got stuck in a deep ravine and by the time we had dug it out, night had fallen.

Cyrintha, a young South African woman working for De Beers, was an amazingly competent driver. But even she knew when to call it a day.

To add to our misery at having drawn a total blank, the heavens opened on the drive back to the lodge and we returned soaked to the skin.

We were luckier next day. In the course of the afternoon, we heard that the pack had been sighted at least 20 kilometres from the area where we had been searching the previous evening.

We bundled into the vehicle, drove to the spot where the dogs had last been seen.

Wendy was just getting herself organized with the aerial when out of the corner of my eye I caught sight of a large animal, a bit bigger than a fully grown Alsatian, with a barrel chest and long legs running fast along a diagonal about 80 metres ahead of us.

The markings on the chest and body were unmistakable.

That first dog was followed by four more. Wendy knew them all by name. "There's Crab, there's Carrot," she called out as they ran by. "They're chasing an impala."

Moments later they had vanished in the bush.

Wild dog pack-size can vary from two adults with pups to up to fifty individuals depending on – among other things – the available area and prey densities. Wild dogs are susceptible to rabies and canine distemper. They can be killed by lions, leopards, hyenas and other wild dogs. One of the original Venetia population, a male dog named Ringo, died after being gored in the throat by a warthog.

"Hyenas carried off his carcass to a cave," Wendy told us. "Ringo still had his radio collar on when he died and for months afterwards we would pick up the signal. There was no way we were going to try to go into that hyena den to bring back the collar!"

The long-term plan is for the Venetia reserve to link up with nearby Mapugubwe National Park, thereby expanding by another 18,000 hectares the area available for the project.

This initiative forms part of a much larger scheme to create a transfrontier protection area, the Limpopo-Shashe Peace Park linking all three countries (Botswana, Zimbabwe and South Africa) in the Central Limpopo Valley.

"From the wild dog point of view, and for conservation in general in this part of Africa," Wendy Collinson told us, "it would be brilliant if it goes ahead."

First published on the *Daily Telegraph*'s Earth website
6 May 2008

21

Stanley Johnson Joins the Crowds at Glastonbury

As dawn breaks on my first Glastonbury morning, I find myself wandering through a still-sleeping encampment like Henry V before the Battle of Agincourt. Around me are tents, tens of thousands of them, stretching as far as the eye can see.

There is indeed something almost medieval about the setting and the eye is ineluctably drawn to those great, towering pavilions where the live musical performances – the festival's very *raison d'être* – take place. Even on a drab grey morning, the huge red and gold canvas structures stand out like great beacons on the plain, pennants flying and banners streaming.

Two hours later, I had worked my way round most of the site. Some 150,000 people are expected in Glastonbury this year and I would say that by now most of them were here. Add another 30,000 helpers and you begin to understand the sheer logistical triumph of the event.

In the early hours, when gentlemen of England still lay abed, I watch convoys of forklift trucks shunting piled-high boxes of baps to different dispersal points around the valley.

A mind-boggling 1.25 million gallons of waste have to be collected from 2,802 lavatories over the three days of the festival.

With it all running like clockwork, I began to wish my own introduction to Glastonbury had been quite so smooth. But for that, I have no one to blame but myself. A day earlier, as I had queued with several hundred other festival fans at the entrance, the heavens opened.

As I stood getting literally soaked to the skin, I found myself admiring the wisdom and foresight of the young men and women waiting in line with me. They had ponchos, cagoules, anoraks and plastic macs. Some had umbrellas. I had rushed out of the door to catch a taxi to Paddington station without even a kerchief to cover my head.

I endured the torrential rain for about half an hour, tempted to abort the mission entirely. I had no dry clothes in my kitbag, just the one-man tent that I had purchased the previous day.

Irritated, I put the bag on the ground and gave it a kick. Spray flew and the zip popped open. It was the work of a moment to pull the tent out of the bag and over my head. When Clara, the *Daily Telegraph*'s photographer, called me on my mobile to ask where I was, I replied: "Look for me in the tent."

"Which tent?" she asked.

"I'm wearing it!" I said.

Well, that tent certainly did me proud. When I bought it, a young man in the shop had explained which poles went through which holes and what to do with the webbing tapes and flysheets. Of course, I hadn't followed a word.

It was after 11pm, with the rain still sheeting down when I finally found a patch of grass recently vacated by cows.

My wife, before I left home, had given me one of those miner's lights you wear on your forehead, to leave your hands free. But still I had no real idea what to do. Did you start with the inner tent or the outer? Two of the poles were blue but one – I could see it with my Scargill lantern – was red. What did this mean?

I was about to give up and simply roll myself in plastic, hoping to survive the night, when Clara once more appeared and took pity. Phew! Thanks to her stunning efficiency, I got at least five hours' sleep.

So the next morning, as the camp gradually awoke around me, I determined to make the most of the festival that is probably without equal anywhere in the world.

I am not well-versed in these matters but even I know that this year's race card is definitely up to scratch.

At 11am on Friday, with Kate Nash performing at the opening session, I was in front of the famous Pyramid Stage, snapping my fingers and singing alongside kids young enough (almost) to be my grandchildren. They knew every line, and the entire festival line-up.

"How do you know so much about it all?" I was truly impressed.

"It's our world. Of course we know," they replied.

Those girls can probably pitch a tent in a storm as well.

First published in the *Daily Telegraph*, 29 June 2008

22

Journey to Anatolia:
Looking for Blonde Ancestors

In the summer of 1961, when I was still an undergraduate at Oxford, I rode a BSA 500cc twin-cylinder Shooting Star motorcycle across Asia, following in the footsteps of Marco Polo. As our small expedition (there were three of us on two machines) powered across the high plateau in the heart of Turkish Anatolia, I had no idea that I would be passing less than 100 miles from my ancestral home: the village of Kalfat, about 100 miles north-east of Ankara, in the province of Cankiri.

To tell the truth, when I was growing up I didn't know a great deal about my Turkish ancestry. My father, an Exmoor farmer, didn't talk much about it. My mother filled in some of the details but not many. She told me that though my father had been born in England (in 1909), his mother – Winifred – had died as a result of complications following the birth. She also gave me the impression that my father had never seen his father, Ali Kemal, a Turkish journalist and politician.

"During the First World War," my mother explained, "Turkey was on the other side. It wasn't possible for your grandfather to visit his English family. Then, after the War ended, your grandfather was assassinated. So your poor father really grew up as an orphan. Your father's mother was half-English and half-Swiss. When his mother died, he and his sister were brought up in England by their English grandmother."

Three years after that motorcycle ride across Asia, a few more bits of the jigsaw fell into place.

After Winifred died, my grandfather, Ali Kemal, married again. His new wife was Sabiha, daughter of Zeki Pasha, the Grand-Marshall of the Army under Sultan Abdul-Hamid. Their son, Zeki Kuneralp, joined the Turkish Diplomatic Service and in 1964 was posted as Ambassador to London.

As far as I was concerned, I was only too delighted to profit from my uncle Zeki's presence in London to find out more about my Turkish links. I visited him more than once at the ambassador's residence in Portland Place, London. I remember him once talking to me about Kalfat, the Anatolian village where Ali Kemal's father, Ahmet Hamdi, had himself come from.

"You should try to go there one day," Zeki said.

I had taken two-year-old Boris along with me on that occasion. Zeki inspected Boris's blonde hair approvingly. "The blonde gene comes from Kalfat," he told me. "If you ever go there, I'm certain you will find some blonde Turks there even today."

"I will go there one day," I said. "I can promise you that."

Well, it has taken me forty-five years to fulfil that promise. With Boris's election as Mayor of London on 1 May, there has been a surge of interest in his Turkish origins and I have found myself, as the proud father, in the position of having to field some of the more detailed enquires. When the editor of the *Mail on Sunday* suggested that, rather than speculate on what Kalfat was like and whether there were still any blonde Turks to be found there, I should actually go and visit the place myself, I jumped at the chance.

Should I call my trip to Kalfat a pilgrimage? Well, why not? It was certainly one of the most moving experiences of my life.

Remembering my own experiences in the sixties, I had been expecting that the journey from Ankara to Kalfat would be along a dusty pot-holed road across a parched Anatolian plateau, so I was agreeably surprised to find that not only was the metalled road in perfect condition, but the landscape was remarkably green, almost lush, as a result of recent rain.

Zeki Kuneralp's younger son, Selim, who has followed in his father's footsteps as a diplomat, came with me that day on my "pilgrimage", as well as two friends of his whom he had invited to accompany us on the trip: Suat Kiniklioğlu, the member of parliament for Cankiri, and Ismail Karaduman, director of the Kalkat Foundation, an organization devoted to promoting the well-being of Kalfat's citizens.

As we drove over the hills that morning, Selim filled in some of the background for the benefit of his guests.

"My cousin, Stanley, and I share a grandfather, Ali Kemal, and of course we share a great-grandfather, Ahmet Hamdi, Ali Kemal's father. Ahmet Hamdi lived in Kalfat, but around 1850 he left the village to go to Istanbul. He set up a candle factory there in the days before there was electricity. With candles being needed for mosques as well as houses, Ahmet Hamdi somehow acquired a monopoly and became a rich man. He was very loyal to Abdul Aziz, the Sultan of the day, so maybe that helped. Ahmet Hamdi's son, Ali Kemal, was born in 1869. As far as we know, Ali Kemal never went to Kalfat and Ahmet Hamdi never went back once he had left."

"Does the Mayor of Kalfat know we are coming, Selim?" I asked.

"There may be a small reception party," Selim replied.

This turned out to be the understatement of the year. The total population of Kalfat is probably around 2,000 and a high proportion seemed to be waiting for us that morning as we drove into the village. They had gathered in front of the Mayor's office, ready to greet Selim and me. I must have shaken hands a hundred times that morning. As a matter of fact, as is the Turkish custom, I was frequently embraced on both cheeks.

The Mayor of Kalfat, Ő Karaağaç, made a speech of welcome in Turkish. My knowledge of that language being shamefully slight, Suat Kiniklioğlu, the local MP, translated for me.

"He's saying how much the people of Kalfat welcome you and your cousin Selim here today. They are particularly proud about Boris becoming Mayor of London. He hopes that Boris himself may be able to come to Kalfat one day soon and he wonders if it might be possible for Kalfat to be twinned with London!"

117

I made a brief speech in reply, which Suat translated for the benefit of the rapt audience.

I was very sorry, I said, that Boris himself had not been able to come. I had spoken to him by telephone that morning and he had sent his very best wishes. My cousin, Selim and I, felt honoured beyond measure by the reception we had received.

I ended my remarks with one of the few Turkish expressions I know. "*Teshekur ederim. Chok teshekur.*" Thank you. Thank you very much. They were simple but heartfelt words.

As I stood there, surrounded by men (yes, all men) who under other circumstances might have been my compatriots, I felt profoundly moved. More than a hundred and fifty years ago my great-grandfather had made the journey from Kalfat to Istanbul. Now his direct descendant was the first Conservative Mayor of London.

My reveries were interrupted when Suat turned to me.

"Stanley-*bey*," he asked, "the mayor would like to know whether you want to see Ahmet Hamdi's house and to meet the family."

I couldn't believe my ears. I hadn't remotely imagined that Ahmet Hamdi's house might still survive or that my own relatives would still be around.

The whole village wanted to follow us down the street but the Mayor waved them back. A reduced band of twenty or thirty of us walked a couple of hundred yards past the mosque, then turned right to come to a stop on a piece of open ground.

Many of the houses in Kalfat today are of fairly modern construction. Turks don't seem to be as sentimental about old pieces of masonry as we are. Many of Kalfat's present residents have worked in Germany and, perhaps as a result of this, have been quite happy on their return to pull down their old homes and replace them with something more modern.

But the house we found ourselves standing in front of was of a kind I recognized from my previous trip through Anatolia, a solid stone and wood construction, with a splendid balcony. (The Turks have a saying: "A man without a tummy is like a house without a balcony!") Standing immediately next to it was another even older house in a state of some disrepair.

A Turkish family was waiting to greet us. I recognized one or two of them as people I had already greeted that morning in the line-up outside the Mayor's office.

Suat listened to the introductions, then summarized for me

"These are Ahmet Hamdi's relatives, members of your Turkish family. This is Ahmet Demir, this is his wife, Aslihan Demir. This is Ahmet's father, Behir, and his wife. Behir's father was Riza and his grandfather was Haci Ahmet. They call him Haci because he made the *haj* to the Holy Places. Haci Ahmet's father, Ali, was probably Ahmet Hamdi's brother."

Suat saved the best till last. "The family is still known in the village by the name they used to have before Ataturk introduced surnames to Turkey?"

"And what is that?"

"*Sarioglangil* ... the family of the blonde boys."

It got better. Ahmet and Aslihan Demir had a three-year-old son, Őmer Berkay Demir. Young Őmer was presented to me. I held him in my arms while we had our photo taken. The sun shone from behind the minaret. Its rays caught the fine-spun white-gold hair. I remembered then what my uncle Zeki had said about finding blondes in Kalfat. On the evidence, there was a whole clan of blondes here and one way or another they were all related to me.

We went from house to house in Kalfat that day. I must have laced and unlaced my shoes more times than I remember. At each stop we would be fêted with tea, yogurt or baklava.

The hospitality did not end there. The Mayor of Kalfat laid on a tremendous lunch for us in a protected forest area to which he had invited the Governor of the nearby town of Orta, Fatih Őzdemir, and other dignatories. The Governor presented Selim and me with a badminton racquet, since Orta was that weekend to be the site of Turkey's national badminton championships. And later that day, in his formal setting of his own office, Mayor Karaağaç gave me an *ibrik*, the traditional copper vessel used to hold the water with which the faithful wash themselves five days a day before prayer.

I flew from Ankara to Istanbul on the way home. The journey across Anatolia which had taken my great-grandfather twelve days in 1850 took less than an hour. I was met at Istanbul airport by Selim's older brother, Sinan, a publisher. We spent the afternoon together tracking down some of the post-Kalfat landmarks of the Ahmet Amdi story.

In Istanbul, so the story goes, Ahmet Amdi bought and married a young Circassian slave girl called Nanife Feride. And it was in this city, in the Suleimanye district, that their child, my grandfather, Ali Kemal, was brought up, together with his sisters.

Towards sunset on my last night in Turkey, Sinan and I walked down the famous Pera Street (now known as Istiklal Çaddesi or Independence Avenue). It was here, on 4 November, in a barber's shop near the Cercle d'Orient Club, that my grandfather Ali Kemal was abducted.

"He was smuggled by boat that same night over the Sea of Marmara to Izmit," Sinan told me, "then brutally murdered on the orders of Nureddin Pasha."

Today, Ali Kemal remains a controversial figure in Turkey. He opposed Turkey's entry into the First World War and was forbidden to speak out or publish while it lasted. After the war, he effectively signed his own death warrant by refusing to leave Istanbul even after the Sultan himself had fled. He was only fifty-three when he died. If he were my age, he would have already been dead some fourteen years.

I have learned recently that, contrary to what I had long believed, Ali Kemal actually did see something of my father, at least in my father's early years. Apparently, after my grandmother's death, the family lived together in Wimbledon for a year or two before Ali Kemal returned to Turkey.

My father never in my hearing mentioned any first-hand

memories of his own father. But that Ali Kemal himself knew and cared deeply for his son I now realize is not in doubt. Apart from that sojourn in Wimbledon, there is the evidence of his novel *Fetret* which was published before Ali Kemal died. Written in Turkish, the book tells the story of the relationship between a father and his son and of the father's vision for the kind of country in which he hopes his son will grown up.

One of the dignitaries present at the lunch we had that day in the forest near Kalfat was a former MP called Hakki Duran. As the ceremony drew to a close, Hakki Duran brought out a plastic bag bulging with books. Amazingly, all of them had either been written by, or were about, Ali Kemal. One of them was *Fetret*. I took the book in my hands. It was not an original copy but a recent paperback reprint. A selection of photographs had been added.

It was the strangest feeling to see, that day in Anatolia, family photographs of my own father, Wilfred/Fetret, as a child together with his elder sister, Celma, which I had never seen before.

But what struck me most was the uncanny resemblance Wilfred/Fetret had to the blonde Turkish boy, Ömer Berkay Demir, whom I had held in my arms just a few hours earlier.

Written for the *Daily Mail*, June, 2008

23

Africa's Boundary-Breaking Safari Park

The Tuli Block, sometimes called "Botswana's best-kept secret", is a great sweep of land at the confluence of the Limpopo and Shashe rivers. Climb to the top of one of the high *kopjes* in the middle of the block and you will see the mopane veld stretching to the far horizon, broken only to the south by the dark forests of the Limpopo Valley.

Tuli is the heart of the Limpopo-Shashe Transfrontier Protection Area – or Peace Park. The park, the result of an agreement between Botswana, South Africa and Zimbabwe, will allow animals to roam unchecked across national boundaries in a vast area of southern Africa.

Just getting to Tuli is an adventure. After a five-hour drive north from Johannesburg, you leave your vehicle with police at a tiny border post on the banks of the Limpopo, then pile into a makeshift cable car before being winched across the swirling water. Because of late rains this year, Kipling's "great grey-green greasy Limpopo" lived up to its billing. As you ride across in the metal cage, you are just a few feet from the surface of the river, keeping a wary eye out for lurking crocodiles.

We were met on the Botswanan side by Richard Modeme, a guide who for the past fifteen years has worked for the Mashatu Game Reserve, a private company that owns about 30,000 hectares within the Tuli Block and runs the Mashatu Main Camp as well as the Mashatu Tent Camp. Hoping to be as close to Africa's wildlife as possible, we chose the tents.

Over the next six days Richard became a firm friend. He woke us at 5.30am, ready for the morning's first game drive at 6am. He drove us each day with impeccable skill and courtesy in our open-top four-wheel drive. He brought us back in time for brunch – about 10.30am – and took us out again for the late-afternoon excursion. He always made sure, when the sun was close to setting, that we were parked in some auspicious spot – in the shade of a giant thousand-year-old baobab tree, for example – where it would be safe to get out and enjoy a ritual sundowner.

Because the space is so vast and the number of visitors so (relatively) few, you can drive anywhere you like, terrain permitting. On two successive mornings, we encountered a pride of lions. There was just one other vehicle in the area on the first occasion. On the second, the only company we had were hyenas, jackals and vultures drawn by the carcasses of the elands the lions had just killed.

The time we spent with the elephants was altogether special. Not long ago, elephants had been virtually shot out in Tuli. Now there are probably 1,400 elephants in the Central Limpopo Valley and as many as 600 in the Northern Tuli Game Reserve, including Mashatu.

On our last morning in the reserve, we must have seen well over 100 elephants. First we saw two troupes, each consisting of about forty animals, coming from different directions to drink at the Majale River, a tributary of the Limpopo. Then, when we couldn't believe there were still more elephants waiting to be seen among the mopane and leadwood trees, we came across another, smaller herd.

Indeed, we found ourselves surrounded by elephants on all sides, including mothers suckling calves and one huge bull who clearly had other things in mind. He gave us a cursory glance, then lumbered off in pursuit of a female. "She'll give him a good run for his money," Jeanetta Selier, the game reserve's resident biologist, told us. "But if she's ready, she'll let him catch her."

Lion, elephant, leopard, cheetah, zebra, kudu, eland, impala, giraffe, waterbuck, warthog, hippo: apart from rhino, Tuli has most of what you could want to see as far as the land mammals of southern Africa are concerned. It also has an amazing variety of bird-life. If you are looking for the kori bustard, Africa's heaviest flying bird, go to Tuli. The lilac-breasted roller, Botswana's national bird and another denizen of Tuli, so enchanted King Mzilikazi of the Matabele that he decreed that he alone could adorn himself with its feathers.

Miraculously, wild dogs, southern Africa's most endangered carnivore, have been reintroduced to the area. Seeing a wild dog hunting in the mopane veld in Africa is equivalent to, say, seeing a blue whale in the middle of the Pacific. You just don't believe it is ever going to happen. Well, it did. One evening, as Richard was casting about for a good spot to crack open the cool-boxes and fix our sundowners, we found ourselves watching, amazed, as a score of wild dogs, hunting as a pack, criss-crossed the surrounding terrain.

Forgoing our evening drinks, we followed the pack as closely as we could without disturbing them and, when darkness fell, Richard's assistant, Ona, stood up at the back of the vehicle shining a spotlight. We didn't see how that particular expedition ended. Wild dogs can hunt for hours without stopping and, in any case, dinner was waiting for us in the *boma* (enclosure) back at the camp.

Tuli is magnificent, but it stands for so much more. I had read about the Peace Park before I arrived, but you can understand the extent of the vision only by seeing the place for yourself.

If the three countries involved can now move ahead with the plan, the Limpopo-Shashe Transfrontier Protection Area will ultimately include national parks, privately owned ranches and communal land in an extraordinary act of political, social and ecological cooperation.

Over dinner, with the stars of the Southern Cross shining overhead, Jeanetta gave us her appraisal: "This is a tremendous visionary concept, which could set a new pattern for wildlife management in southern Africa. We're all ready to go forward, but events in Zimbabwe, as you can imagine, are holding things up."

The Mashatu Tent Camp is a stone's throw from the Zimbabwe border. As I gazed across the stream-bed towards the official frontier, I found myself wondering whether Robert Mugabe and his henchmen knew or cared what a priceless asset they were putting at risk.

First published in *The Times*, 27 September 2008

24

Road to Shangri-la

There were relatively few foreigners present at the coronation last month of Jigme Khesar Namgyel Wangchuck as Druk Gyalpo, or King of Bhutan, and I am ready to bet that not one of them actually walked 65 kilometres over the mountains to attend that extraordinary event. But my wife, Jenny, and I did precisely that. Admittedly, we had not planned it that way.

Back in June when we made the arrangements to visit the Himalayan Kingdom of Bhutan, the precise date of the coronation was still under discussion. Soothsayers still needed to be consulted and entrails examined. So our aim at the time was simply to trek from Paro (where the plane from Delhi would land) to Thimpu (the capital) and to do some sightseeing once we got there.

The plan was for us to have a couple of days to acclimatize in Paro, before heading off over the mountains. I work at the top of our house in London and Jenny has a study on the ground floor so I emailed her the details of the trek.

"I don't think we're going to do any very high-altitude stuff," I wrote, "so I'm sure you'll be OK."

Men are from Mars, women are from Venus. Jenny pinged an email back.

"I see we're camping at 3,750m on Day 3. How high is that?"

"Not quite sure of the actual altitude in feet," I replied. "Should be a piece of cake anyway."

Well, some pieces of cake are more edible than others.

Trekking in Bhutan is not like trekking in Nepal. Everything you need is carried on horses, donkeys or mules rather than by porters.

To help Jenny and me across the mountains from Paro to Thimpu required the assistance of our guide, Sonam Norbu, an engaging and humorous twenty-five-year-old Bhutanese from the east of the country, one head cook, named Kunzang, one assistant cook, Tashi, one horseman, Tshering, and seven pack animals, namely three horses, three donkeys and one mule.

Jenny and I met our full team, pack animals included, early one morning at the agreed rendezvous. As vantage points go, this was superb. The Paro valley stretched out below us, dominated by the magnificent Paro Dzong. The *dzongs*, found throughout Bhutan, are unique Bhutanese fortresses, built in commanding defensive positions and used for both civil and religious purposes. For the next hour, as we climbed up through the forest, the image of the *dzong* down in the valley below grew steadily smaller. Eventually, as the path entered the trees, it passed from our view.

Our travel guide's itinerary had spoken of a "long but not steep" climb for this first day's trekking. "Long" and "steep" are really subjective terms. I have to admit that Jenny and I found the going tough. One might have thought that with seven pack animals at our disposal we might somehow have managed to grab on to a passing horse's tail. But that's not the way it is. In Bhutan the horses don't accompany you as you climb. Each morning you just walk out of the camp, leaving your team to pack everything up. You don't have to dismantle the tents or even roll up your sleeping bag. That's all done for you. You might have been trekking for two or three hours before you hear the tinkling bell of the lead horse coming up fast behind you.

This is the moment to step aside, unhook your water bottle and take a deep swig, as the animals pass. Our horseman, Tshering, brings up the rear. The paths over these hills are narrow. To the untutored eye, the way is often not clearly marked, with several options on offer.

I ask Sonam, our guide, how the horses keep to the track.

"They know the way," Sonam replies.

Sometimes, we pass a convoy coming in the opposite direction. Once I noted that the lone horseman had a sling in his hand.

Sonam elaborates: "If the horses go in the wrong direction, the horseman can fire a slingshot at the lead animal to set it back on the right track."

On the whole, we didn't do much talking that first day. Jenny and I were seriously winded. As the track got steeper and rockier, we found ourselves counting out the paces.

"98 ... 99 ... 100," I would pant. "OK, let's do another hundred before we pause."

By the time we reached a spot of level ground where Tashi had spread out a copious lunch, I was ready to admit – at least to myself – that it would have been advisable to have spent a bit more effort getting into shape before we left London. We could have climbed up to the top of nearby Primrose Hill once or twice, for example.

In many ways, the first day was the worst. Even if we had been fit, it was not easy going. The fact is, with horses the dominant means of transport in these parts, the narrow paths get quite churned up. They can be slippery as well as rocky.

We camped the first night at almost 3,700m, just below the 16th-century monastery of Jili Dzong. We might still have been in the 16th century except for the fact that, in the stillness of the evening, we could hear the sounds of a transistor radio, the monks' only contact with the outside world. At that altitude it was seriously cold. The food warmed us up a bit. My notebook records that we had noodles, pork, broccoli, rice and potato curry, followed by apple custard. But still, that first evening, Jenny and I felt totally exhausted. By 8pm we were inside our tent and tucked up in our sleeping bags. As we lay there, we could hear the voices of our team outside, as dinner was cleared away and the horses hobbled for the night.

"We only hobble the naughty horses," Sunam had explained during supper, "the ones who may lead the others astray."

Jenny had packed some head-torches. We switched them on, like miners' lamps, to study the next day's itinerary. I tried to sound encouraging.

"It's downhill all the way tomorrow."

Jenny was not reassured. "Downhill can be even harder. It can put a tremendous strain on the knees."

"Just lengthen your poles," I advised.

Bhutan is the country that famously has, as its national goal, the pursuit not of ever-increasing Gross National Product (GNP) but of Gross National Happiness (GNH). As we began the second day of our trek from Paro to Thimpu, I began to glimpse the reality behind the slogan. We walked through tiny villages that had never seen a car (there mostly aren't any roads in Bhutan anyway), where quantities of green and red chillies were spread out to dry on the roofs of the houses, and teams of oxen pulled wooden ploughs around the small terraced fields. We came to a watermill where the wheat was being ground into flour. A small boy showed us how the system worked and I wanted to give him a dollar. Sonam gave him a stick of chewing gum instead. "It will be more use to him," he said.

At a tiny hamlet called Jedika, where we stopped for lunch, the women were washing clothes in the stream below an ever-turning prayer wheel.

"The water is always turning the wheel. It never stops," Sonam explained.

"Who earns the merits then?" I asked. By then we had been in Bhutan long enough to know that in this deeply Buddhist country the accumulation of merit is a vital consideration – at least if you want to avoid being reincarnated as, say, a dog in the next life.

"The man who built the prayer wheel over the stream earns the merit," Sonam explained.

The sun shone brilliantly that day, as it did throughout the whole of our trek. The scenery was spectacular. Though we were walking down through forests of fir trees, we almost never lost sight of the distant Himalayan peaks, many of them rising to over 6,000m.

Whereas Nepal has been invaded by mountaineers, Sonam explained that Bhutan has closed its mountains to adventurers of every sort.

"Why so?" I asked.

"Out of respect for the gods," Sonam replied as though this was the most obvious thing in the world.

We spent most of our third day climbing once again. That's the way it is in Bhutan. Up 1,000m , then down 1,200m , then up, say, another 1,250m. Late in the afternoon, when we were heading for the campsite at Phajoding, another 16th-century mountain monastery which actually overlooks the Thimpu Valley, we saw two golden eagles, circling on the thermals. At one point they soared almost directly above us and I grabbed my camera. I caught a distant image of one of the birds as it powered overhead. I know the resulting photo won't win a prize, but still it means the world to me.

Gross Personal Happiness! That's how I would describe that moment on the mountain pass, as the golden eagles flew overhead with the valley of Thimpu spread out far below and the sun beginning to set on the far mountain peaks.

We spent the last morning walking down to Thimpu. After a while, the conifers gave way to deciduous trees. Can you have a cacophony of colour? I'm not sure, but that's how it felt. The forests were streaked with autumn hues. I shall never forget the pink bloom of the Himalayan cherry trees we saw that morning on our way down.

Around two o'clock that afternoon, when we had reached more or less level ground and the horses were being unloaded for the last time, I learnt some astonishing news. The Bhutanese authorities, who keep a close track of all visitors to this mountain kingdom, had apparently spotted my name on some list and while we were up in the mountains had decided that I was to be issued with a press invitation to the coronation.

Our tour had been arranged by Choki Dorji of Blue Poppy Tours and Treks; his English wife, Naomi, came out in person to the mustering point on the outskirts of Thimpu to inform us of the sudden change in plans.

"The Prime Minister is holding a press conference this afternoon at three o'clock and you're expected to attend. The coronation itself is actually going to take place tomorrow in Thimpu Dzong."

I have to admit that I reacted to this development with mixed emotions. On the one hand I was delighted to be issued with a press pass to what would undoubtedly be a unique event. Though King Jigme Singye Wangchuk, King Jigme Khesar's father, had stepped aside in 2006, the handover would not be complete until this week's ceremonies were over. We couldn't have timed our arrival better.

On the other hand, I had absolutely nothing suitable to wear. Apart from a pair of black leather shoes that I had thrown into my case at the last moment, trekking gear was all I had.

"Can I buy a suit in town?" I asked Naomi.

Naomi looked doubtful. "The Bhutanese don't do suits, and even if they did, I am not sure they would have one to fit you."

There was no time to sort out the problem that afternoon. While Jenny went to the hotel, I went to the Prime Minister's press conference. Though a fair number of Bhutanese journalists were present, as far as I could see the international contingent consisted of Reuters' New Delhi correspondent, a German lady from *Glamour* magazine, and me.

Sitting in the second row of the stalls, I was able to observe the Bhutanese Prime Minister Lyonchhen Jigme Yoser Thinley at close quarters. Though Prime Minister Lyonchhen has vast experience of Bhutanese politics, he has actually only been in his present job since March this year when Bhutan's new constitution came into force.

His reverence for the institution of monarchy was almost palpable. He started by explaining the key role of the previous king, Jigme Singye, the current king's father.

"The King gave us democracy. Democracy has come to Bhutan not by the will of the people, but by the will of the King."

He went on to assert that the new king would be a unifying force: "The King will be the force to ensure the long-term sustainability of democracy."

Someone – was it the lady from *Glamour* magazine? – asks the Prime Minister how he intends to promote Gross National Happiness in practice.

"Gross National Happiness," replies the PM, "is never far from our minds. With every project we undertake, we ask ourselves, will this project enhance the happiness of our people?"

Cynic that I am about much of politics, I nonetheless found myself engaged at that moment in what Samuel Taylor Coleridge once called "the willing suspension of disbelief". I had seen enough of Bhutan so far – the beauty of the country, the demeanour of the people, the reverence for tradition and the Buddhist way of life, the deep-rooted respect for and veneration of the monarchy – to be ready to concede that the Prime Minister truly, madly, deeply meant what he said.

None of that, of course, helped me in my key dilemma of what to wear at the following day's ceremony where, so the Prime Minister announced, the press would have unique privileges. We would be admitted to a special platform in the courtyard of the great Thimpu Dzong and would have an unrivalled view of the arrival both of the dignitaries and of the king himself as he made his way to the throne room. Later in the day, another vantage point had been prepared so that we could witness at close quarters the passage of the royal party across the courtyard to the temple where the ceremony would continue.

Happily, Yeshey Dorji, Bhutan's Foreign Secretary who had been sitting alongside the Prime Minister for the press conference, came to my aid.

As I left the room at the end of the conference, he signalled to an aide, who presented me with a carefully wrapped parcel. "You may find this useful tomorrow," Yeshey Dorji said tactfully.

I have no idea how he knew that I was several sizes larger than the average Bhutanese, but he obviously did. When I got back to the hotel and unwrapped the parcel, I found a magnificent Bhutanese *gho*, the national dress, first introduced in the 17th century and a must for all formal occasions. All the trimmings were there too: the long white scarf to be worn over the left shoulder, the white shirt with the long sleeves that you fold back on to the outside of the *gho*, the belt to pull it tight, the long socks to keep the draught off bare legs.

Sonam, our guide, came to the hotel at six o'clock the next morning to help me dress. I didn't begin to understand the subtleties: how much white shirt could be glimpsed at the neck of the *gho*, how deep the skirt could drop below the knee without giving offence. Was it OK to wear underpants? (I decided it was.)

By 7am I was on the viewing platform in the *dzong*'s courtyard, together with the rest of the press corps. We watched as Pratibha Patil, the President of India, arrived, followed by Sonia Gandhi, president of India's Congress party. Next came the ancillary royals, notably King Jigme Singye's four wives, all sisters. (Apparently, a fifth sister was also invited to become his wife, but she politely declined the honour.) At 8.30am there was an extra stir of excitement as the young king, Harvard and Oxford educated, took his seat on the dais next to his father.

I looked at King Jigme Khesar Namgyel Wangchuck sitting on his throne, surrounded by his family and courtiers. I took in the staggering beauty of the setting: the trumpeters on the roof of the *dzong*, the giant tapestry, or *thondril*, hanging from the tower in the middle of the courtyard. I watched the masked dancers perform their rituals before Their Majesties. A line from *Hamlet* came into my mind as I watched – "There's such divinity doth hedge a king ...". I have to admit that I couldn't help thinking at that moment that Shakespeare had got it right.

King Jigme Singye Wangchuck was only sixteen when he acceded to the throne in 1972 and only fifty-two when he handed over to his son. Jigme Khesar, the new king or *Druk Galyo*, is only twenty-eight, still unmarried. Who can tell when the next coronation will be? It might be half a century from now.

Will Bhutan, that magical mountain kingdom, the Shangri-la archetype, still be the same fifty years hence? Will it have managed to retain the qualities that make it unique among the nations of the world? Will the pursuit of Gross National Happiness remain the official goal?

Though sandwiched between those giants of our time, India and China, Bhutan, with barely 700,000 people, has so far miraculously managed to retain its own unique identity. Will it continue to do so?

From what I have seen I am sure that, under the constitution developed and sponsored by his revered father, the new king's government and parliament, and indeed the vast majority of the Bhutanese themselves, will do their level best to ensure that this is the case.

And if in the end they don't succeed, it will – I suspect – not be through their own fault. It will be a result of global forces, largely beyond their control. Bhutan versus the Rest of the World? I know which side I'm on.

First published in the *Independent Magazine*,
Saturday 6 December 2008

25

The Far Side of the World

I have visited Australia half a dozen times since my older sister, Hilary, and her family went to live there in 1969, but up till now I have never had a chance to visit Tasmania.

Last month, however, as deep snow fell on London's streets, my wife and I spent a fortnight travelling around Australia's magical offshore island. We must have driven almost a thousand miles while we were there. Such a distance, of course, is a mere bagatelle to those used to the vastness of mainland Australia, but in Tasmania a thousand miles goes a long way.

I find myself wondering why on earth I waited so long before heading across the Bass Strait. As a holiday destination, I would have to put Tasmania right up there among the world leaders.

Take the weather, for example. Most days the sun shone and a light wind blew. While other parts of Australia, notably the state of Victoria, experienced scorching heatwaves and the worst bush fires in decades, the temperature in Hobart when we landed was a comfortable 20–23°C. And it stayed that way for the rest of our time on the island.

In the nature of things, you are never far from the sea in Tasmania and most days I was able to swim. On the southern coast (we visited both Bruny Island and Tasman Island), the water is admittedly bracing, and only slightly less so on the eastern coast, but when you go up to the north coast to stay, for example, in the little village of Stanley, the water feels almost Mediterranean.

Of course, Australia is an outdoor country. But in Tasmania, with only half a million people in an area the size of Ireland, outdoors has a special meaning. One of the high points of our visit was the four days we spent on the Freycinet Peninsula, on Tasmania's east coast.

This is a place of sugar-white beaches and crystal seas, secluded rocky coves and granite headlands splashed with flaming orange lichen. One side of the peninsula looks out on to Oyster Bay; the other is bounded by the waters of the Southern Ocean.

Over the course of our time there, Jenny and I walked the whole length of the peninsula, now protected as Freycinet National Park. Apart from the spectacular scenery, Freycinet is a haven for wildlife. We saw sea eagles and dolphins, black swans and rare crested terns. One afternoon, walking back to our eco-lodge in the forest behind the beach, we saw one lone king penguin standing on the foreshore. It was in the last stage of its moult, living off its fat, before returning to the sea.

For me, as an environmentalist, Tasmania was seventh heaven. After Freycinet, we drove to Cradle Mountain in the heart of a World Heritage area and then on to Corinna, a tiny settlement, once a mining village, on the banks of the Pieman River at the southern edge of the Tarkine Forest, the world's second largest temperate rainforest.

My motto has always been: "If you can't swim in the sea, swim in a river." Unlike Queensland or the Northern Territory, where you run the risk of being eaten by a crocodile, there are no such lurking dangers in Tasmania's rivers.

One afternoon I took a kayak and paddled a few miles downstream to where the Savage River joins the Pieman. A century and a half ago, there was a mini gold rush here. Now there are only half a dozen houses in Corinna. If you are lucky, you get to stay in an old miner's cottage. Tasmania's human history, of course, goes back far beyond the sealers and the whalers, the miners and the "piners" (who sought out the high-value Huon pine). Like other states in Australia, Tasmania has begun to realize the richness and importance of its Aboriginal past. The Tasmanian Museum and Art Gallery in Hobart contains an Aboriginal gallery which celebrates 2,000 generations (around 35,000 years) of Aboriginal history, as compared with the eight or ten generations (200 years) that have passed since the arrival of the Europeans.

Looking back, what astonishes me is how much there is to do and to see and, because of the relative compactness of the place, how easy it is to get around. To sum it up: the natural environment is without equal, the Tasmanian food and wine (particularly the Pinot Noir) are superb, while its cultural and historical aspects are now recognized as being of major importance. The day we spent at Port Arthur, for example, the site of the former penal settlement, was both fascinating and moving. As a West Countryman, I was struck by how many of the convicts seemed to come from Devon.

In spite of all the sombre associations, there is, in the end, something uplifting about Port Arthur. Many convicts eventually earned their freedom. Van Diemen's Land was in due course renamed Tasmania. A grim past has been replaced by a glorious future.

First published in *ES Magazine*, Monday 16 March 2009

26

The Wandering Star:
In Search of the Albatross

I saw my first albatross on 12 January 1984. It was a day I shall never forget. I had been invited by the British Antarctic Survey (BAS) to join their research and supply vessel, the *John Biscoe*, as it made its annual visit to the series of research stations which Britain maintains in the Antarctic.

We had left Punta Arenas, the most southerly town in Chile, to head south across the fearsome Drake Passage, which separates the tip of the South American continent – Cape Horn – from the Antarctic Peninsula.

It had been a bumpy crossing, to say the least. As the *Biscoe* left the relative shelter of the Magellan Straits, we encountered mountainous seas and gale-force winds. My own personal survival technique was to tie myself to a chair, anchor the chair firmly to some immovable object, and then sit quite still, with my eyes firmly fixed on the wildly gyrating horizon.

On the morning of the fourth day I ventured out on deck to discover that the sea was much calmer, resulting, I imagined, from the drop in temperature as we steamed ever further south. Though it was still the Antarctic "summer", you could see bits of ice in the water – "bergy bits", the *Biscoe* crew called them – and even the occasional iceberg.

Around 10 o'clock that morning, with the binoculars glued to my eyes, I saw for the first time dead ahead of us the towering white cliffs of Antarctica. As the *John Biscoe* approached – we were heading for our first landfall at BAS's Faraday station on Galindez

Island – those white cliffs grew taller and taller until the ship was, literally, dwarfed by huge walls of ice.

The Antarctic seabirds seemed to sense that this was a special occasion – for us, at least – because they were out in force. Cape pigeons, otherwise known as pintado petrels – white with black markings on the wings – skimmed across the surface of the water. Then, further astern, sweeping in wide arcs into the wind, before rising and banking to turn, I saw a pair of black-browed albatrosses.

For me, that first sight of those magnificent birds was a truly uplifting moment. The albatross sings to the soul. No wonder it has for centuries been the source of inspiration and the stuff of legend. As a child I learned by heart, as so many of my generation did, Samuel Taylor Coleridge's *Rime of the Ancient Mariner,* and as I stood there on the frosty deck I found myself reciting whole chunks of verse learned in my prep school days on wet Sunday afternoons.

> The ice was here, the ice was there,
> The ice was all around:
> It cracked and growled, and roared and howled,
> Like noises in a swound!
> At length did cross an Albatross,
> Through the fog it came;
> As if it had been a Christian soul,
> We hailed it in God's name.

Those birds stayed with us more than an hour, sometimes far out to sea, sometimes swooping close to the stern of the ship. The black-browed albatross is not the largest albatross; that honour belongs to the southern royal species. But with its wingspan that can extend to almost 3 metres, it still seemed to me to be dramatically large. Once, one of the birds passed almost directly overhead, and even without the binoculars I could see the bright orange-yellow bill and the black shadowing round the eye which gives that particular species its name.

That was the first but not the last occasion on that voyage when I saw albatrosses. My notes record that I observed on various occasions several different species: including grey-headed, sooty, yellow-nosed and wandering albatrosses.

I think I got a special kick out of seeing the wandering albatross. Part of the reason was the wonderful Latin name the taxonomists have given the bird – *Diomedea exulans*. Exultant! That is exactly the right image. Partly, it was the sheer size of the animal. The wingspan of the wandering albatross lies between 2.5 and 3.5 metres and its body length is almost 1.5 metres. In some parts of the world, whole families occupy rooms not much bigger than that!

As the *John Biscoe* finally headed north again at the end of our tour of Britain's Antarctic bases, a wanderer stayed with us virtually the whole day. I wrote in my notes: "The day turned into a murky evening, but in the mist I could see the wandering albatross I had first spotted that morning. It was still with us, a magnificent sight, swooping around the ship just above the water, then soaring away from us with two beats of its giant wings. I wondered how long it would stay with us and whether it enjoyed flying as much as I enjoyed watching it."

I was fortunate on my first trip to Antarctica in 1984 to have been able to visit Bird Island, near South Georgia, home to some of the most significant albatross colonies in the world. BAS has a base on Bird Island – so Peter Prince, then the station commander, came over to the *Biscoe* in a Zodiac boat, and took us ashore. As we came in through the kelp beds the fur seals were poking their heads up like otters or little dogs begging.

We climbed the hill and headed west across the island. Our guide for the day was one of the Bird Island scientists, a young man called Ben Osborne. "The albatrosses hatch now and up till the end of March," I recorded him telling us. "The adult bird weighs about 10 kilos, but its chicks can go up to 16 or 17. They put on so much weight that they become great swollen balls of fat. Add Bird Island and South Georgia together and you've got maybe 10 per cent of the whole world population of wandering albatross." About half the world's grey-headed albatrosses also breed on South Georgia. We saw many of them that day.

To stand there on that grey, blowy day looking across the plateau at the great mass of nesting albatrosses was one of the high points of my first Antarctic trip. I have seldom in my life felt more privileged than at that moment when I was able to observe, literally, thousands of those great white birds on their nests, almost mythical creatures which seemed not the least bit disturbed by our presence. This was their world, not ours.

Some of the birds weren't nesting, but strutting around singly or in groups, sometimes spreading their wings and lifting their heads, as they engaged in courtship rituals.

"Over there," said Osborne, "is a display group. There are some males and females who simply don't seem to pair up. They go along in an unmarried state for quite a long time. Display is all part of the pairing-up business when they're ready for it. The youngest breeding birds are about nine and they live till well over forty."

Our guide caught a wanderer with a long pole with a crook on the end and held it by the beak to demonstrate the bird's extraordinary wingspan. "Ten to twelve feet for a big male," he told us. "White tail feathers. The older they get, the whiter they get. Look at the tubes, the nostrils at either side. The giant petrel has its tube on top."

By then we had more or less reached the most westerly point of Bird Island. This must surely be, I thought, one of the most amazing places on earth. Wherever I looked I could see the great birds, perched on their nests amid the tussock grass or displaying on the green sward of the plateau. It was a mind-blowing sight.

Almost a quarter of a century later, I had the chance to go back to the Antarctic Peninsula, this time as a tourist on board a well-appointed cruise ship, the *Antarctic Dream*. Remembering my earlier experiences, I spent hours on deck, or in front of the plate glass windows of the observation lounge, looking out for the first exhilarating sight of an albatross on the wing.

The first part of our journey followed much the same route as we had taken in the *John Biscoe*, except that we set out from the Argentinian port of Ushuaia, instead of Chilean Punta Arenas. And for once the Drake Passage was relatively calm. But even though, this time round, I was able to concentrate without being distracted by seasickness, the sad truth is that things have changed – and I did not see a single albatross until the very last day of our voyage when, as we made our way back up the Beagle Channel, a lone bird started to follow the ship, banking and swooping and gliding over the grey waters.

I did not on this occasion have a chance to revisit the great albatross breeding colonies in South Georgia, Bird Island or the Falklands. But I did have a chance to talk to experts, both on board the *Antarctic Dream* and subsequently in the UK. The consensus view seemed to be that, yes, there were far fewer albatrosses around and that several, if not most, species of albatross were endangered and some even threatened with extinction.

The good news is that the level of international concern for the plight of the albatross is rising rapidly. Several of the people I spoke to suggested that if I really wanted to find out what was going on I should head to Hobart, capital of the Australian island of Tasmania.

"That's where this story is playing out," my old friend Rob Hepworth told me. Hepworth is the Executive Secretary of the Convention on Migratory Species. The Convention encourages the setting up of special arrangements for the conservation of various threatened species. In that context, an international Agreement on the Conservation of Albatrosses and Petrels (ACAP) had recently been signed and ratified by more than a dozen states with interests in the Southern Ocean.

So I headed for Hobart and, the day after my arrival, went to ACAP's office in Salamanca Square. Warren Papworth, a fifty-year-old Australian who serves as ACAP's Executive Secretary, reviewed that global status of albatross populations for me. "There are nineteen albatross species currently listed by ACAP, fifteen of which are classified as threatened with extinction," he told me. "Four species are currently recognized as 'critically endangered', five are 'endangered', six are 'vulnerable' and four are 'near-threatened'."

We were joined by Dr Rosemary Gales, a marine scientist working for the Tasmanian Department of Primary Industries and Water, who serves as Convenor of ACAP's Status and Trends Working Group. "Albatross are among the most threatened species of bird in the world," she told me, flashing up a series of slides to make the point. I learned that as long ago as 1993, Dr Gales had reviewed the global status of albatross populations and the factors affecting them. She had concluded that mortality associated with commercial fishing operations had become the most serious threat facing these birds.

The key issue then was "albatross by-catch", in which the birds are caught by long-lines targeting tuna, toothfish and other species. More recently, trawl fisheries have also been identified as a major threat, the birds being attracted by discarded fish and offal only to be caught on trawl cables and drowned.

If I learned that morning about the gravity of the situation in conservation terms, I also learned about the important steps being taken to address the problem. "Above all, we have to work with the fisheries' management organizations," Papworth told me. So much depends on the willingness of the fisheries to cooperate. In the case of trawl fisheries, as for the long-line fisheries, there are technical solutions, which can make a huge difference to the survival of albatross and other seabirds. If the fishing vessel, for example, can arrange its affairs so that it separates the discard phase from the catch phase, the number of birds clustering round the stern of the fishing vessel and becoming entangled in the warps can be dramatically reduced.

While I was in Tasmania, I also talked to Graham Robertson, who works for the Australian government's Antarctic division and who for some years has been a leading figure in the effort to develop "mitigation" measures. As far as the long-line fisheries are concerned, they revolve around the way in which the hooks are baited, the rate at which the line sinks, and the effectiveness of counter-measures, such as "tori" streamers, which are designed to deter birds.

Graham Robertson believed that as far as seabed (or "demersal") fisheries were concerned, important progress had been made, at least within the framework of the Convention for the Conservation of Antarctic Marine Living Resources (CCAMLR). This is a treaty with teeth. Mitigation measures can be mandated and enforced, although the problem of illegal, unreported and unregulated fishing remains. Another problem is that albatrosses range far and wide, and certainly into latitudes where CCAMLR does not run. That is why the work of ACAP and its ability, actual or potential, to influence fisheries-management organizations is so vital.

Apart from ACAP, CCAMLR and the Australian Antarctic division, there is another major Hobart-based plank in the international effort to save the albatross: the Albatross Task Force (ATF), set up under BirdLife International's seabird programme. I had dinner one night with its coordinator, Ben Sullivan, who told me that one of the Task Force's main objectives is to increase the number of observers on fishing vessels. "The long-term solution," he said, "is not to discharge offal when you're trawling. We try to put our people on board the boats themselves. Actually, we don't call ourselves observers, we call ourselves instructors. We are two years into the programme now. We try to work with the fishing industry, but we need the support of government too."

As it happened Sullivan was leaving Hobart the next day to fly to London to attend a reception Prince Charles was hosting at Clarence House. He paid tribute to the part Prince Charles had played in launching the Task Force in 2006 – and hoped that its members would be having a special meeting with Prince Charles before the reception. They certainly deserved it, I reflected.

The day after my meeting with Sullivan, I was browsing in a Hobart bookshop when I came across a magnificent new illustrated book for which Prince Charles had written a moving introduction: "I remember so well when I was in the Royal Navy," he wrote, "standing on the deck of a fast-moving warship in one of the southern oceans, watching an albatross maintaining perfect position alongside for hour after hour, and apparently day after day. It is a sight I will never forget, and I find it unthinkable that we could extinguish them forever, never to be resurrected. But unless action is taken, that is exactly what will happen."

As Sullivan put it to me: "We have made huge progress as far as the demersal long-line fishery is concerned within the CCAMLR area. But there is still a long way to go in implementing it outside the CCAMLR's Antarctic catchment area."

Even if you do solve the problems associated with fisheries – and it's a big "if" – there are still the other threats to deal with. Gough Island, for example, a United Kingdom Overseas Territory in the South Atlantic, is home to the Tristan albatross. This species is now critically endangered, not by fishing, but by "supermice". These are ordinary house mice, which arrived on the island on sailing ships decades ago and have developed into monster rodents that burrow into the albatrosses' nests and eat the hapless chicks while they are still alive.

Since Britain's Foreign and Commonwealth Office is directly responsible for Gough Island, one can only hope someone puts a note on David Milliband's desk with an urgent sticker on it saying: Action this day!

The waved albatross in the Galápagos is also critically endangered. A couple of years ago I had a chance to visit Española Island and spent a magical morning watching the birds there. This is the only viable population of waved albatross in the world and, of course, it is one of the main attractions in the extraordinary Galápagos Archipelago. I can't help feeling that the ever-growing number of visitors to the island, however well-regulated they may be, must inevitably be having an impact.

Probably no other bird ranges so far and wide as the albatross, yet its nesting areas are few and far between, mostly on small sub-Antarctic islands. The problems of predation and disturbance can be very real.

During my time in Hobart, I also met Dr Heidi Auman, a remarkable young woman who, before coming to Australia to work with ACAP, had spent seven years on Midway Island in the Pacific Ocean. She showed us a series of slides, demonstrating the horrendous accumulation of plastic debris in the ocean and its impact on marine life.

The world's largest colony of Laysan albatross, she explained, is to be found on Midway. "The adult birds ingest the plastic accidentally while feeding out at sea, then regurgitate it to feed the chicks. The chicks can feel full, but they can be slowly starving to death."

At a meeting of the UN Convention on Migratory Species held in Rome last winter, when I was planning my trip to Tasmania, I met Barry Baker, an Australian wildlife expert who works with ACAP. "But will I actually get to see some albatross if I come to Hobart?" I asked.

I was ready to go to Tasmania to talk about albatrosses, but I wanted to meet some too! I didn't want just to speak to people in offices. I wanted to get out on the water, to catch once again the majesty of the bird in flight.

I had done my homework. I knew that there were important albatross breeding colonies on at least three small islands off the coast of Tasmania. "What about Pedra Branca and Mewstone? Can't I get there from Hobart?"

"We could get you out there in a boat all right or even a small plane," Barry replied. "You could go round the islands but you wouldn't be able to land. Even if it was physically possible, and that would depend on how rough the sea was, I don't think the authorities would allow it."

Of course, I understood what Barry was saying. Pedra Branca and Mewstone islands, off the southern coast of Tasmania, together with Albatross Island, off Tasmania's north-eastern tip, are home to the whole world population of the Shy albatross. Around 12,000 pairs nest on those rocky surfaces. They have enough to contend with as it is without having to deal with curious visitors.

In the event, I was able to get my "fix" before I finally left Tasmania. On two consecutive days, the boat guide Robert

Pennicott took me out on the Southern Ocean in one of his high-speed vessels first developed for the New Zealand Navy. The first day we set out from Bruny Island, and the second from Tasman Island. Knowing my interest in seeing albatross, in whatever shape or form, Robert ensured that we headed out on to the high seas as well as hugging the coast with its dramatic towering cliffs.

On both days, seals, dolphins, sea-eagles and gannets were among the many marine species on show. And, yes, on both days we saw albatrosses too: both Shy albatrosses, their breeding ground close at hand, and Buller's albatross, whose breeding ground is in New Zealand's sub-Antarctic islands. Yet again, I was transfixed by the sheer beauty of these birds as they skimmed and soared, swooped and banked above the waves.

Pennicott's vessels have powerful engines. I suspect they could hit 50 or 60mph if they tried. Once, just for the hell of it, he turned up the throttle and, for a moment, we drew alongside one of the great birds as it dipped down towards the crest of a wave. Then it nonchalantly gave a slow beat of its wings and accelerated away from us into the distance. We didn't stand a hope of catching up with it ... even if we had wanted to.

First published in the *Independent*, 11 April 2009

27

Gorilla-Watching in the Congo

In Mbeli Bai, a 15-hectare clearing in the heart of the Republic of Congo's equatorial rainforest, the New York based Wildlife Conservation Society (which runs the Bronx and Central Park zoos) has been studying the life and habits of some 135 western lowland gorillas who visit the *bai*, or marshy clearing.

For the past fifteen years, for up to ten hours a day, WCS scientists have been watching and recording what happens on this expanse of green swampy vegetation. They know every gorilla by sight and by name. The insights they have gained into the behaviour and social structure of these amazing animals are pathbreaking in scientific terms.

As Thomas Breuer, the German scientist leading the WCS team at Mbeli, told me over a beer in camp one evening: "The *bai*, as you will have seen, has large deep pools of water among the swampy ground. One day I saw a female gorilla leave her baby behind at the edge of the pool while she went off to look for a stick to test the depth of water." Breuer's was the first ever report of tool use by wild gorillas.

What's truly special here is that the scientists open up their mirador – the observation deck at the edge of the *bai* – to visitors, and share their knowledge of the gorillas with those who come here.

I do not wish to diminish the thrill of trekking gorillas in Rwanda or Uganda or even in the eastern Congo (Democratic Republic of the Congo). But the special excitement of watching gorillas in Mbeli Bai in Congo Brazzaville is that these animals are unaware of observers. They are not "habituated", used to the close presence of tourists or researchers. At Mbeli Bai you are looking at one of the world's most extraordinary animals without any distorting filter.

The other reason I found gorilla-watching at Mbeli Bai – in the Nouabalé-Ndoki National Park – so satisfying was that there was no sense of the pressure of time. Most organized gorilla trekking gives you an hour with the gorillas (if you are lucky enough to find them) and when that hour is up, you head back to camp. At Mbeli Bai, you have all day. At 8am on our first morning, we climbed up the steps of the mirador to find a group of gorillas already there. "That's Khan's group," Breuer told us before disappearing to his look-out station on the roof.

I looked Khan up in the handy catalogue. "Khan is an extremely large-bodied silverback with an enormous crest and monstrous neck muscle. Khan has tiny eyes, pointed ears and a large scar on the left part of his upper lip. His nostrils are large and pointed. Date of birth unknown."

As I watched the mighty animal, seated on his haunches less than 180m away, I reflected that the WCS catalogue entry was apt. If ever there was an example of raw, concentrated power, this was it.

There were ten gorillas in the *bai* that first morning. Besides the great silverback, there were three adult females, two with infants, and a smattering of immatures and juveniles. Khan's group did not return during the rest of our time at Mbeli Bai. But on each of the three subsequent days, we saw a different group of gorillas, each with its own silverback leader. We saw almost fifty gorillas over four days.

Mbeli Bai is remote. From Brazzaville, the capital, there is an hour's flight to Ouesso, followed by a five-hour ride in a motorized pirogue (dug-out canoe) to WCS headquarters at Bomassa. We were still on the river, with an hour of daylight left, when it began to rain. It rained harder and longer than I would have believed possible. When we finally disembarked, stiff and tired and soaked to the skin, we found that all the spare clothes we had were wringing wet – and didn't dry out for days.

In camp, our guide told us "this is no country for sissies". The insects are also a problem. Each morning before we set off through the forest to the *bai*, he would intone: "Let us spray!" On the return journey, we found that our plane to Brazzaville had been cancelled and we were twenty-four hours late returning to the capital, so I missed my flight back to England.

But these are just the hazards of travelling in the Congo Basin. The great rainforests of central and western Africa contain one of the richest stores of biodiversity on earth, not least in the form of the Western Lowland gorilla which, in spite of the ravages of the Ebola virus, poachers and loggers, still exists in substantial numbers (possibly in the tens of thousands) in these regions. If ever there was a journey where the rewards far more than outweigh the hardships, the trip to Mbeli Bai is it.

First published in the *Financial Times*, 16 May 2009

28

See Kenya by Balloon Safari:
The Greatest Wildlife Show on Earth

As they pumped hot air into the giant balloon, its dark shape swelled against the lightening sky.

The first rays of sunlight caught the top of the balloon, just as a full moon was dropping behind the plateau that bounds the western edge of the Mara Triangle – the north-western part of Kenya's Masai Mara game reserve.

Our pilot that morning was an American, Mike McGrath. He came from Chicago to visit the Masai Mara in 1988 and has stayed in Kenya ever since.

He works for a company called Skyship, which proudly boasts it can treat you to the "greatest wildlife show on earth" by taking you on an early-morning flight in a balloon over the plains.

I am sure the bold assertion is right. If you are lucky enough to be in the Mara when the migrating animals are there – the exact timing depends on the rains – make sure you build the balloon ride into your safari. It's an unbeatable experience.

As you rise into the air, you gaze down at the vast expanse of plain. As far as you can see, indeed right up to the Serengeti itself on the other side of the Tanzanian border, the grassy plains are black with animals.

The sheer numbers are mind-boggling: more than a million and a half wildebeest or gnus, half a million zebra, another half-million topis, eland and Thompson's gazelle.

With the sun behind us, the balloon cast a great shadow on the plains as we passed 50–100ft overhead. When the pilot fired the burner, the whoosh of igniting flame often caused a mini-stampede.

Standing in the balloon's basket, we could hear the thunder of hooves and the squeals and rumbles of the herd.

As we floated downwind, we seemed to open up a path in the sea of animals below, like Moses parting the waters of the Red Sea.

Normally, a balloon ride in the Mara can last up to an hour. Seeing how fast our shadow was travelling across the plains, I couldn't help realizing that we must have caught the wind.

"How fast are we travelling?" I asked Mike.

"Around 40 miles an hour," he replied. "Actually, we are making pretty good time this morning. In another minute or two we could be crossing the border into Tanzania, which isn't a good idea. They're not very keen on unannounced visitors."

After that, things happened very quickly. "Sit down in the basket and hold on to the ropes!" Mike shouted. "Watch out for the bump!"

I'd barely had time to clench my buttocks before the basket hit the ground with a mighty thwack. That wasn't the end of it. We bounced hard and high, two or three times, before our craft finally came to a stop and we were able to crawl out on to terra firma.

Later, when the safari trucks had caught up with us and we were sitting around a long trestle table enjoying a champagne breakfast, Mike made light of the experience.

"One time," he said, "when we were being dragged along in the basket, we scooped up a 10ft python. Another time, we picked up the rotting carcass of a wildebeest."

Of course, he sounded nonchalant, but I could tell that he'd had his work cut out that morning. "I would have given you guys more warning," he half-apologized, "but frankly I was too busy trying to spill the air from the balloon."

If that balloon ride was the first unforgettable feature of my four days in the Mara, the second was the extraordinary sight of wildebeest and zebra crossing the Mara River in the teeth of a small army of waiting crocodiles.

As far as timing goes, we were extremely lucky. My guide, Abdul Karim, told me that people can sometimes wait for nine hours for the animals to cross.

"The water is very low this year. The crocodiles are easy to see in the water so the animals turn back," he explained. "They crowd on the bank but just won't go in." I almost found myself feeling sorry for the crocodiles.

The previous night we had stayed in a tented camp near the Tanzanian border. We were working our way back up north and were within striking distance of the river below the Mara Serena Lodge when Abdul, our driver as well as our guide, exclaimed: "The animals are crossing."

We must at that moment have been two or three miles from the river. The ground sloped down in front of us to the edge of the water and rose up again on the other side. On the distant slopes, Abdul had seen the animals massing. A cloud of dust rose from thousands of hooves.

On our side of the river, a dozen vehicles had already arrived. As Abdul nudged our Toyota Land Cruiser into a splendid vantage point almost directly above the crossing, we saw a crocodile lunge at the hind leg of a wildebeest as it splashed, panic-stricken, through the water.

The croc failed to get a good grasp of its prey and the wildebeest wrenched itself free to make a dash for the safety of our bank.

After that, there was a lull in the action. On the far side of the river, we could see the animals – led, it seemed, by the zebras – coming down to the water, even taking a step or two across the rocks, then catching sight of the crocodiles and withdrawing to the safety of the bank, only to be jostled and harried by other animals hoping to cross.

Oddly enough, it was a lone zebra that broke the deadlock. By now, half a dozen crocodiles were almost directly in the path of the migrating animals. With water levels so low, we could see virtually the whole length, breadth and height of the massive reptiles. If we could see them from where we were, the migrants certainly could.

But the lone zebra seemed to have thought it out. He didn't try to dash past or even – heroically, on quick and dancing feet – over the crocodiles. Instead, he went downstream, round the back of them. An end-run, if ever there was one. Out of danger, he scampered up the bank.

That splendid solo effort was the signal for a sudden rush of animals. They came thick and fast – so thick and so fast that it seemed that even the huge, snapping jaws of the crocodiles were going to miss their mark.

The death we witnessed that morning by the Mara River had almost a balletic quality to it.

This might be nature red in tooth and claw, but still there was a terrible beauty about the way one crocodile managed to seize a young zebra, catching it by its throat, while three or four other crocodiles – hungry giants, all of them – swivelled into action in a stunning display of teamwork.

Within a minute they had forced the whole zebra under water. With the reptiles now otherwise occupied, the way was clear for a mass crossing to take place.

Sitting in our Land Cruiser, Abdul and I and my friend Toby Fenwick-Wilson, formerly one of Africa's top guides who is now in charge of Sanctuary's lodges in East Africa, found time to reflect on the noble sacrifice we had just witnessed.

"One zebra has died," Toby explained, "but in the meantime, hundreds, perhaps thousands, have made it to the other side."

"And what is that zebra's heavenly reward?" I asked. "Seventy-two virgin zebras?"

Abdul, who is a Muslim and who missed out on most of the meals including the champagne breakfast (it was still Ramadan while I was there), seemed to enjoy that one.

The great migration is, of course, the most spectacular attraction of the Masai Mara, which extends over 153,000 hectares. Its inner core of 64,500 hectares is designated a National Reserve.

But leaving aside the wildlife, the Mara has everything else you could wish for. I stayed at the beautiful Sanctuary Olonana tented camp, perched on the bank of the Mara River, with a small pod of hippopotamus grunting and dousing only a few yards away.

I saw elephants, giraffes, lions and baboons by the score. And, on one excursion, a male leopard stalking a warthog. We had to get back to camp before the gates closed, so missed the denouement.

If birds grab you more than mammals, the Mara is rich indeed. Eagles, vultures, herons, kingfishers, plovers, wheatears – the Mara has them all. And if you have a guide as good as Abdul, you'll learn quickly how to tell a hawk from a handsaw.

What makes the Mara so special, of course, is that it is not a reserve that operates against the interests of the local Masai people. On the contrary, the inner National Reserve is itself divided into two parts: one third is run by the Trans-Mara Town Council and two thirds by Narok Town Council.

It is not a question, I was assured, of badly needed tourist dollars being siphoned off wholesale to Mr Big in Nairobi with no trickle-down effect for the locals.

On my last day, Toby, Abdul and I paid a visit to a Masai village. I was greeted by a delegation of the women, who decked me out in traditional beads and sang songs of welcome.

We stooped low to enter their huts, bought some carved animals, and watched a Masai fire-maker coax a flame from a piece of wood he twirled between his hands.

Trite, of course. Horribly trite. But if the Masai have bought in to the idea of the reserve (and they seem to have done), it is largely because of the very real economic benefits the tourist trade brings them.

I am sure there are eco-activists in London NW1 who will throw up their hands in horror at the thought of my balloon ride, at least in terms of its impact on global warming and so on.

But believe me, without tourists like me, the Masai will begin to question what is the real value, to them or indeed to anyone else, of one million wildebeest and half a million zebra.

The herds of Masai cattle are there, just outside the reserve, longing to leap across from the parched pastures of the villages on to the lush grasses of the Mara. You see them from the air in the little plane back to Nairobi.

The eco-activists, the "socially aware" non-governmental organizations, might argue that even if the Mara is lost, there is always the Serengeti to fall back on.

Well, I'm afraid nothing could be further from the truth. This is one colossal ecosystem. If the Mara goes, the Serengeti goes too. As the song goes, you can't have one without the other.

So I am proud to have taken that wonderful balloon flight, even if we did have a hairy landing. It helped to make my brief trip to the Masai Mara one of the most amazing experiences of my life.

First published in the *Mail on Sunday*,
Sunday 27 September 2009

29

Rescued by HMS *Albion*
and Home by Sunset

HMS *Albion* approached Portsmouth Harbour last night in time for the sunset. We could see people waving from the rooftop terraces as the great ship drew near to the quay to tie up virtually next door to HMS *Victory*, Nelson's flagship. Helicopters buzzed overhead.

My wife Jenny and I were in the crowded bow of the ship watching the proceedings with most of our fellow evacuees when my mobile phone rang. "Is that Mr Johnson? This is BBC News. Where are you standing? If you look at the helicopter overhead and wave your arms, we ought to be able to pick you out."

It was the end of a journey that began on Thursday last week in the Galápagos Islands. Jenny and I had been travelling there when we heard the news that a volcano in Iceland had erupted. We were booked to fly from Ecuador on an Air Iberia flight to Madrid. The Spanish airline was still flying.

"Do you have a plan for when we get to Madrid?" Jenny asked me.

"Not as such," I replied.

There were already several hundred people queuing at the Air Iberia information desk when we arrived in Madrid after our ten-hour flight from South America. Spain had become a magnet for travellers from all over the world, desperate to set foot on the continent of Europe. They had come from America, Asia, Africa, even Australia.

Trains to Paris were fully booked for days, we were told. If you tried to hire a car, you might have to pay thousands of euros. For returning UK citizens, the dilemma was particularly acute. Even if

– miraculously – you made it to the Channel ports, you still had to cross the Channel itself. Or you could stick around in Madrid and wait for the skies to open again.

We made a quick calculation. Just to get in front of the harried official at the information desk would, we reckoned, take at least a day or two at the rate the queue was moving. So we headed for Madrid's central bus station instead.

"*Vamonos*!" I urged the taxi-driver.

There were two seats left on the 4.30pm bus to Santander, in the north of Spain. Our great good fortune was to find five fellow Brits seated near us at the back of the bus. Janet and Rosemary, making their way back to Britain overland from Morocco, had teamed up with Andrew doing much the same. Kelly and Scott had attached themselves somewhere along the line to form a nucleus of five.I wouldn't say that any of the group was particularly sanguine about the chances of making progress. BlackBerries and iPhones blipped and bleeped. As our bus cruised along the Autovía, suggestions came in from all sides.

"The best hope," Janet said, "may be Brittany Ferries. It looks as though they may be taking bookings for Thursday."

Thursday! That didn't sound too bad. After all, it was almost Tuesday already.

"Thursday 29 April, I mean," Janet sighed.

One intriguing gobbet of information emerged on the journey. Scott had a military background with the elite Pathfinders. He had already served two tours in Afghanistan and was due to rejoin his unit within days.

"I just heard," he told us, "that they may be sending HMS *Albion* to Santander to pick up some of our soldiers returning from Afghanistan."

Our spirits rose. Suddenly, our mad dash onto the bus seemed to make sense. If they were going to pick up British soldiers in Santander and carry them back home to Blighty, maybe they would have room for a few civilians as well. Our bus rolled into Santander at around 10pm. As we drove along the quayside, we looked out for

HMS *Albion*. The consensus among our little core group was that if HMS *Albion* had already arrived in Santander, the ship should be easy enough to spot.

Next morning, as our taxi drove down the Avenida de la Reina Victoria towards the dock, we saw a grey shape looking enormous against the still handsome Santander waterfront. The vessel was so vast that it dwarfed all the other traffic on the water. As we got closer, we saw men and women in camouflage uniform on the deck. The HMS *Albion* had indeed arrived! Our boys and girls were already on board!

We jumped out of the cab, hauling our luggage with us to the dock gates. There must, I suppose, have been fifty or sixty Brits there that morning, all hoping against hope that somehow room would be found for us too, in addition to the two hundred or so people who were being brought up from Madrid under the auspices of the British Embassy there. And I was on board!

Soon after HMS *Albion* had put out from Santander into the Bay of Biscay, I found myself being invited to tea by Commander John Gardner, the executive officer in charge.

I told him that, as we stuck our nose through the closed gates on the Santander quayside, we had been afraid that we would be left behind. Commander Gardner said masterfully: "I was not prepared to leave any Brits on the jetty if I could possibly help it."

The maximum number of people the *Albion* is meant to carry is 1,150. With 489 military personnel to be taken on board, and with the ship's own complement of 375, the scope for "others", such as ourselves, to be "rescued" was well defined. In the event, the *Albion* sailed with exactly 1,150 souls.

When, later that afternoon, I walked round the vehicle deck with Commander Gardner on a tour of the ship, I found myself talking to two captains from the Army Medical Corps. If the journey my wife and I had made to get to Santander had been long and eventful, theirs had been doubly so.

"We left Camp Bastion on Monday," Capt Katie Miéville told me, "to fly to Kandahar. Then on Wednesday we flew to Cyprus to wind down for a few hours. Thursday morning we took off from Akrotiri for Brize Norton, only to be turned back an hour and a half into the flight. We took off again yesterday for Zaragoza in southern Spain, then were bussed up to Santander, arriving after midnight."

I feel humbled to have been involved in whatever small way with this great ship at this time. We were unexpected guests, yet everyone on board treated us with astonishing warmth and courtesy. If you said "loos" when you meant "heads", they didn't make a meal of it. If you didn't grasp the geography of the ship at first sight (with no less than fourteen decks it is easy to end up in the wrong place), there was always someone to set you straight.

If the volcano cloud had made life difficult for people like my wife and me, spare a thought for our soldiers in Afghanistan. Outside the sick bay, I talked to the doctor in charge. "The aeromed chain," he told me, "had been severely disrupted because of the volcano. If we couldn't have flown gravely injured personnel back to Britain, we would have had to send them to the States." The news that the flying restrictions had been lifted gravely mattered in this case.

Minutes later, the sun set over Portsmouth harbour. The last command Jenny and I heard before we went down to pack our bags, broadcast over the Tannoy, was: "ATTENTION UPPER DECK! FACE AFT AND SALUTE THE SUNSET!"

I am not sure whether my wife and I were really among the intended targets of this broadcast instruction but we heeded it anyway, snapping to attention with a crisp salute. As a way of showing our gratitude to the Royal Navy, to the ship's company, to the soldiers who travelled with us, to the diplomats who helped organize this "mini-Dunkirk", and – last but not least – to our lively and good-humoured fellow-evacuees whose experiences may have been every bit as dramatic as ours, that symbolic salute seemed the very least we could do.

First published in the London *Evening Standard*, 22 April 2010

30

Me Stanley, You Jane

There are at least two good reasons for going to Kigoma, a dusty Tanzanian town situated on the eastern side of Lake Tanganyika, about 25 miles south of the Burundi border. First, it was here, on 10 November 1871, that Henry Morton Stanley famously met David Livingstone. A mud-hut museum in nearby Ujiji contains a larger-than-life plaster of Paris model of the two men and other flyblown memorabilia. Second, Kigoma is the jumping-off point for the amazing Gombe National Park, where, in 1960, at the age of twenty-six, Dr Jane Goodall first began to study the behaviour of chimpanzees in the wild. She was sent there by Dr Louis Leakey, the renowned palaeontologist, who spotted her potential. "He watched me, he saw how I behaved with animals, he realized that I didn't care two hoots about the things that lots of girls care about – clothes, hairdressing. He saw I was very tough and I could make do with very simple things: every day we had just one cupful of water for washing. He also realized I had an absolute passion for animals."

Fifty years on, it's hard to think of any long-term wildlife research that has achieved such great recognition. The fact that chimpanzees are our closest living relatives, sharing 99 per cent of our DNA, has made insights into their behaviour and social structures especially relevant. "They can be loving and compassionate, and yet they have a dark side," Jane has said.

Goodall has been criticized by the scientific establishment for giving the chimps names, not numbers; for distorting their behaviour by feeding them bananas; and indeed for having no scientific training. Her fans, however, argue that it was her fresh approach and empathy that enabled her to make new discoveries in the field. "There's no sharp line dividing us from the rest of the animal kingdom," she maintains. It was she who learnt that chimpanzees not only use tools but also make them, for instance, stripping twigs to "fish" for termites. This challenged many scientists' belief that we humans are unique in our tool-making abilities.

I have seen chimpanzees in the wild in Kibale, in Uganda, and in the Ngamba Island sanctuary on Lake Victoria. But for me Gombe has long been a kind of Mecca. To track Jane Goodall down was no mean feat. She travels for more than 300 days a year, campaigning for conservation. So when I learnt that she was to visit Gombe, I asked to meet her there.

I flew into Dar es Salaam, and after a night's recuperation at the magnificent Kilimanjaro Hotel Kempinski, I continued on to Kigoma. And finally, there she was, on the veranda of the Jane Goodall Institute (JGI) headquarters. "Stanley, I presume?" she joked. Then she gave me a great bear hug and invited me in for a cup of tea.

Anyone who has read Jane's books, particularly *In the Shadow of Man*, her account of her early years at Gombe, will know how she first came here. But to hear her retell the tale right there at Gombe made it especially piquant.

Brought up in Bournemouth after her parents' divorce, Jane left school at eighteen, took a secretarial course and a couple of different jobs, before jumping at the chance to stay at a schoolfriend's parents' farm in Kenya. There, in Nairobi, she met Dr Leakey, who was the curator of what is now the Nairobi National Museum, and was offered, with one other girl, the opportunity to accompany Leakey and his wife, Mary, on one of their annual palaeontological expeditions to Olduvai Gorge in the Serengeti plains.

It was Leakey who told Jane about a chimpanzee population at Gombe, suggesting that she might undertake an unprecedented study of them in the wild. In those days before women's liberation, the proposal must have been highly unusual. The (then colonial) authorities certainly felt so. They were not happy about an unaccompanied white woman camping for months in the bush. But Jane had wanted to live with animals since reading the *Tarzan* books as a child, and she had the support of her mother, Vanne, who told her: "If you work hard and really want something and never give up, you'll find a way."

"Louis Leakey helped find the funds to finance my first field work," Jane recalled. "But the authorities wouldn't let me set up camp on my own." Fortunately, Vanne was able to come with her. Her presence at Gombe during Jane's first stint in 1960 was absolutely central. Vanne helped out in many ways, looking after the camp while Jane was in the hills, running a clinic for nearby villagers, above all just being there. "I still have some of my mother's ashes in a dried-milk tin at the camp," Jane confided. "I'm planning to scatter them in her favourite places at Gombe."

We journeyed across the lake to Gombe itself, joined by a guide, Bernard Gichobi, and by Dr Anthony Collins, a director of her institute, who has worked with Jane since the 1970s, but still manages to look after his wife and family in north London. "It's hard," he confessed as the boat got underway, "but somehow, after so many years, I feel more at home here than in England."

Lake Tanganyika is the second deepest lake in the world, containing 17 per cent of the world's fresh surface water. It is bounded to the west by the Democratic Republic of the Congo. Over the years there have been frequent incursions, even invasions, by refugees both from the Congo and from Burundi. The signs of population pressure are obvious: hillsides denuded of vegetation; dramatic gullies where the exposed soil has been eroded from the hills in heavy rains. At the boundary of the park, however, the change is dramatic. At last you see the luxuriant sweep of trees that you expect of a tropical rainforest.

Jane and Anthony were to stay in the house Jane and her first husband, the photographer Hugo van Lawick, built in the early

1970s. They divorced, and in 1975 she married Derek Bryceson, a former RAF hero and director of Tanzania's national parks. Five years later, he died of cancer, a tragedy that is still raw.

I was staying a few kilometres away in the Gombe Forest Lodge, a privately run tented camp. Jane and Anthony came up there in the boat. After sunset, we lit a fire on the beach and opened a bottle of whisky. We looked out over the flat-calm surface of the lake to the lights of a line of fishing boats, extending as far as the eye could see, and I found myself thinking about the ripple effect of the Jane Goodall phenomenon. The importance of Jane's research certainly helped to ensure Gombe's designation in 1968 as a national park. This in turn increased the protection not just for Gombe's chimpanzee population, but for other denizens of the forest – baboons, monkeys, egrets, herons, eagles, vultures – and, crucially, for the forest itself.

Last December Jane was in Denmark at the Climate Change Summit. "A lot of things went wrong in Copenhagen – or didn't come right – but I think everyone recognized how vital the forests are. I was with Chief Almir of the Surui tribe from Amazonian Brazil. We were part of the South-South Initiative, which trains indigenous and local people to monitor their forests using Google Android cell-phones. This information goes straight up to a satellite. It will enable them to prove they are indeed protecting their forests and thereby qualify for international assistance."

What an extraordinary journey it has been for her! The twenty-six year old dragging up her boat on to the shore, with "one ex-army tent, one pair of lousy binoculars and a couple of tin mugs and plates", has turned into a star of the international circuit. Hectic as her life now is, she doesn't want to be known simply as "the chimpanzee lady". In 2002, Kofi Annan, the then secretary-general of the UN, appointed her, with other notable personalities, as a Messenger of Peace. She told me: "I was the only one who actually showed up in New York for the ceremony."

As the whisky bottle went round again, Jane remembered the moment in May 1975 when the Congo exploded into their lives.

"It was the middle of the night. The kidnappers came in by boat, parked on the beach down there" – she waved towards the spot. "They grabbed four of the students. They sent one of them back almost at once with a message. The parents came out. I think money was paid, because the next two were released. I think the figure was $250,000. But the fourth didn't come back for some time."

She was evidently deeply marked by that event. In practical terms, it meant she had to give up full-time residence at Gombe. "We had to go: the authorities wouldn't let us stay." But even without the abductions, one wonders how long Jane and Hugo could have remained. Kidnappers were not the only menace. They had a son, Grub, to bring up, and Gombe is not safe for an infant. Jane had noted early on that chimpanzees were omnivores. She showed me "Grub's cage": a wire-netting enclosure, it was designed to protect the boy, but was not a long-term solution.

Later, Anthony was to tell me how Frodo, a male chimpanzee, once grabbed, killed and partially ate a village woman's child.

Next day, I took a trek up through the Gombe hills to find a group of chimpanzees located by trackers earlier that morning. "That's Freud," Anthony told me. "He used to be the alpha male, but he's been supplanted by Ferdinand. And here comes Frodo, watch out!" I had put my backpack on the ground and Frodo was out to get it. He had also been an alpha male and was now making a bit of a comeback.

A mother and daughter chased each other around a tree. Groups of chimpanzees called to each other across the clearing, "pant-hooting". The alpha male shook the trees and the females submitted to his will. "If they don't come at once," said Anthony, "Ferdinand will beat them up."

When we met up with Jane, we gave her a full account of the day's events. The last chimpanzee of those she first met in 1960 died three years ago, so she has known all 106 of the current Gombe chimpanzees since their birth. Her thinking about her extended family has evolved over the years. If she ever idealized them, she has moved on. She has witnessed terrible internecine fighting, as one group all but obliterated another. She watched a deadly rampage as one female took her daughter on a killing spree, murdering and devouring any infant chimpanzees they came across.

When we told her that Frodo had charged my backpack, she shook her head. "I'm afraid to go out now if Frodo's around. He makes a beeline for me and tries to knock me down. He almost killed me once, dragging me to the edge of a cliff and pushing me over. Mind you, I think he knew there were trees that would block my fall."

Despite such fears for her safety, even today she insists on walking the hills alone, hour after hour. I remarked that nobody wants to hear on the news that she is dead. She smiled. "It would be quite a story, wouldn't it? I wonder what it would do for the cause of conservation, 'Jane Goodall killed by chimpanzee!'"

It would be more than a personal tragedy. Goodall is still desperately needed, not just in Tanzania, but in the wider world. While we were in Gombe, the US announced a grant of $5.5m to her institute, to support community development in more than a score of villages, extensive forest regeneration and corridors linking Gombe with other areas with important wildlife populations including chimpanzees. The new grant is intended to build on, and to expand, JGI's programme of community-based conservation, known as Tacare (Take care: Lake Tanganyika Catchment Reforestation and Education).

"It has changed the attitude of every village around Gombe," Jane said. Local people are eager to protect the animals they now view as "their" chimpanzees from the bushmeat trade.

The culmination of her life's work lies in mobilizing rising generations. Twenty-one years ago, sitting with young Tanzanians on the terrace of her house in Dar es Salaam, she conceived the idea of the Roots and Shoots programme, aimed at encouraging children all over the world to develop their own clubs and associated projects. Today it has a network of tens of thousands of participants in more than 100 countries. And she continues to campaign with evangelical zeal.

That night at dinner, she said: "Think of the most beautiful tree you know. Then think of how that tree began. When little shoots try to reach the sunlight, they can break through the cracks in the wall. Actually, they can bring the wall down."

We all knew what Dr Jane Goodall DBE meant. We raised our glasses. "Happy fiftieth anniversary, Jane," we chorused.

First published in the *Sunday Times Magazine*, 23 May 2010

31

Return to Machu Picchu

My wife and I originally planned to travel to Peru in February this year, a journey that had to be postponed owing to the floods and landslides in the Andes. Sections of the railway linking Cusco to Machu Picchu had been washed away. Since there was – and is – no road into Machu Picchu, thousands of tourists had to be evacuated by helicopter. When Jenny and I finally left England for Peru, at the end of March, Machu Picchu had not yet officially reopened for business. But we planned to spend a few days in the Amazon region first.

If you have time, take a detour – as we did – to Puerto Maldonado, the pampered approach to the Inca trail. If you don't have time, make time. We spent four days at Inkaterra's amazing Reserva Amazonica, a jungle eco-lodge on the Madre de Dios River about 9 miles downstream of Puerto Maldonado, near the border with Brazil. The lodge offers a full range of tropical forest experiences – day and night-time expeditions into the jungle – as well as the longest canopy walkway I have ever been on. From a height of 90ft you find yourself looking down on the monkeys in the trees. While we were in the forest, word came through that the vital sections of the railway track had been reopened. So we flew from Puerto Maldonado to Cusco, staying once again at another magnificent Inkaterra hotel, La Casona, an elegant colonial building next to the museum of pre-Columbian art and a stone's throw from the main square.

As we checked in that evening, I couldn't help remembering the last time I had visited Cusco and the Sacred Valley. It was,

I realized, almost exactly fifty-one years ago. In May 1959, I was halfway through my gap year (though that phrase had yet to be coined) and walking down Bishopsgate, in the heart of the City of London, when I noticed a discreet bronze plaque outside a building. It read: "H. Clarkson, Brazil (Shipping) Ltd." I entered the building and asked to see the managing director.

"The MD's in a meeting," I was told.

"Don't worry. I can wait." I made it clear that I would wait till October if I had to, since the Oxford term didn't start till then.

Eventually, when I met the MD, he told me rather gruffly to write down what I wanted and leave the letter with his secretary. So I wrote: "Dear Mr Glen, I would like to work my passage to Brazil on one of your boats. Yours sincerely, Stanley Johnson." The secretary suggested I should put "ships" instead of "boats".

A few days later the MD sent me a letter telling me that I wouldn't be able to work my passage. Instead he offered me the owner's cabin on an iron-ore carrier bound for Brazil provided I was ready to pay a nominal "victualling" charge of £1 a day.

That trip to South America remains a high point in a lifetime of travel. And the culmination of a memorable journey was the visit to Machu Picchu, that magnificent Inca site in the Peruvian Andes, at a time when, as a tourist destination, it was still virtually unknown.

It is strange how chance encounters can shape one's life. Drinking a caipirinha one day in a bar on Copacabana Beach in Rio de Janeiro, I ran into a young man who told me that if I had time to spare I should really "do the Incas".

"But the Incas," I protested, "are in Peru, aren't they – the other side of the continent?"

That was about all I knew then about the Incas. I didn't know about the great wealth of archaeological treasures in and around Cusco and the neighbouring regions. I don't think I had even heard of Hiram Bingham, the American professor-turned-explorer who in July 1911 "discovered" Machu Picchu in the high jungle of the Peruvian Andes and named it, unforgettably, the "Lost City of the Incas".

But I heard enough that night in Rio to know that Peru was where I wanted to go. A few days later, I boarded a little wood-burning steam train that chugged its way across the heart of the Mato Grosso in Brazil to Corumbá, on the Bolivian border. I hitched a ride on a Bolivian military plane from Santa Cruz to La Paz, then took a local bus up on to the Altiplano, the great grassy plains surrounded by ice-covered mountain peaks, home to great herds of llamas, alpaca and vicuña. I crossed Lake Titicaca, the world's largest high-altitude body of water, into Peru and took another local train from Puno to Cusco.

Nowadays, of course, Cusco, the former capital of the Inca empire, is recognized not only as the jumping-off point for the visit to Machu Picchu but as an extraordinary cultural and architectural treasure in its own right. When the conquering Spaniards demolished its monuments and temples in the 16th century they used the stones to build the cathedral, churches, monasteries, convents and other structures of the present-day city. The mighty Inca ruins of Sacsayhuamán, which I visited in 1959, today still dominate the skyline above the town. The Incas moved boulders weighing 80 or even 100 tonnes into position, building great Cyclopean walls, which because of the system of interlocking stones have been virtually earthquake-proof where other structures have collapsed.

I spent only a night or two in Cusco in 1959 before taking a steam train down through the Sacred Valley, following the Urubamba River, to Machu Picchu. I was the only foreigner, indeed the only tourist, as far as I could see. I was surrounded by peasants carrying livestock and other produce to the market. I must have broken the journey at some point, because among my old photographs I have a picture of my younger, thinner self, perched on the terraced hillside at Pisac, another Inca wonder.

Fifty-one years later, Jenny and I were not able to repeat exactly the itinerary of my gap year travels. Because of the recent floods and landslides in the Peruvian Andes, we couldn't board the train until the wayside stop of Piscacucho, a long way down the Sacred

Valley. Piscacucho is, in fact, only 17 miles from Machu Picchu, which is located at the end of the Sacred Valley, but it seemed much farther.

The Urubamba River that day was still in spate, spraying the embankment with foam and debris; the track was still fragile, in some places visibly crumbling, and the driver understandably proceeded with caution. We took well over an hour to cover the distance. I would not have had it otherwise. If you look down, as the train winds its way slowly through the mountains, you can see the foaming river, only a few feet below. If you look up, through the glass panels in the roof of the carriage, you can see the mountain peaks and the circling hawks.

In 1959, I was the only tourist on the train. In April, when my wife and I went there, all the compartments were packed, with passengers being limited to hand luggage. And the little station that serves Machu Picchu has itself been transformed. From my earlier visit, I remembered a tiny wayside stop, where you disembarked to climb up to the citadel. Today, the town (known as Aguas Calientes or Machu Picchu Pueblo) has more than 2,000 people. I can't recall where I spent the night when I first went there but, since I was travelling on a shoestring, I am sure it was a fleapit hostel. Today you can stay in splendour at the five-star Inkaterra hotel on the edge of town or in the Sanctuary Lodge Hotel right outside the entrance to the archaeological site.

In 1959, there weren't any other tourists in Machu Picchu. I look at my old photographs and I cannot see a single human being. Today, if you stand on Machu Picchu ("Old Mountain") and take a wide-angle shot of the ruins with Huayna Picchu ("Young Peak") as a backdrop, you will on an average day find scores, if not hundreds, of tourists in view.

If there weren't any tourists in 1959, there weren't any tourist guides, either. Looking back I rather regret that. We certainly benefited from having a knowledgeable escort this time around.

At the end of our first morning in Machu Picchu, we found ourselves standing in front of a tall circular structure with three trapeze-shaped window openings looking out to the east.

"This is the Sun Temple," our guide, Ivanov, told us. "At precisely 7.22 on the morning of the winter solstice [21 June], the sun will shine through the central window to illuminate that huge white granite rock."

I knew from my photo album that I had seen precisely the same structure in 1959, without understanding the astronomical significance.

I suggested to Ivanov that if the Incas had been anything like the Aztecs they would have marked the occasion with a sacrificial victim or two. Ivanov shook his head.

"We don't find any evidence of human sacrifice at Machu Picchu. At Cusco, however, there is such evidence. It was regarded as a great privilege to be chosen as a sacrificial victim. Upper-class families competed for the honour!"

We learnt such a lot that day. Ivanov told us, for example, that the alignment of the great Inca towns reflected iconic images of Andean wildlife. Cusco, he told us, is designed in the shape of a puma and "the Incas built their great citadel of Machu Picchu in the shape of a giant condor so that, at death, they could fly to the Milky Way".

Later that day, we met a party of British hikers who had completed the arduous Inca Trail, hiking for four days through the mountains to reach Machu Picchu. I took out my notebook and accosted one of the walkers.

"Hello," I said. "I'm from the *Daily Telegraph*."

She told me that her name was Maxine Heasman and that she worked in a civilian capacity for the police in Esher, Surrey. Completing the Inca Trail had been an exhilarating experience. Hard work, too. "At times I have been in tears," she said. "It was the hardest thing mentally and physically I have ever done. No amount of advice before you leave England can prepare you for it."

Our guide left us after lunch to return to Cusco. Jenny and I spent the afternoon walking around the ruins. As the early crowds dispersed, I found myself reliving the grandeur, mystery and excitement of the place I had known in my younger days. In the whole world, there is nothing quite like Machu Picchu. Even 5,000 tourists a day can't change that.

Will I go back again? You bet I will. I have promised myself that, some time before that giant condor flies me off to the Milky Way, I will return. With any luck, I will still be fit enough to hike through the mountains along the Inca Trail, and sleep under the stars.

First published in the *Daily Telegraph*, 12 June 2010

32

Endangered Spaces: Can Our Wildest Places Survive Tourism?

Eco-tourism – is this now fashionable concept basically a contradiction in terms – on a par, as cynics might say, with "business ethics" or "compassionate conservatism"? "Adventure travel" is, of course, a concept as old as the hills, even if some of our greatest adventurers, such as Captain Scott, took great pains to proclaim their serious scientific purposes.

Nowadays, much "adventure travel" is given a deliberately green tinge. Organizations like Earthwatch send young (and increasingly frequently old) people to the four corners of the earth to study and protect endangered wildlife of every sort and, yes, to enjoy themselves in doing so.

But just how realistic is it to imagine that increasing numbers of people can visit the wild places of the earth, and the animals, trees and plants that live there, without destroying them? Oscar Wilde famously wrote that "each man kills the thing he loves". Have we reached, or are we approaching, the limits of sustainable wildlife tourism? Should there be a strict rationing of visitors in sensitive areas? Should "return visits" be banned? Should there be total no-go zones?

There are no easy answers to such questions, but it is important that they should be asked. Take the Galápagos Islands, for example. Historically, British visitors have formed the second largest group. Even with the recession, there were still 14,000 British visitors last year.

When I first went to the Galápagos, 600 miles off the coast of Ecuador, in 2006, I did ask myself whether it was altogether appropriate to visit, but the sheer excitement of being offered a bite at this incredible cherry won the day.

During that first trip to the archipelago, I spent ten days on board a sixteen-berth schooner, sailing from island to island. For me, as for most visitors, the love affair began as soon as I stepped off the aircraft. The astonishing thing about the Galápagos is that you actually do get to see what you hope to see. If you are lucky, you will come across most of the famous birds that intrigued Charles Darwin when he landed there 175 years ago next month. You will see blue-footed boobies and frigatebirds, Galápagos hawks and flightless cormorants. You may swim and snorkel among huge Pacific Green turtles and whitetip reef sharks. You will meet giant tortoises well over 100 years old and still going strong.

This relatively benevolent relationship between man and nature didn't always exist. Vast depredations of Galápagos wildlife occurred in previous centuries. Tortoises were captured in their thousands by passing ships. The surrounding oceans were virtually emptied of whales. It is only really since 1959 when the Galápagos was established as a national park and, subsequently, as a World Heritage Site, that a proper framework has been created for safeguarding this paradise. But since then numbers of human residents and visitors have boomed.

When I first visited, some 500 cruise ships were already offering the Galápagos as a destination and some of those ships would be carrying hundreds of passengers. Nor was the problem confined to people on boats. It might not yet have been a backpacker's dream, but when I walked through the main town of Puerto Ayora on Santa Cruz Island, with its agencies offering " Galápagos Adventure Tours", I could see the potential for disaster. An explosion of short-stay visitors might overwhelm the capacity of the authorities to manage. It would also dramatically increase the risk of alien species being introduced.

Even if the authorities had the knowledge and the means to control mass-tourism, would they have the political will? In the early years of the new millennium, the islands had seen a high rate of immigration from the Ecuadorean mainland, and as many as 30,000 people now lived there – most of them involved in the tourist industry. Pressures to increase the ceiling on the number of tourists permitted to visit the islands (then about 120,000) were already being felt.

But the island's uniqueness draws visitors back again and again, myself included. I returned to the Galápagos this summer, keen to see it with fresh eyes after being asked to chair an event for the Galápagos Conservation Trust. My wife and I travelled on board the MV *Eclipse*, which carries a maximum of forty-eight passengers. Crucially, from our point of view, there were the three Ecuadorian naturalists on board: Javier, Tommy and Daniel. Day after day, they escorted us to the different sites on land. If we were snorkelling, they led the way, using hand gestures to point to giant starfish, slow-cruising sea turtles, and marine iguanas plucking seaweed from the rocks, or Galápagos penguins flashing past at speed in search of their prey.

In the evening, as we sat in the lecture room, they elaborated on key themes. "The Galápagos," Javier told us, "is one of the most important nesting areas for the Pacific green turtle." As we disembarked, he warned us to stay clear of the areas of the beach above high-water mark where the turtles had already laid their eggs. "There are five important marine turtle nesting sites in the Galápagos," he explained.

For me, this was a profoundly emotional moment. For the last several years I have served as an ambassador for the United Nations Environment Programme's Convention on Migratory Species (CMS). Within the framework of the CMS, the countries that border the Indian Ocean and the South-East Asia region have already reached an agreement to protect all species of marine turtle. Now the CMS and other bodies are considering what measures can be taken to protect marine turtles in the eastern Pacific, many of whose populations are under threat.

It is clear that the Galápagos, as a key breeding location for marine turtles, will play a vital part in any such agreement.

Ali Kemal, my paternal grandfather, who was assassinated in Turkey in 1922. He was Minister of the Interior under the last Sultan, Mehmed VI. *See* chapter 22.

Wearing a magnificent Bhutanese *gho* at the coronation of King Jigme Khesar Namgyel Wangchuck, in Thimpu, Bhutan. *See* p.133.

Bhutan's new King Jigme Khesar Namgyel Wangchuck makes his way to the throne room in Thimpu Zhong. *See* chapter 24.

Tarkine Forest, Tasmania, is the world's second largest temperate rainforest. *See* p.136.

Nouabalé-Ndoki National Park, Republic of Congo: There were ten gorillas in the *bai* that first morning. *See* p.148.
Photo credit: Thomas Breuer

A sudden end to a balloon safari in Masai Mara, Kenya, as the basket hit the ground with a mighty thwack. *See* p.152.

Wildebeest and zebra crossing the Mara River, Masai Mara Reserve, Kenya. One crocodile managed to seize a young zebra. *See* p.154.

Troops mingling with "rescued" passengers on board HMS *Albion* on the approach to Portsmouth Harbour. *See* p.160.

A mud-hut museum in Ujiji near Kigoma, Tanzania contains a larger-than-life plaster of Paris model of Stanley and Livingstone. *See* p.161.

Frodo used to be the alpha male and still displays aggressive behaviour. *See* p.165. *Photo credit*: Jane Goodall Institute

With Dr Jane Goodall, at Gombe, Tanzania. More than fifty years after she first arrived to study chimpanzees at Gombe, Jane continues to campaign – for wildlife and for people – with evangelical zeal. *See* p.167.

Returning to Machu Picchu after fifty years I learnt that the Incas built their great city in the shape of a giant condor so that, at death, they could fly to the Milky Way. *See* p.172.

Prime Minister Putin, World Bank President Robert Zoellick and Chinese Premier Wen Jiabao at the Global Tiger Summit, held in St Petersburg, Russia, November 2010. *See* p.185.

Off the Kamchatka Peninsula, Russia, the crested auklets gather on the water in huge flocks. *See* p.191.
Photo credit: Heritage Expeditions

With Jenny at the Taj Mahal. We arrived well before the crowds began to gather and walked in the cool of the morning through the beautiful Moghul gardens. *See* p.195.

Standing there on the critically important Bachas beach, I truly felt that I was in on the ground floor.

But it's the giant tortoises that are perhaps the most famous of all the Galápagos wildlife. Today it is estimated that the islands' giant tortoise population stands at about 15,000 individuals divided into eleven subspecies. The largest population is on the volcano of Alcedo on Isabela Island.

How are the giant tortoises faring after the depredations of earlier centuries, when whalers, pirates and sailors used to take giant tortoises on board to provide fresh meat and oil? Darwin notes that the crew of the HMS *Beagle* collected between 600 and 800 tortoises in just a few weeks. The introduction of goats and rats hastened the process of decline.

If you want a poignant reminder, go and visit "Lonesome George" in the grounds of the Charles Darwin Research Centre just outside Puerto Ayora on Santa Cruz Island. The tortoise given this nickname, who could be more than eighty years old, is the last of his subspecies, the Pinta tortoise. While his plight is a sad reminder of what we risk losing, the giant tortoise breeding programme has been very successful in bringing other subspecies back from the brink.

But the "elephant in the living room" – tourism – remains. On my first visit, the idea of huge people-carriers anchoring off the islands and disgorging boatloads of passengers had sent shivers down the spine of conservationists around the world. Nor was it clear what benefit to the local economy such visitations would bring. One of the great advantages of a small-scale Galápagos cruise is that a well-equipped vessel carries its own expert guides. And a well-arranged itinerary provides plenty of time for those experts to brief interested passengers on the threats and challenges the islands face. On my second visit, it was Tommy who summarized for us the current situation. He gave us the good news first.

Thanks to a moratorium inspired – in part at least – by a campaign led by the Galápagos Conservation Trust, the menace of large cruise ships has, at least for the time being, disappeared. But what about the explosive growth of other kinds of tourism? In 1991 tourists had numbered 41,000. Annual visitors now number around 170,000.

"Ship-borne tourists are not a major threat to the visitor sites. These are relatively well managed," Tommy explained. "The National Park authorities are in strict control of the number of visitors and of their itineraries."

He went on to point out that new guidelines were being introduced. Whereas, in the past, a seven-day circuit of visitor sites, largely confined to the inner islands, had been the norm, in the future it would become the exception. Instead of returning again and again to the same limited number of sites, the tourist vessels would have to range further afield, calling at sites so far infrequently visited.

"The biggest challenge now," Tommy said, "is the rapid increase in the number of people coming to Galápagos for reasons other than a wildlife cruise. Whether they are here for two days to cross it off a list of must-see sites, or simply to sit in the sun, their number and their activity is much harder to control." He added that the risk of invasive species remains the biggest threat. The Galápagos Islands now have 748 species of introduced plants, outnumbering the approximately 500 species of native plant. "However tough your quarantine measures, there is always a danger."

As Tommy continued his lecture that evening I couldn't help thinking about those amazing giant tortoises, which so attracted Darwin's interest when he visited the Galápagos 175 years ago. How ironic, how banal, it would be, I thought, if the rampant spread of blackberry bushes (now considered to be one of the most serious threats as far as invasive species are concerned) finally caused the demise of the giant tortoise! Clearing the invasive plants is one of the Galápagos Conservation Trust's most important projects. And it wasn't just a matter of ripping the offending plants out. "Most invasive plant species," explains Toni Darton, the chief executive of the trust, "come via people's gardens. That's why we are supporting a project to encourage residents to swap their introduced choices for native Galápagos species."

If I am lucky enough to make a third visit to the Galápagos before I am borne away on the back of a giant sea turtle I hope to be able to report more good news. The Galápagos, it seems to me, is a kind of test case for managing other vulnerable sites of natural beauty, though few perhaps will rival the Enchanted Isles in terms of their scientific, natural and environmental interest.

I know that many people have been dismayed that UNESCO has recently removed the Galápagos Islands from the "most threatened" list of World Heritage sites (in 2007, UNESCO mentioned tourism as one of the main threats to the Galápagos ecosystem); but, looked at another way, this is really good news, not bad. It means that solid progress has been made, and that more progress can be expected in the future. Tourism will be an inevitable part of the Galápagos future but, I hope, it can evolve to a point beyond where we are now, and each visitor can nurture the land they love without destroying it.

First published in the *Independent*, 23 August 2010

33

What Does the Future Hold for
the Inuit People of Baffin Island?

For three days this month, Iqaluit, the capital of Nunavut, one of Canada's Arctic territories, was the venue for this year's Canada-UK Colloquium. The Colloquium, involving politicians, diplomats, civil servants, academics and experts of various kinds depending on the subject under discussion, meets each year in an appropriate location to discuss matters of common interest. Because this year's theme has been "The Arctic", the choice fell on Iqaluit.

It's not an easy place to get to. Iqaluit is located on Baffin Island. It used to be called Frobisher after Sir Martin Frobisher, the Elizabethan buccaneer who – in 1576 – sailed into the sound now known as Frobisher Bay believing he had found the fabled "Northwest Passage" and a new route to China.

By air, it is 1,300 miles from Ottawa. You cannot reach Iqaluit by car. There are some roads, and cars, in town. The longest, indeed the only significant stretch of tarmac, serves to connect Iqaluit with a settlement a couple of miles away where the Hudson's Bay Company once had a trading post.

The population of Iqaluit is just over 7,000 and 60 per cent are Inuit. Their ancestors, the Thule people, are thought to have migrated to the region a thousand years ago from Alaska. With 770,000 square miles, Nunavut is one fifth of Canada, and half the size of Western Europe. Nunavut's total population is around 33,000 people, with 84 per cent of them being Inuit. That works out at one person every 23 square miles.

In some ways, the very existence of Nunavut as an Inuit homeland is a miracle. The tale of official dealings with Canada's indigenous peoples over the past 250 years makes for sorry reading. Although King George III's Royal Proclamation of 1763 asserted that the Crown would in future obtain lands required for settlement only through treaties negotiated in public with Indian nations, these guarantees were honoured more in the breach than the observance. In the 1776 Declaration of Independence, Thomas Jefferson raged against the Royal Proclamation, the English and the Indians.

"The English King has excited domestic insurrections among us, and has endeavoured to bring on the inhabitants of our frontiers, the merciless Indian savages whose known rule of warfare is an undistinguished destruction of all ages, sexes and conditions."

The Canada-UK Colloquium is fortunate in having as its chairman Tony Penikett, a former premier of Yukon, who had been intimately involved in the negotiation of Yukon's land claims. In his view, it is vital for all those engaged in Arctic matters in Canada to have a clear understanding of the issues of sovereignty and "ownership". He explains: "In the US, in the 1820s and the 1830s, the Cherokees went three times to the Supreme Court. The Court concluded that the Royal Proclamation of 1763 had force and that the US government had an obligation to make treaties. George Washington thought that the requirement wouldn't endure. And in Canada, treaty-making was largely forgotten until British Columbia's Thomas Berger went to court on behalf of the Nisga'a in 1969–71."

The Nisga'a, Penikett continues, won their battle. The Court's verdict took the establishment by surprise. The then Prime Minister, Pierre Trudeau, is reputed to have said: "Your people have a lot more rights than I thought you did."

Following the Nisga'a victory, the three Canadian Arctic territories (Yukon, Northwest Territories and Nunavut) have – after years of negotiation – all settled their land claims, the Nunavut

Land Claims Agreement, for example, finally having been ratified in 1993. The legal certainty which has followed has been immensely important in assuring Canadian and international business that the Arctic is a place they can invest in without facing years of litigation. Over the next decades, we are likely to witness a scramble for Arctic resources equal to any seen in the past.

It is estimated that, of the world's undiscovered hydrocarbon resources, 13 per cent of oil, 30 per cent of natural gas and 20 per cent of natural gas liquids could lie in the Arctic. Okalik Eegeesiak, the president of the Qikiqtani Inuit Association (QIA), explains that "the Sverdrup Basin is entirely within the area under QIA jurisdiction in the Nunavut land claim. The Basin is estimated to contain 17.4 trillion cubic feet of recoverable natural gas and 334 million barrels of oil."

There is another factor which makes the prospect of a new Arctic "resources rush" a near-certainty: the impact of climate change. In the past fifty years, average annual temperatures in some Arctic regions have risen by up to 3°C. As temperatures rise, and waters become free of ice, opening up areas so far hard to reach, the practical possibilities of exploiting Arctic wealth are significantly increased.

Inuit leaders such as Eegeesiak are aware of the inherent ironies. If global warming has opened up the Arctic, it has also made the Inuit's traditional daily life that much more difficult. Those difficulties will increase. How will the seals pop up through a hole in the ice as the hunter waits and watches, when all the ice has gone? And what is happening to the caribou herds?

"This new interest in the Arctic contains contradictions," Eegeesiak says. "Contradictions like the fear of climate change on the one hand and on the other hand a keen desire to exploit oil and gas resources that up to now have not been reached."

Even assuming the Inuit had both the will and the authority to say "no" to a new wave of Arctic exploration, why should they? It could be argued that for many of them, particularly the younger generation, it may already be too late to return to the traditional way of life exemplified by *Nanook of the North* (Robert Flaherty filmed this famous documentary in the Canadian Arctic in 1920–21). It could also be argued that equally noxious (in climate terms) developments would anyway simply take place elsewhere. Unless some scheme could be put in place to compensate for the "non-exploited energy resources" (such as those currently under discussion to compensate communities and countries for "forests not cut down"), it is hard to see how Inuit and other native peoples could afford to forgo benefits that the development of Arctic resources will bring.

These benefits are real, not notional. They include jobs, obviously, particularly jobs in the Arctic energy sector as it opens up. They include vitally needed improvements in housing, health and social welfare. Some of the most disturbing statistics we heard were those related to suicide. It is above all the young who are "suiciding". With suicides occurring at rates around 120 per 100,000, Nunavut is possibly the suicide capital of the world.

One thing that struck me in Iqaluit is how non-pushy our Inuit hosts were. Perhaps it is a cultural thing. Or perhaps they have just been beaten down by centuries of colonialism, including domestic colonialism. As Eegeesiak says: "At a policy level, Inuit need to be included as equals in any dialogue about developing our lands and around our waters."

Why do these people, who have learnt over hundreds of years to live in harmony with nature and to manage their own resources (as we have not), have to ask to be "included as equals" in discussions about developing their own lands? Surely the snowshoe should be on the other foot?

Unless the land claims agreements are fully and correctly implemented, the Inuit may, I fear, turn out to have sold their birthright for a mess of potage. I pick up a local newspaper as the Colloquium ends. It is printed both in English and Inuktitut. The lead story is about the federal government's plans to carry out seismic testing in Lancaster Sound, located between Devon Island and Baffin Island, and forming the eastern portion of the Northwest

Passage. The QIA has sought an injunction on the basis that the testing would cause irreparable damage to wildlife and impair the Inuit's ability to hunt in the area. (The area is a habitat for narwhal, beluga and bowhead whales, as well as for seals, walrus and polar bears. Seabirds flock to Lancaster Sound in the hundreds of thousands.)

But the real shocker, as far as I'm concerned, is that apparently the Inuit hadn't even been consulted. Maybe we need another Royal Proclamation to set matters straight. The Queen is, after all, still Queen of Canada!

First published in the *Independent*, 19 November 2010

34

With Friends in High Places, is There Hope for the Tigers?

At the end of November 2010 I attended the first ever "Global Tiger Summit", held in St Petersburg, Russia. This was an intriguing and important event for a number of reasons. Chief of these, from my perspective, is that thanks in part at least to the decisions reached in St Petersburg the prospects for the survival of the tiger in the wild may be measurably improved.

Over the last century, tiger numbers have plummeted from about 100,000 to less than 3,500 tigers in the wild today. Three sub-species of tigers have already completely disappeared and the fate of the other six is at stake. The last decade alone has seen a decline of almost 40 per cent in tiger numbers and habitat as a result of human-made threats, such as, in particular, habitat loss, illegal wildlife trade and poaching and human-tiger conflicts.

Why will the St Petersburg Summit make a difference to the fate of the tiger? It is easy to be cynical about the motives of world leaders but I found myself, during those few days in St Petersburg, ready to give them at least the benefit of the doubt. The key role in the preparatory process was played by the World Bank. Two years ago, World Bank President, Robert Zoellick, alerted to the fact that the tiger was on the verge of extinction, devoted time and energy to setting up a Global Tiger Initiative so as to bring together all thirteen Tiger Range Countries (TRCs) at a series of preparatory meetings. The outcome of those meetings was an action plan, known as the Global Tiger Recovery Programme, whose objective is to reverse the dramatic decline in tiger populations around the world, so as to achieve a doubling of tiger numbers by the year 2022.

Of course, there have been tiger recovery action plans in the past. Some of them, like Indian Prime Minister Indira Gandhi's Project Tiger, have at first seemed to be successful in stemming the decline in tiger populations only – for one reason or another – to run out of steam. But the GTRP seems to be the first truly comprehensive document, built from the bottom-up on realistic national tiger conservation plans and projects.

Under the draft GTRP, which was presented to the St Petersburg summit for agreement, the thirteen Tiger Range Countries "agree" to strengthen international collaboration to protect the majestic Asian wild cat. Monitoring will be improved to help restore the species' habitats and its trans-boundary corridors. Halting poaching and illegal trade of tigers and tiger products is a core component of the conservation strategy. Creating incentives for local people to protect tigers and strengthening wildlife law enforcement and legislation will be vital to achieve the ambitious targets. Conflicts occurring between tigers and local communities will be reduced by involving local people more actively in biodiversity protection.

During the discussions of the draft GTRP in St Petersburg, numerous delegates pointed out that the tiger has played a very important role in Asian nature and culture for centuries. Almost half of the world's population, 3.3 billion people, live in the countries of the tiger's distribution range in Asia. Therefore immediate and effective steps are necessary to create an economic and ecological balance matching the interests of these states towards a safe future for the tiger.

Tigers, being on top of the food chain, have an important umbrella function to maintain the biodiversity of their habitat. As such they maintain the biodiversity of the region, contribute to a healthy ecosystem and generate tourist revenue for economies through tiger watching and safaris.

The Terai Arc Landscape between India and Nepal, for example, shows how conservation efforts to save the tiger have also resulted in increased benefits for the endangered rhino and other animals in the region. The ecosystems in these countries support tigers, their prey and a vast amount of biodiversity. Any efforts to conserve the tiger as an umbrella species will also ensure that the rich biodiversity of these areas is protected.

Even if the leadership of the World Bank was absolutely crucial in developing the global tiger initiative, the effort could only have come to fruition with the whole-hearted "buy-in" of the Tiger Range Countries themselves. This buy-in was to a large extent achieved in the run-up to St Petersburg and the momentum was maintained at St Petersburg itself. Indeed I cannot recall another occasion when so many heads of government have gathered together to endorse an action plan for the conservation of a single non-human species. And this is where Prime Minister Putin's own commitment to ensuring the success of the St Petersburg Global Tiger Summit was absolutely crucial. In a very real sense, he made it happen.

Rather like Robert Zoellick himself, Vladimir Putin seems to have had his own "on the road to Damascus" conversion to tiger conservation when in August 2008 he visited the Ussuri Nature Reserve in Russia's Far East and participated in a scientific programme, involving the tagging of the Siberian or Amur tiger, of which only 400–500 remain in the wild. Putin himself is reported to have aimed the tranquillizing dart, thereby earning global headlines: "Putin shoots tiger!" Russian colleagues I spoke to in St Petersburg assured me that Putin is genuinely an animal-lover and though he, as any other politician, is no doubt aware how these macho moments will play in the public mind, his deep-down conservationist motives should not be questioned.

Be that as it may, one thing is certain: Putin and Zoellick working together attracted an astonishingly high level of participants to St Petersburg. On the last day of the meeting, we were bussed in a snowstorm from St Petersburg to the Konstantinovsky Palace on the grey, frigid shores of the Gulf of Finland. The line-up on the dais that morning included, besides

Mr Putin and Mr Zoellick, Premier Wen Jiabao of China, as well as the prime ministers of Nepal, Bangladesh, and Laos. All of them made speeches, some better than others. Who, I asked myself, except Putin, could have delivered that line-up? Getting Premier Wen Jiabao, for example, to St Petersburg on what was literally a one-day visit almost wholly dedicated to tigers was frankly staggering.

Another reason for optimism about the outcome of the St Petersburg meeting is in my view the continued commitment that is being shown by the World Bank. The Tiger Summit adopted a Declaration that, among other things, invited the World Bank to continue with the Global Tiger Initiative. In his own remarks to the Tiger Summit, World Bank President Robert Zoellick stressed the readiness of the World Bank to administer a "tiger trust fund" and to contribute to that fund as well as funding conservation programmes directly in the Tiger Range Countries, and encouraging others to do the same. The price tag on the Global Tiger Recovery Programme amounts to US$350 million spread over five years. When 80 billion Euros are being spent to save Irish and other banks, US$350 million could, frankly, be characterized as chickenfeed.

There was one other reason why I came away from St Petersburg with a sense of optimism. I attended the Global Tiger Summit as the Ambassador of the United Nations Environment Programme's Convention on Migratory Species (CMS), together with my colleague Aline Kuehl, one of CMS' Scientific Officers. (The CMS' Executive-Secretary Elizabeth Mrema had unfortunately been detained on official business at CMS headquarters in Bonn.) During the course of the St Petersburg meeting Aline and I were able to meet Russian Environment and Natural Resources Minister, Yuri Trutnev, as well as Deputy Minister Igor Maydanov. We pointed out that the CMS fervently hopes that the Russian Federation will soon become a party to the CMS, thus facilitating interstate agreements about trans-boundary movements. I don't often have the opportunity to report, as a journalist, on my own speeches, so here goes! This is what I said at the conclusion of my remarks to the Global Tiger Summit in St Petersburg on 22 November.

"In this context, I would just like to say how much Mrs Mrema, the Executive-Secretary of the CMS, and my CMS colleagues welcome the interest which the Russian Federation is currently showing in becoming a party to CMS. It is not just a matter of tigers. Many of the species of interest to CMS, some of them covered by specific agreements within the CMS framework, are to be found in the Russian Federation. Many of the migratory birds, which fly around the world, begin or end their journeys in this mighty land. Many of the marine mammals originate in or pass through Russian waters on their way to other parts of the ocean. The sockeye salmon I saw in the rivers of the Kamchatka Peninsula earlier this year spend a life at sea. So I just want to say that the red white and blue flag of the Russian Federation is a flag the CMS, which now has 114 members, will be very proud to fly in its atrium in Bonn."

I much hope to be able to report in due course to *Open Democracy Russia* that the Russian Federation has indeed joined the United Nations Environment Programme's Convention on Migratory Species and that Russia, building on Prime Minister Putin's tiger initiative, is now taking the lead in seeking international protection measures, not just for tigers, but for a host of other endangered migratory species as well.

First published on *Open Democracy Russia*
website 21 December 2010

35

Russia's Wild Kamchatka Peninsula

The remote "ring of fire" in the easternmost part of Siberia is full of wildlife, best seen up close by small ship.

A volcano was venting a cloud of dust into the atmosphere as we came into land at Petropavlosk-Kamchatsky, though the pilot of our Aeroflot Boeing 767 seemed unfazed.

The Kamchatka Peninsula, which drops like a giant pendant from the easternmost part of Siberia and is a ten-hour flight from Moscow across eight time zones, has more volcanoes – about 300 – than any other region on Earth. And twenty-nine of them are active. As we lost height, I could see the great conical shapes pushing up through the cloud base below us, the peaks catching the late-afternoon sun.

Our ten-day voyage on board the *Spirit of Enderby*, from Avacha Bay on Kamchatka Peninsula to the Kuril and Commander Islands – and back – was a journey around a ring of fire. Many of the volcanoes we saw were more than 3,000m high, rising steeply from the sea to snow-capped summits. You can explore this territory by land, but the infrastructure is limited, the distances long and the roads and hotels poor. A cruise by small ship, with good accommodation on board, makes much more sense.

If physical beauty is one of the characteristics of the region, the abundance and the variety of wildlife is another. In terms of its biological richness and diversity, this is one of the most extraordinary parts of the world I have visited. It's a trip that could easily be justified in terms of its whale watching interest alone. The thrill of being in a Zodiac surrounded by a pod of killer whales (or orcas) as they hunt for Steller sea lions or sea otters takes some beating.

On our last full day at sea, when we were heading back from the Commander Islands to Kamchatka, we must have seen a score of humpback whales, at least as many killer whales and a handful of sperm whales. A few days earlier, in Olga Bay, we spent a morning following a group of grey whales. When a grey whale comes to the surface and blows just a few feet from your small inflatable boat, you hold your breath. You can smell the whales' breakfast.

On the north-west cape of Bering Island we parked our Zodiacs and hiked across the dunes to visit a vast colony of northern fur seals. More than 5,000 females and their pups had been herded into harems by jealous males. Young male pretenders lurked off shore and from time to time tried to seize a piece of the action, only to be hurled back into the water by irate bulls.

But perhaps most remarkable is the marine bird-life. On the craggy cliffs of the Kuril and Commander Islands, guillemots, puffins, fulmars and auklets abound. At Ariy Kamen, a rocky outcrop a few miles west of Bering Island that we reached in our Zodiacs, we were greeted by thousands of birds. On another occasion, as we circled Toporkov Island in the southern Kurils, Adam, our on-board naturalist, informed us nonchalantly that the most recent estimates put the population of crested auklets at "over a million pairs".

More than a million pairs! We watched enthralled from our boats as, towards evening, the auklets began to gather on the water in huge flocks. "Rafting" is the term the birders use. Then, as dusk fell, the sky darkened further as the birds took off from the water to settle on the cliffs for the night.

Don't overlook the terrestrial mammals: Kamchatka is famous for its bears and the Kamchatkan subspecies of brown bear is the second largest in the world. There are thought to be 10,000 bears throughout the peninsula – and with a visit scheduled to the Kronotsky Biosphere Reserve, which extends over one million hectares, you have high hopes of seeing one. We spotted one sunning himself on the tundra. He loped off before we could get close. It was one of many magical sights on a voyage filled with unforgettable wildlife.

First published in *The Times*, 15 January 2011

36

Return to India: Tigers and the Taj Mahal

I first visited India in the late summer of 1961, driving a motorcycle down the Grand Trunk Road from Kabul to Delhi. With two friends, Tim Severin and Michael de Larrabeiti, I had set off two months earlier from Oxford, planning to follow Marco Polo's route across Asia to China. Marco Polo had entered China through the Wakkan corridor in northern Afghanistan, but we had found the route impassable so we rode on down into India instead.

Though we left England with two motorcycles, one of them had been severely damaged in a crash in Iran and we had to leave it behind. So we all piled on to the remaining bike. As we drove south through the Khyber Pass, then on through Peshawar and Amritsar to Delhi, dodging buffaloes and sacred cows, we must have looked like some multi-limbed Hindu god.

Of course, we were desperately disappointed to have failed in our main objective but there were compensations. Seeing the Taj Mahal was one.

I can remember even now, at a distance of fifty years, the sheer excitement of that first glimpse of the Taj as we drove into the centre of Agra. This was – and is – a monument stunning beyond words. We parked our motorcycle in the shade of a banyan tree, found a willing guide, and spent an hour or two walking round, feeling totally gobsmacked. I still have the notes I made at the time. I see that I jotted down the famous lines by the Bengali poet, Rabindranath Tagore, who described the Taj as a "teardrop on the face of eternity".

Perhaps more intriguingly, I also noted a comment about the mausoleum by one Lady Sleeman, as relayed by our guide. "I would die tomorrow to have such another over me," Lady Sleeman is supposed to have said. Later, I found out that Lady Sleeman was the wife of Major-General Sir WH Sleeman, General Superintendent for the Suppression of Thuggee in India, known by the nickname "Thuggee Sleeman"!

I have visited Agra three or four times since 1961 and for me the Taj Mahal comes as close to perfection as any building I have ever seen. Can one ever tire of it? I suspect not. As I grow older, I must be getting more emotional. On this visit I found myself not only overwhelmed by the sublime architecture, but unconscionably moved by the narrative behind it.

Was this the greatest love story of all time, I asked myself, as I watched the sun rise over the Taj's great white central dome? Mumtaz Mahal, Shah Jahan's second wife, died while delivering their fourteenth child. "On her deathbed," our guide told us, "she asked two promises from her husband. The first was that he would never marry again. The second was that he should build a monument peerless in concept and beauty which would symbolize their eternal love for each other."

As far as the first wish was concerned, Shah Jahan – fifth of the Great Mughal Emperors, he ruled India from 1627 to 1658 – already had three other wives (including a Hindu and a Christian one) and a harem numbered in the thousands, so agreeing not to marry again was perhaps not such a great act of self-denial as it might at first appear. But it was Shah Jahan's determination to observe the second promise that enabled Agra to achieve in the 17th century the peak of its glory. Shah Jahan invited designs from the famous architects of the world. Ultimately, the Persian Ustad Ahmad Lahauri was nominated.

For twenty-two years Shah Jahan closely supervised the construction of the magical building on the banks of the holy Yamuna River. He neglected the affairs of state; he virtually bankrupted the treasury.

The construction of the Taj Mahal was finally completed in 1648 and the mortal remains of Empress Mumtaz Mahal interred beneath the dome.

We were so lucky that morning in Agra. Sometimes – let's be frank – air pollution in what is now a large industrial city can affect visibility. The clear lines of the Taj can be shrouded in mist. But for our visit the weather was absolutely stunning. We arrived well before the crowds began to gather and walked in the cool of the morning through the beautiful Moghul gardens. I remembered the inscription I had once seen on the gates of a Moghul garden in Lahore, in what is now Pakistan: "If there be any paradise on earth, it is here, it is here, it is here."

Shah Jahan fell ill in September 1657. Taking advantage of this opportunity, one of his sons, Aurangzeb, took over the throne and imprisoned him in Agra Fort. Today, when you visit the fort, you can stand by the window from which, for the last ten years of his life, Shah Jahan was able to gaze at the wonder he had created, not much more than a mile away, on the bank of the holy river. He was still a captive when he died, in 1666, to be entombed alongside Mumtaz.

For my money, Agra is the pinnacle of the Golden Triangle. Our tour took us, of course, to Jaipur and Delhi as well.

Nowadays, Jaipur is gaining considerable prestige as the location of an international literary festival. We arrived in the town a week before the festival and could well understand the success it is having as a venue for the literati and indeed the glitterati. This is a fascinating, beguiling place. Jaipur is actually one of Rajastan's youngest cities, having been founded in 1727 by Jai Singh II of the Kachchwaha royal family.

At its heart lies Jai Singh's original capital, known as the Pink City. Our guide explained: "Jai Singh decreed that the city should be painted pink to welcome the Prince of Wales when he visited Jaipur in 1853. Pink is the colour of hospitality!"

Of course, not everyone got to go out in the wide streets of the new town to welcome His Royal Highness, the eventual Edward VII.

One of the most striking buildings in the city is the Hawa Mahal, the place of winds, a tapered construction with 953 latticed windows, which permitted royal women to observe ceremonial processions without themselves being observed.

We spent two days in Jaipur and could easily have spent several more. The Amber Palace, Jaijargh Fort, the Albert Hall Museum – these are sites that would benefit from longer visits. For those of a scientific or mechanical turn of mind, Jaipur's Astronomical Observatory must be uniquely interesting. Maharajah Jai Singh was not only an inspired town planner and soldier of note, he was also an astronomer of distinction and the colossal instruments – eighteen in total – that you can see in the observatory still perform today the functions for which they were designed.

The official title of our tour was "Tigers and the Taj". Though we had seen the Taj under the most perfect conditions, we had not yet seen the tigers. When India gained independence from Britain in 1948, there were 50,000 tigers. Now there are possibly fewer than 2,000. I had had the good fortune to see tigers in the wild in India on a previous trip, but this was my wife Jenny's first visit.

En route to Jaipur, we had visited Sariska National Park. A few years earlier, Sariska had suffered an epidemic of poaching and a total wipe-out of the tiger population. Five tigers were subsequently brought in from another national park, Ranthambore, but one of those, alas, had died. I told Jenny not to have too high expectations. "You may have to settle for a footprint."

Our guide explained why. "The average male tiger has a range of 11 to 15 square miles. The average female ranges over 7 to 11 square miles." Needles and haystacks came to mind. Well, we were lucky. We didn't see any tigers in Sariska, but we did in Ranthambore.

Ranthambore is one of the loveliest of India's national parks. With its 10th-century fort perched on a hilltop looking out over deep forests, it is straight out of Kipling's *Jungle Book*. Though in the nineties poaching led to a collapse in Ranthambore's tiger population, it seems that since then there has been a recovery.

When we arrived at our lodge, just outside the boundaries of the park, we were briefed by a ranger: "We believe there are about thirty tigers in Ranthambore today." We went out four times in the canters – open-sided vehicles riding high off the ground for good viewing. We enjoyed the magical setting: the lakes, the battlements, and the jungle backdrop. We saw a mass of wildlife – monkeys, peacocks and an abundance of sambar deer and spotted deer, herons and kingfishers – but the tigers remained elusive.

From time to time a tracker would point out a print, but this would be followed by a shaking of the head and a clicking of the teeth. "*Acha*! This is not a fresh print. Tiger was here this morning. Now gone very far!"

Finally we came to the end of our last ride on our last day in Ranthambore. I was sitting up front with a tracker, Shivraj, next to me. Shivraj was deeply despondent. It was as though he felt his own honour was impugned by his inability to produce a real live tiger for us.

Then, as we were getting ready to call it a day, a message came through on the radio that a tiger had been seen at a waterhole a few miles away. With our driver, Vijay, breaking the speed limit by a considerable margin, we careered off through the forests only to find that the tiger, if there was one, had moved on.

Finally we had to head for home, still lickety-split, since we were out of time and the park gates had already closed. We were travelling, I guess, at almost 30mph on a bumpy track when we were all but sideswiped by a Jeep containing a party of tourists. What interested Shivraj, as we took rapid evasive action, was that the Jeep wasn't heading for the exit; it was heading towards another part of the forest.

"Follow that Jeep!" Shivraj told the driver.

So we belted after the Jeep and, as luck would have it, arrived a few minutes later at a fork in the road where three or four vehicles were already gathered. A female tiger came out of the bush and crouched in the road right alongside one of the vehicles. We could hear her growling. Seconds later, a male tiger followed her.

The female's growls grew into snarls. By now I was standing up, holding on to the windscreen, trying to focus my camera. "They are going to mate," Shivraj whispered to me. "That's why the female is snarling."

I would like to report that we saw the tigers mating, but suddenly Shivraj told the driver to reverse and beat a retreat.

"We are illegal here!" he told me as we drove back. "This is Route No. 5. Ours is Route No. 4. If the park officials catch us, our canter can be impounded, and the rangers can be suspended and fined."

We drove back to the lodge, tired but happy. Like the Battle of Waterloo, it had been a damned close-run thing.

Our last days were spent in Delhi. Actually there are at least three Delhis, not just one. There is Old Delhi with the Red Fort and the Jama Mashjid, Humayun's Tomb and the Qutub Minar. There is New Delhi, so much the creation of Sir Edwin Lutyens and Sir Herbert Baker. Then there is the Delhi of post-independence India – the teeming, bustling city that is literally bursting at the seams. With a population of 14 million, it is the third-largest city in India. There are seven and a half million vehicles on Delhi's roads, with 900 new vehicles being registered every day.

I could not help thinking how much had changed since I first rode into the city as a twenty-one-year-old on my motorcycle. Yet the magic was still there. If I could find that old 500cc BSA twin-cylinder Shooting Star somewhere in the back streets of the city, I would be quite ready to roar off into the sunset.

Once you have seen both tigers in the wild and the Taj Mahal in all its glory, what else counts?

First published in the *Mail on Sunday*, 20 February 2011

37

Taking on Kilimanjaro

"*Polé, polé*". In Swahili this means "Slowly, slowly". Old hands will tell you that if you are planning to climb Mount Kilimanjaro in Tanzania, the highest peak in Africa and the world's highest free-standing mountain, *polé, polé* is the way to do it. Particularly if, as I am, you are halfway through your seventy-first year.

I had heard tales before I set out last month of how such supremely fit people as former tennis champion Martina Navratilova had failed to make it to the top.

Google "climbing Kilimanjaro" and you get a whole litany of things that can go wrong, from altitude sickness to acute pulmonary or cerebral oedema. Someone is bound to suggest that you update your will before you leave for Africa. My advice is don't worry.

I am not saying this is a total cakewalk. It isn't. There are some long days' walking and climbing and the assault on the summit can indeed be daunting, as can the long descent.

For the averagely fit septuagenarian, however, I would say climbing Kilimanjaro is totally doable. I would go further. From my personal perspective, the week I have just spent climbing up 18,651ft has been one of the most memorable of my life.

If you don't actually enjoy climbing Kilimanjaro you are wasting your time and money. I knew right from the start that I had the right formula.

Although I am sure that I could have arranged for some travelling companions I decided not to. I wanted to be free to set my own pace or, more accurately, to follow the pace set by my guide without having to worry if it was too slow or too fast for someone else.

I didn't want to find myself idly chatting about which film would win the most Oscars or whether the Lib Dems would pull out of the Coalition. Solitude, of course, is a relative term. Besides myself, my party comprised a guide, a cook, four porters and even a waiter.

The rhythm of our days on the mountain was straightforward. I had decided to approach Kilimanjaro from the Kenyan side along the so-called Rongai route. There are six approaches but Rongai is less-frequented and one of the most delightful.

Entering Mount Kilimanjaro National Park at Rongai Gate soon after lunch on day one, we spent our first afternoon walking up to Simba Camp at 8,612ft.

With the team having gone ahead to pitch the tents and prepare the evening meal, my guide Elibariki Simon and I took a leisurely uphill stroll through the rainforest.

That is one of the extraordinary things about climbing Kilimanjaro. In the space of four days you pass through tropical rainforest into a zone of heath and moorland. Then as you rise above the 13,120ft contour you continue through a kind of lunar landscape before ascending beyond 16,400ft into the summit zone.

That first afternoon in the rainforest we must have seen at least twenty black-and-white colobus monkeys, with their extraordinary long capes of white hair and flowing white tails, leaping from tree to tree. The same number of blue monkeys was also evident as well as a chameleon and a variety of sunbirds.

I found myself adopting a defensive strategy. Even if I don't make it to the top, I said, I will have had a wonderful outing in one of Africa's most astonishing national parks.

One of the advantages of taking a wholly tented approach to Kilimanjaro is that you are not bound by anyone else's timetable. You don't have to observe check-in and check-out times as you do if you take the Marangu route where you have to move from hut to hut under a strict timetable.

I never felt the advantage of our choice of route and mode of travel (tents plus porters) more keenly than at the end of day four when we made the final push for the mountain's summit.

We reached Kibo Camp 3,000ft from the summit at about 5pm. Elibariki poked his head into my tent to give me final instructions: "Dinner at six. Then you sleep until eleven."

It seemed a long time. "Eleven tomorrow morning?" I queried.

"No, this evening; we start climbing at midnight."

Eli was as good as his word. We left Kibo Camp for the final push to the summit at exactly midnight. With a full moon shining on the mountain we had no need of head torches as we scrambled upwards, although we carried them with us just in case.

At about 6.30am the sun rose above Mawenzi Peak, Kilimanjaro's lesser twin. We were already high above the clouds.

At 10am we reached the rim of the mountain and from Gilman's Point we were able to look down into Kilimanjaro's ice- and snow-covered crater.

Mission accomplished.

Eli helped me unfurl the banner of the Gorilla Organization, whose chairman I am. So far we have raised almost as many UK pounds for gorilla conservation as the altitude (in feet) I climbed.

As importantly, Eli helped me safely back down the mountain. Although I didn't experience any kind of altitude sickness at any point on the mountain my feet were certainly tired and aching when, at around 2pm, we made it back to Kibo.

This was where taking the tent-only option paid off. If we had been "hutting" rather than "tenting" we would have had to vacate our berths after the briefest of rests to trudge on down that same day to the next camp at Horombo – three or four more hours' steady walking. This on top of a stint that had begun sixteen hours earlier when we first set off for the summit at midnight.

Staggering into camp I put my foot down. "I'm not going on down to Horombo," I told my guide. "Not today. I'll do it tomorrow. I am going straight to sleep in my tent. Here and now."

Which is exactly what I did.

First published in the *Sunday Express*, 31 March 2011

 38

Survival of the Cutest

For as long as I can remember, I have wanted to see a giant panda in the wild. Not in a zoo. Not in a research station. In the mountains of central China, the only place on earth where they survive. Giant pandas once inhabited much of China, but nowadays they are to be found in only three provinces: Sichuan, Shaanxi and Gansu. In the mid-1980s, I visited Sichuan, taking a cargo boat down the Yangtze through the Three Gorges. While my fellow passengers filled their breakfast bowls with rice from a pail, I'd pop up on deck with my eyes skinned, hoping that, just as the sun was rising, I might see a giant panda having its own breakfast on the banks of the river. No such luck.

WWF, formerly the World Wildlife Fund, which celebrates its fiftieth anniversary this year, adopted the panda as its emblem in 1961, but the Chinese had long before then recognized it as a national symbol. Chinese postage stamps are issued with the giant panda image. Wherever you go, shops and street markets are full of cuddly panda toys. But all these are poor substitutes for the real thing.

My wife and I visited China in 2001, but that trip took in Shanghai, Beijing and other east coast locations – not panda habitat. I then decided to concentrate on other endangered animals, such as the gorilla. At the end of February this year, I had just returned to Britain from climbing Mount Kilimanjaro to raise funds for the Gorilla Organization when the telephone rang. It was a specialist travel agent based in Cirencester, inviting me to see the giant panda in the wild.

"We're planning to take a small group to Shaanxi Province," said Paul Craven, who would be leading the trip. "In the Qinling Mountains you have some of the highest density of pandas in the whole of China. It's hard work, mind you. How fit are you? Some of the peaks are over 3,000 metres. We'll be pushing through the forests from dawn to dusk. There'll be snow on the ground. Of course, that can make the tracking easier."

Frankly, he made Kilimanjaro sound like a cakewalk. Paul admitted that he himself had never seen pandas in the wild, though he had once seen panda poo in a Sichuan reserve, and chewed bamboo shoots.

"The panda eats shoots and leaves!" I commented – the sum total of my knowledge of the elusive creatures at that point.

Ten days later, we landed in Xi'an, capital of Shaanxi province. Joining Paul and me were Robin and Mary, and Keith, who was travelling on his own.

His wife was quite happy not to come on this one, he told me. "My wife feels the same," I said. "It's a bit of a long shot, isn't it?"

Giving Xi'an's terracotta army a miss (when you've seen one terracotta warrior you've seen them all), we headed for the hills with a local Chinese guide, Cheng. He stood, microphone in hand, at the front of the minibus as sleek black new Chinese-made Nissans and BMWs overtook us on both sides along a new highway. "Xi'an is 100km from the Qinling mountains. The mountains form a watershed between north and south China. The water that falls on the northern slopes flow into the Yellow River. The water that falls on the south side flows into the Yangtze River."

The motorway started to snake through the mountains. Some 500 bridges, tunnels and viaducts cut through panda territory. Our first three days were to be spent in Changqing Nature Reserve, the last five in Foping Nature Reserve. Though not contiguous, both are key habitats for the Qinling giant panda, which some experts are claiming is so distinctive as to merit being called a subspecies in its own right.

Though so much has changed in China, some things have remained the same. Water buffalo are still used to plough the fields; the eaves of village houses are laden with cobs of maize, hung out to dry in the chill air. The friendliness of the people amazed me. Gone was that sense of being a stranger in a strange land. If you smiled, they smiled back. If you waved, they waved back. Maybe this spirit of goodwill is as new to them as it is to us.

In Changqing we saw at least a score of crested ibis, a bird that only a few years ago was on the verge of extinction. And we saw lots and lots of panda poo. Giant pandas eat for more than twelve hours every day, but most of what they eat is undigested. Researchers can examine the bite marks on the bamboo stalks in the droppings and work out how many pandas there are and where they live.

After three days, I had begun to think that droppings were all I was going to see. Soon after eight each morning, we headed off for the hills with two guides, Zhang and Qi. Before it was declared a nature reserve in 1995, Changqing had been logged, and there were still old tracks through the forest. If you were lucky enough to find one, this could make progress easier. But sometimes you just had to put your head down like a charging bull and hope your rucksack did not become fatally snagged in the undergrowth.

From time to time Zhang or Qi would examine some droppings and shake their heads. Our escort, Cheng, interpreted the gestures for us. "They say this is two-week-old poo, maybe older." Late one afternoon, we saw a pile of panda poo that looked very fresh. We gathered round excitedly, taking out our binoculars. "Watch for a movement in the bamboos," Cheng whispered. "They shake the bamboo as they eat." Once, we heard a rustling below us as we paused by a ravine, but it turned out to be a pair of golden pheasants pecking among tree roots.

My mood that night was despondent. There hadn't been an official survey of giant pandas in China since 2004, when experts came up with a total of 1,600 – 1,600 in the whole of China! Would our luck be better in the next reserve? Paul tried to boost our spirits. "Foping is around 300 square kilometres. It's thought to have nearly 100 giant pandas. That's almost a third of a panda to each square kilometre."

"At this point," I told him, "I'll settle for a quarter of a panda, or even an eighth."

Our minibus took us to a mountain pass, from where we walked 8 kilometres to the Foping research centre. At dinner we mixed with research staff and other eco-tourists, including a party from Canada led by Tom, who wore a badge saying "Grizzly Bear Tours". "Our grizzlies are hibernating at this time of year," Tom explained. "Giant pandas don't hibernate. Apart from eating shoots and leaves, they sleep – around ten or twelve hours a day." Matthias, a Swedish photographer for *National Geographic*, told me that two days earlier he had seen a panda – from a distance. I shook his hand and took his photo. I could always say I had met a man who'd seen a panda in the wild, even if I hadn't seen one myself.

Our first full day in Foping was perfect for tracking. The sun shone as we headed towards the first of the several valleys we would explore. The panda is on the whole a solitary animal. The general rule is one valley per panda. We were joined by guides He, Pu and Hu. Pu and Hu were authorized to scout in the mountains around and above us. If they spotted a panda, they would summon us by mobile phone. It seemed a fine system, but the call from the spotters never came.

Pu and Hu were still out in the field when Paul checked his watch. It was around 6pm and the sun was beginning to set.

We were heading back to base camp when suddenly Cheng passed me on the narrow track. "They've seen a panda in a tree!" he hissed. "Go back! Back up the hill!"

We retraced our steps and he gestured that we should go down a slope through the bamboo, then up the dry bed of a creek. Mary saw it before I did – a large white mass of fur, 40ft up a tree, almost directly above us. Moments later, I too saw the animal. From time to time, it waved a paw but otherwise it remained motionless. Our presence seemed not to bother her in the slightest.

But the best was yet to come. March is mating season for pandas. Seconds later, a fully grown male panda poked its head out of the bamboo twenty yards away and gazed balefully at me. The size of the animal stunned me (an adult male can reach 5ft when standing and weigh more than 20 stone), but so did the fact it was there at all. Not only was there a female panda directly overhead, but a large male panda, looking decidedly grumpy, was heading in my direction. I was so shocked I completely screwed up on the photography front. I pointed my camera at the approaching male, tried to press the button for the zoom, but somehow turned the camera off instead.

Two days later, I found myself in WWF's Beijing office being briefed by Chang Youde, a panda specialist. "In the 1970s the first national panda survey in China estimated that there were 2,459 individuals in the wild," he told me. "In the 1980s, orders were issued to prevent poaching, selling and smuggling of rare wildlife. In the 1990s, the giant panda was one of the top fifteen conservation priorities in China. And in the 2000s, the total number of nature reserves reached sixty-two, covering 71 per cent of the giant panda population and 57 per cent of its habitats."

But that means 43 per cent of the giant panda's habitat and 29 per cent of its population remain less effectively protected. There are around eighteen populations of giant pandas. Even if commercial logging had been brought under control in protected areas, habitat fragmentation and degradation continued as a result of road construction, mining, dam building and mass-tourism. WWF's reason for helping to conserve the giant panda goes far beyond the species itself.

Its objective is to protect the landscape where the pandas live, thereby also protecting the thousands of other species living alongside them, and the natural resources and ecosystems on which, ultimately, humans also depend.

"This is our vision," Youde told me. "By 2030, a viable giant panda population lives in well-managed forests of the upper reaches of the Yangtze River, which in turn provides ecological services to the people living in its vicinity and further downstream." That vision means so much, not just for the future of the panda and the people of China, but for the rest of the world too.

China's phenomenal economic progress has brought tremendous environmental pressures – but the Chinese government is attempting to redress some of the damage. Reforestation, and saving and enhancing biodiversity, are goals of its environmental strategy. To the Chinese, the giant panda is far more than an evolutionary curiosity. It is a unique, necessary component of the country's environmental rehabilitation plan.

The WWF works alongside the Chinese authorities to integrate all the giant panda's habitats into a network that is part of the wider landscape. Youde clasped my hand. "Let's join hands to protect this beating heart, its functional ecosystems like forest, grassland, wetland, lakes, and their relevant key species at landscape level, so we can leave a living future for giant pandas."

"How far is the Chinese government committed?" I asked Su Chunyu, a very senior official in the Ministry of Forestry, who works in a large Soviet-style building. Among all the bustle and glitz of modern Beijing, these symbols are a reminder of the all-encompassing power of the Chinese government. There was a time when a panda hide could be sold for $10,000. Su shook his head emphatically.

"There is no trade in panda skins. It is completely banned." I was not surprised to hear him say this – trading in panda skins carries the death penalty.

There will be no trophy hunters either, no rich Americans coming over with high-powered rifles. The Chinese government will see to that, too.

Men like Su Chunyu and Chang Youde realize that saving the giant panda is China's own responsibility and opportunity. It is part of the battle to save China itself from the scourge of development.

First published in the *Sunday Times*, 17 April 2011

39

The Inambari Dam in the Peruvian Amazon

When Hylton Murray-Philipson, the green financier, writes to me, I sit up and take notice. Five years ago he invited me to stay with his friend Tashka for a long weekend. I was delighted to accept, though the logistics of the trip were complicated. Tashka is the paramount chief of the Yawanawa tribe. The Yawanawa tribe live in the heart of the Amazon forest, in the state of Acre, Brazil, not far from the Brazil-Peru border. Hylton and I flew from London to Sao Paulo, then on to Rio Branco, the capital of Acre. Then we took a small plane to Tarauaca, landing in a grassy clearing in the jungle. After that we canoed up stream for a couple of days before reaching Tashka's village. Some weekend!

That Yawanawa excursion wasn't just a jaunt. On my return I wrote an article for a national newspaper about how the Brazilian authorities were proposing to tarmac the BR364 all the way from Rio Branco to the border with Peru. The highway, I reported, would have a severe impact on the Yawanawa tribe, whose territory was virtually adjacent.

Now Hylton was writing to me about another threat to the Amazon – the projected Inambari Dam in Peru.

In the interests of transparency I reproduce here the full text of Hylton's email to me of 18 December, 2009. "Thought you might like to see this," he wrote.

Even if the sender of the attachment had not been Hylton, I would – I am sure – have been riveted. The report Hylton forwarded with his email described in more detail a major hydroelectric development in Peru. The Inambari Dam was to be the first of a series of dams in the Peruvian Amazon to be financed by Brazil with by far the largest part of the hydroelectric energy generated being exported to Brazil. The dam, producing 2,000 MW, would be the fifth largest in the whole of South America.

There was another reason why I took Hylton's email seriously. By a strange coincidence I was actually planning a trip to the Peruvian Amazon within the next few weeks en route to the Andes and the Galápagos Islands. My wife and I had already booked in to stay a couple of nights at Inkaterra's famous Reserva Amazonica, the "eco-lodge" set in the heart of the Peruvian Amazon on the Madre de Dios River, downstream from the town of Puerto Maldonado. Was the Inambari dam-site anywhere near Puerto Maldonado, I wondered?

A few minutes with a map in front of me provided the answer: "Up to a point, Lord Copper". As far as I could tell the Inambari dam-site was to be situated at the junction of the Inambari and Madre de Dios rivers, around 80 miles from Puerto Maldonado. I was intrigued to note that Puerto Maldonado itself was not very far from the territory of Yawanawa tribe, which I had visited with Hylton. It just happened to be on the Peruvian side of the border.

I rang up our obliging travel agent. Could she give us one more day in the Peruvian Amazon?

Laura sounded sceptical. "Are you sure you can get from the lodge to the dam-site and back all in one day? That's a lot of ground to cover in that part of the world."

To tell the truth, for virtually the whole of my life I have been fascinated by the Amazon. In my gap year, I criss-crossed Brazil, ending up in Brasilia at a time when the city, which is now the nation's capital, was just a red scar in the jungle. I must have been back to the Brazilian Amazon half a dozen times since then. The lure of those great rivers and the seemingly endless forest is irresistible.

"I'll give it a go," I replied.

In the event, landslides and torrential rain in the Andes earlier this year, forced us to delay our trip to Peru. My wife and I landed in Lima around 6pm on 29 March. Alfredo Novoa-Peña, who had been alerted via email by Hylton, met us in our hotel around 9pm.

Given the time-difference between London and Lima and the fact that we had changed planes in Madrid, Jenny and I had been travelling for around nineteen hours so we were perhaps not at our most sparkling. Alfredo made up for it.

A former Peruvian ambassador to Germany, and now president of the Peruvian renewable-energy association, he was clearly himself renewably energized by the prospect of the looming battle. As we sat in the lobby, sipping our first pisco sour of the trip, he expanded on the briefing Hylton Murray-Philipson had previously supplied. Brazil and Peru had already signed a memorandum of understanding, allowing Brazil to study, finance, build and operate six hydroelectric plants in Peru, including the Inambari Dam, with most of the energy destined for Brazil, but many Peruvians were opposed to it. As far as the Inambari Dam itself was concerned, 40,000 hectares of land would be flooded, including part of the buffer zone of one of Peru's most important national parks. Up to 12,000 persons would be displaced. The downstream effect of the dam on the flow of the river had still to be assessed. Above all, Alfredo Novoa-Peña rejected the whole concept that Brazil, "in its imperialistic way", as he put it, could somehow buy up the Peruvian Amazon and exploit it for its own benefit.

He told me: "We do not want, we will not accept, we firmly reject the Brazilian model for the Amazon region. Over my dead body are we going to allow that. My last granddaughter is my inspiration. I am speaking on her behalf."

Early next morning, my wife and I took the plane to Puerto Maldonado. Though there had been clouds over the Andes, which we had to cross on the way from Lima, as we began our descent into the selva, the vast green forest that is Peru's Amazonian territory, the weather cleared. Looking out of the window at the landscape below, I began to understand what the fuss was all about. One of the reasons that this issue of hydroelectric power in Peru's "high forest" has become a political hot-potato, is because

Peru has so many potentially excellent dam-sites, conveniently located on rivers which debouch from the steep mountain valleys onto the plains. From an engineering point of view, you can get a big bang for your buck.

If Alfredo Novoa-Peña, and his allies, are convinced that Peru is making the wrong decision, that the sale of these precious natural resources to finance the explosive growth of its big neighbour, Brazil, cannot be justified, others take a different view. Peru, they say, is a poor country. It cannot afford to pass up a major economic opportunity and the resulting revenues that will flow into national coffers. A stable source of hydroelectric power can also, they argue, transform the lives of thousands of people living in the towns, villages and settlements of Peru's Amazon region.

My travel agent had been right to query the feasibility of making a quick "side-trip" from Inkaterra's Reserva Amazonica 12 miles down the river from Puerto Maldonado all the way to the Inambari dam-site and back in a single day. To tell the truth, I too had my doubts, even though I was determined to do my best to get there. I had imagined I would be spending hours lurching in a 4-wheel drive vehicle along dirt roads, returning to the Inkaterra lodge well after midnight or even later. In practice, the trip to Inambari was a good deal easier than I had anticipated.

Around 7am the morning after our arrival at the lodge, I took the boat back upstream to Puerto Maldonado where Naturaleza, Brazil's vigorous and well-respected nature protection organization, has an office. Forewarned by Alfredo, the director of the Puerto Maldonado office, Hector Vilchez, welcomed me warmly. I was left in no doubt that his team viewed the Inambari project with the greatest misgivings. But his English wasn't good enough, nor was my Spanish, for prolonged conversation. Fortunately, Hector Vilchez had designated a young Peruvian anthropologist, Daniel Valencia Samamé, to act as my guide and interpreter.

By 10.15am, Daniel and I had left Puerto Maldonado to head in a more or less south-westerly direction on the road to the

Inambari dam-site. If I had been expecting an unmade-up track slicing through the forest, I was agreeably surprised. Though single-track, the road was tarmacked and for the most part in good condition. Every few miles, huge billboards had been erected.

"*CORREDOR VIAL INTEROCEANICO SUR: PERU–BRASIL!*", the signs grandly said.

Daniel explained: "This is going to be the route of the Great Inter-Oceanic Highway which will connect the Atlantic and the Pacific Oceans. In Peru, the work has already started. But the bridge over the river in Puerto Maldonado still has to be built. And in Brazil, the road to the border still has to be completed."

Suddenly, it all became clear to me. When Hylton and I had been visiting the Yawanawa a few years earlier, we had been campaigning against the hardtopping of the BR364 and the damage it might do to the indigenous populations in the area. Now I realized that the BR364 was not just a Brazilian road. It was a vital section of the Inter-Oceanic Highway!

I found myself looking at the road we were travelling on in a whole new light. Imagine, I said to myself, that the Brazilians actually complete their stretch of road; imagine that the bridge is built at Puerto Maldonado; imagine that Peru in turn continues to upgrade the highway to the coast. What would there be then to stop hundreds of lorries thundering along each day laden with logs and trees as they head from the interior of Brazil to Peru's Pacific ports? The Japanese, I thought, and other Asian "tiger-economies" with their insatiable demand for tropical timber, must be beside themselves with joy at the prospect. As for the potential impact of the road on the rates of Amazon deforestation, well, the prospect was almost too hideous to contemplate. Up till now, all timber from the Amazon has to be exported to the Atlantic coast of South America. If you opened up the Pacific export route, you might as well put a match to the forest and have done with it.

We reached Inambari around 2pm. Daniel and I stood on the bridge across the river, at precisely the spot where the new dam would be constructed, if the project is given the go-ahead. It was

– no doubt about it – a stunning location. Two great rivers meet here, flowing in from two separate Andean valleys. It seemed to my untutored eye that a relatively simple structure, a few hundred feet long, would permit the impounding of a great wall of water with massive hydroelectric potential.

I permitted myself the first joke of the day. "From a technical point of view, Daniel, this dam site is a damn sight better than some other places I've seen."

But of course, as Daniel was quick to point out, this was not really a laughing matter.

In a few weeks' time the Brazilian government will have to give its final decision on the Inambari Dam. By then, presumably, it will have the benefit of the environmental impact study it has commissioned. People like Alfredo Novoa-Peña are sceptical.

"They have only spent US$200,000 dollars on the study. A serious study would cost at least $2 million."

Will the environmental impact assessment factor in all the elements associated with the loss of 40,000 hectares of tropical forest? Will it take into account the transformation that will be wrought by the arrival in the area of hundreds, perhaps thousands, of workers? Will it look ahead, beyond Inambari, to the construction of other dams in the Peruvian Amazon? Already five other potential dam-sites have been identified. Those projects, if they go ahead, may result in a far greater displacement of people than the Inambari Dam itself will. Peru's indigenous tribes – the Asháninka, Shipibos etc. – will certainly be massively disrupted.

And outside Peru? What will the generation of vast quantities of hydro-power in Peru, for export to Brazil, mean for developments in other parts of the Amazon basin? What use will Brazil make of these new cheap energy supplies except to hasten the already scarily rapid transformation of its Amazon territories? And what in turn does that mean for the future of indigenous peoples, not just in Peru, but in the Amazon region as a whole? What does it mean for the fight against global warming, indeed for the future of the planet itself?

The irony is that, if Peru does go ahead with the Inambari Dam, presumably over Alfredo Novoa-Peña's dead body, they will have to flood over 60 miles of the embryonic Great Inter-Oceanic Highway, between Inambari and Puno. That section is not yet built. If they go ahead with the dam, it never will be. And it may take several years to develop an alternative major road through the Andes to the Pacific. Every cloud has a silver lining.

First published in *Papagaio*, 13 May 2011

40

No Passport Needed
For Grassholm's Gannets

When Mike Clarke, the RSPB's chief executive, invited me to join him on a visit to Grassholm and Ramsey Island, I jumped at the chance. I have been lucky enough to visit some of the great seabird breeding areas in the world – the albatross colonies on Bird Island, South Georgia, the penguin colonies of the Antarctic Peninsula, the crested auks off Russia's Kamchatka Peninsula – but in decades of wildlife watching I have never managed to visit the incomparable south-west Pembrokeshire coast. The island of Grassholm alone has 40,000 pairs of gannet, 10 per cent of the total world population.

Right up to the last moment, there was an element of doubt about whether the sea would be calm enough for us to cross from St Justinian. But, in the event, our little venture was blessed with a most glorious day. Landings are no longer permitted in the interests of the wildlife – unless you're part of a scientific team. The science, of course, is crucially important: each year, scores of gannets are tagged and vital information is thereby gleaned about migration patterns and other movements.

As a non-scientist, I was quite content with the non-landing edict, for what I saw from the deck of the boat that morning will stay with me for the rest of my life. Every surface of the rock – for Grassholm is really just a great rock rising sheer from the sea – seemed to be occupied by a nesting bird. At the same time, the sky above and around the island was full of birds, whirling and diving. Of course, there were puffins and guillemots, razorbills and shags as well, but it is the sight of those mighty gannets that will stay with me to my dying day.

Ramsey Island is larger – two miles long and a mile wide. Our hosts were wardens Greg and Lisa Morgan, who have lived full time on the island for the past six years. Landing is permitted, so with the Morgans' guidance, this time on foot, we explored another extraordinary environment. From the cliff-top, you can look down into the coves to the grey seal pups – Ramsey has the largest population of grey seals in southern England.

There are seven or eight pairs of choughs there, and we must have seen three of them that day. "There are only 500 pairs in the whole of the UK," Mr Morgan told us, "and 250 of those are in Wales." It is no accident that choughs are thriving on Ramsey – Mrs Morgan keeps a close eye on the sheep. "They keep the grass short," she explains, "which means the choughs can get at the worms and beetles and other insects they feed on."

There are about 3,500 guillemots on Ramsey Island, and some 1,500 razorbills, but the truly exciting thing for me is that about 2,000 pairs of Manx shearwaters have made it their home. Mr Morgan crouched over a shearwater burrow in the sward, put his iPhone to the mouth of the hole and played the recorded call of the male bird. "If there's another male there, he'll answer the call; if it's the female's turn to take care of the nest, she'll keep quiet." He tried a couple of burrows, but answer came there none.

At the third attempt, our luck changed. Mr Morgan put his hand to the hole and pressed the switch. As soon as the recording had finished, from somewhere in the burrow below us there came an answering call, mimicking exactly the sound that we had just played. It was uncanny. But, I promise you, this was what happened. Mr Morgan stood up. "When that chick finally emerges from the burrow later this summer, he'll fly straight off to South America."

First published in *Country Life*, 22 June 2011

41

Climb Every Mountain!

Don't let anyone tell you climbing Mount Kinabalu, the highest summit in South-East Asia, is a pushover. It isn't.

OK, at the age of seventy-one I admit I'm no spring chicken. But having climbed Africa's highest mountain, Kilimanjaro, two months before heading to Borneo, I was confident I'd take Kinabalu in my stride.

But one thing bothered me. Though its summit is not as high as Kilimanjaro's, the speed of ascent and – above all – descent is much faster. Would I be up to the challenge?

The summit of Mount Kinabalu is known as Low's Peak, after a British colonial secretary who, ironically, never scaled it despite three attempts.

I flew overnight with Malaysian Airways from London to Kuala Lumpur, where I changed planes for Kota Kinabalu, Sabah's capital.

On arrival, I was driven straight to the headquarters of Kinabalu National Park, 50 miles north-east of the city. Around 8am the next morning, accompanied by my Malaysian guide, I began to climb.

"My full name is Masnani," the woman guide told me. "But you can call me Nani."

She was forty-two and had five children, the eldest of whom was eighteen. I told her I had six children, whose ages range from forty-seven to twenty-six. Bonds thus established, Nani offered to carry my rucksack, as well as her own, but I pooh-poohed the idea.

I wouldn't say Nani and I spent a lot of time talking as we forged our way up the trail towards the hut where we, along with other climbers, would spend the night. Frankly, I preferred to save my breath.

That first day we climbed from the Timpohon Gate – at 6,122ft – to the Laban Rata resthouse, an amazing construction built like a Tibetan monastery at the edge of the mountain at more than 10,000ft. In other words, we climbed up almost 4,000ft.

The trail winds up through gnarled tree roots to a mossy world of drifting clouds, orchid-draped trees and rhododendrons.

Then you pass the tree-line and enter a world of sheer granite cliffs and vast, smooth-sided boulders.

It is a bit of a misnomer to say climbers spend the night in the Laban Rata resthouse before tackling the summit. You have a few hours' break and that's about it.

Having been warned by Nani we would be starting on the next stage of our climb at 2.30am, I lay down on my bunk at 9pm. The idea is to reach the summit at sunrise, so the first few hours of the climb would be in darkness.

"Don't forget your head-torch," she had said.

Of course, I forgot my head-torch. Happily, for 20 ringgits (£5) I was able to hire one from the resthouse.

It was money well spent. There were moments during the dash to the summit when you needed to haul yourself up a rope using both hands. In no way would a hand-held torch have been fit for purpose.

There was at least one occasion when, unbalanced by the weight of my rucksack, I found myself swinging wildly over an abyss.

One of the advantages of being a slow climber is that by the time I reached the summit – at 10am, long after dawn – all the other climbers had left.

As I plodded upwards towards the distant, towering peak, I found myself being greeted by a succession of Malaysians, Japanese, Koreans and Chinese on their way back. Most of them wished me luck.

Some, visibly astonished, asked how old I was and when I gave my age I could see they were impressed.

I'm not sure I deserved that respect. It was just such a pleasure to be there. For twenty minutes on a brilliantly sunny morning, I enjoyed the view of Sabah's forests and mountains while, to the west, the blue waters of the South China Sea were clearly visible.

Suffering no ill effects from the cold or altitude, I felt I could have stayed up there for hours, but Nani urged me to start on down.

She was right. Though I had trekking poles, my knees took a hammering and a couple of times I missed my step.

By mid-afternoon we were only half-way down the mountain and by sunset we still had at least two miles to go. I was making heavy weather of it.

The second time Nani offered to strap my rucksack on top of hers, I gratefully agreed. Even so, it was past 7pm when we completed the descent to Timpohon Gate, where, happily, our transport was still waiting.

Of course, you don't need to climb Mount Kinabalu to enjoy Malaysia's first World Heritage site. The Kinabalu Park covers 300 square miles, with an astonishing variety of fauna and flora that crosses four climate zones.

It is home to 1,200 species of orchid and twenty-six species of rhododendron as well as the world's largest pitcher plant. The insect-eating Rajah Brooke's pitcher plants can hold up to six pints of water.

The two days I spent in Kinabalu were a brilliant prelude to a week-long Borneo adventure that included some welcome rest and recuperation in the amazing Shangri-La Rasa Ria resort in Kota Kinabalu, an overnight stay at the Batang Ai Longhouse resort in Sarawak's tropical rainforest, a boat trip to a traditional Iban community and an afternoon at Semenggoh nature reserve, 15 miles south-west of Kuching, Sarawak's historic capital.

I saw five orangutans there, including a mother and infant. Of course, they were not wild.

Semenggoh is home to a rehabilitation centre for animals orphaned due to hunting and deforestation, or rescued from cages where they were kept illegally as pets.

But the aim is to return them to the wild. To see them swinging through the trees of their forest home is a fabulous experience.

Borneo's forests are under threat as never before. Responsible tourism has much to offer as an alternative to the despoilation of its natural resources – particularly timber and palm oil plantations – which is, alas, all too prevalent.

First published in the *Daily Mail,* 12 August 2011

42

Easter Island: The Eyes Have It

I will never forget my first glimpse of Ahu Tongariki. We were driving the cliff-top road on the eastern margins of Easter Island, near the Poike Peninsula. The sun blazed, herds of wild horses roamed the headlands and, far below, big waves smashed against red rocks. Suddenly, a bend – then the statues, fifteen colossal *moai* looming up along their panoramic platform, stony-faced soldiers on parade. This must be one of the wonders of the world – but that afternoon, we were the only people there.

One thousand years ago, when they were raised, Easter Island's stone sentries were less inscrutable. "The *moais* had eyes," explained Beno, my guide that day. "The last thing our forefathers did when they erected a statue was to carve the eye sockets and insert the eyes they had already made from coral. This was a special moment, when the ancestor's *mana*, his soul and spirit, leapt back to life."

Easter Island! I have been longing to go there for half a century, ever since I picked up Thor Heyerdahl's great travelogue *Aku-Aku* – his account of sailing a balsa-wood raft 3,000 miles across the Pacific Ocean to the world's most isolated chunk of rock – and couldn't put it down. It poses fascinating questions. How did the islanders get here, and where was their home? How had their giant totems been carved? How did they grapple them into position? What did they signify? And, above all, why had a thousand-year-old civilization, capable of such artistic greatness, collapsed into a civil war so vicious that its people ended up eating each other? By the time Heyerdahl visited, not a single statue was left standing. Something had gone disastrously wrong.

"How on earth did your people get the statues to the platforms?" I ask.

Beno smiles.

"Maybe they walked on their own."

Since reading *Aku-Aku* I've travelled all over South America. I have seen Machu Picchu, the Galápagos, Patagonia, the Amazon rainforest. But Easter Island remained elusive. Then I read Jared Diamond's 2005 book *Collapse*, the opening chapter of which resembles a detective story.

It is all about the strange events at Easter Island, and how the gobbling up of scarce resources virtually destroyed a once flourishing society. *Collapse* has become a textbook for the environmental movement, and I longed to visit the scene of the crime – to investigate first-hand. Rapa Nui, the "Big Island" of the ancients, is a speck in an awful lot of sea. It's a miracle that those prehistoric Polynesian canoeists found it in the first place.

Today, it has 4,500 residents, one bank and one petrol station. If there were a road encircling the coast, it would stretch just 40 miles. There isn't. But you can ride, hike or explore by 4-wheel drive, and the team from the Chilean-owned Explora travel company devised a plan that went to the very heart of the island's mysteries.

Perhaps the most striking thing about my stay was the passionate young men and women who showed me around – almost all can trace their families back to the island's original eleven tribes. Beno, a descendant of tribal kings, leads me to Rano Raraku, the quarry where nearly all the *moai* were made. Nearly 400 unfinished monoliths sprout from their mother volcano here, a nursery in stone. We hunt for the largest *moai* ever carved – all 69ft of it. It doesn't take much finding: the head alone is more than 20ft tall.

Nobody has really unlocked the secret of Easter Island. Did the islanders cut down trees to make rollers to move the stones? Did that cause the island's deforestation? And did the loss of resources lead to clan conflict, even cannibalism? At one point, the population fell to a mere handful from a peak of 15,000 or more. Yet Rapanui such as Beno are proud of their heritage, and understandably reluctant to sign up to the Jared Diamond theory, which blames the islanders for their own demise.

On my last day, I visit Orongo, the ceremonial village where Rapa Nui's birdman competition took place. After the disastrous upheavals of the past, the island's elders decided on a new method of electing a king. Each year, they gathered at this cliff-top village beside the crater of the Rano Kau volcano. Each tribe chose a champion. Eleven young men then swarmed down the cliffs, swam a mile out to the islet of Motu Nui and waited for the arrival of the sooty terns, which year after year migrate here in their thousands to nest.

The first to find a newly laid tern's egg would race back through the waves and scale the rocks to the top of the crag, carrying the egg on his forehead in a special pouch. Once the presiding priest had certified that this was indeed a sooty tern's egg, the chief of the victorious tribe was proclaimed king, a position he held for the next twelve months.

My guide this afternoon is Nicholas, a young Rapanui whose grandfather helped Thor Heyerdahl to raise upright one of the fallen *moai*.

"So the leader of the victorious tribe became king," I say. "But what was the reward for the young champion who found the first egg?"

"Each tribe brings a virgin to Orongo before the competition," Nicholas explains. "The winner gets to choose one of the virgins. As a matter of fact, he can have all the virgins, as long as he can find a way to keep them. That is his privilege."

He speaks of this extraordinary ritual as if it happens still. Easter Island's totems continued to be chiselled into the 17th century, almost to the time when the first Europeans arrived, bringing smallpox and slavery. The last birdman competition took place less than 150 years ago. And when my plane takes off for the mainland after three engrossing days and nights, I feel I have only scratched the surface of the place.

First published in the *Sunday Times*, 28 August 2011

Climbing Mt Kilimanjaro, Tanzania. From Gilman's Point, we were able to look down into Kilimanjaro's ice- and snow-covered crater. *See* p.201.

My guide Elibariki Simon in Mount Kilimanjaro National Park, who helped me up, and as importantly, down the mountain to Kibo camp. *See* p.201.

Tracking the giant panda in the Qinling mountains, Shaanxi Province, China. "Seconds later, a fully-grown male panda poked its head out of the forest twenty yards away." *See* p.206. *Photo credit*: Paul Craven

With Cheng, our guide, tracking pandas in the bamboo forests, Quinling mountains, Shaanxi Province, China. *See* chapter 38.

The still-to-be-completed Inter-Oceanic Highway in Peru. "If you open up the Pacific timber-export route, you might as well put a match to the Amazon forest." *See* p.212.

Climbing Mt Kinabalu, Sabah, Malaysia. One of the advantages of being a slow climber is that by the time I reached the summit, all the other climbers had left. *See* p.217.

Ahu Tongariki, Easter Island. Fifteen colossal *moai* loom up along their panoramic platform, stony-faced soldiers on parade. *See* p.221.

Rano Raraku, Easter Island. We hunted for the largest *moai* ever carved; the head alone is more than 20ft tall. *See* p.222.

A group of Marquesans performing the Pig Dance on a vast *paepae*.
See p.236.

Hotlin Ompusunggu was presented with a Whitley Award by HRH the
Princess Royal in May 2011. *See* chapter 43. *Photo credit*: Whitley Awards

Midsayup, Mindanao, southern Philippines. Inside the ring two stallions, already lathered in sweat and blood, tried to fight each other to a standstill. *See* p.241. *Photo credit*: Network for Animals

In Tanzania's Serengeti, the riverbanks opposite were, literally, heaving with wildlife as the wildebeest jostled each other before leaping into the foaming tide. *See* p.253.

Etosha National Park, Namibia. Lioness returning to the pride. *See* p.262.
Photo credit: Kathryn Haylett

The average full-throated roar of an Etosha lion lasts for 36.6 seconds and is repeated between four and eighteen times. *See* p.262.
Photo credit: Kathryn Haylett

Madikwe National Park, South Africa. The staggering total of 411 rhinos was poached in South Africa in 2011. *See* p. 257.
Photo credit: Eugene Bothma

British Graves at Spion Kop, Natal. When these young men dug themselves in that morning, they were in a very real sense digging their own graves. *See* p.260. *Photo credit*: Raymond Heron

43

Desperately Seeking Hotlin Ompusunggu

The first time I saw Hotlin Ompusunggu was in May 2011 at the headquarters of the Royal Geographical Society in Kensington. She was one of seven recipients of the Whitley Fund for Nature's Annual Awards. Now in their eighteenth year, the Whitley Awards aim to recognize outstanding contributions to the protection of the natural environment. HRH Princess Anne is the Patron and it is a task she takes very seriously, not least by actually turning up year after year in person to present the prizes.

Hotlin was, as I recall, the fourth or fifth person to be honoured that evening. As she walked up onto the stage of the RGS's Ondaatje Auditorium to deliver a brief acceptance speech and to receive her award, I glanced at a paper containing brief biographies of the prizewinners that had been handed out as we arrived. Hotlin, I noted, was a dentist! She had apparently started a whole new movement in Kalimantan, which is the Indonesian part of Borneo, linking the provision of dental care to conservation objectives.

Dentists for Conservation! The idea sounded totally intriguing. Hotlin had my attention even before she began her speech.

"As a dentist," she began, "I never imagine that I would receive a conservation award. As I am standing here, I remember a twelve-year-old girl, who almost broke her jaw because of chronic bone-related tooth infection. Her father brought her to our clinic a year ago for treatment, because he would not cut down trees from the forest home to Borneo orangutan to pay for his daughter's medical bills. Grateful for her recovery and in return for the care received, he brought us manure to plant trees in our reforestation projects. This project works."

At the end of the ceremony, when all the awards had been presented, Princess Anne made a graceful and witty speech herself, congratulating the winners on their achievements. Having listened to Hotlin Ompusunggu's own remarks, I was not surprised that the Princess Royal drew particular attention to the unusual nature of the Indonesian dentist's work.

"As in all the previous years," Princess Anne commented, "demonstrating the support of local communities is critical to achieving those positive conservation results. It isn't always approached in the same way and perhaps the most important thing about today's winners is underlining the fact that you don't have to be scientifically qualified in biology or natural sciences in order to make a difference. Being a dentist is just as important."

Princess Anne went on to say: "Yes, you need a degree of imagination and you certainly need a degree of persuasion but to use healthcare in its widest form to encourage people to look at their habitat very much more differently, to encourage them to be more constructive in replacing what has been lost sets an enormously good standard for the future and I hope will encourage a lot of people who may say to themselves they are simply not qualified to tackle the problem ..."

During the reception after the ceremony, I buttonholed Hotlin. I had been totally intrigued, I told her, by the project she described. Having been an environmentalist most of my professional life, and having a particular interest in the conservation of tropical rainforests, I wanted to understand more clearly what she and her team were doing out there in West Kalimantan. "When are you going back there?" I asked. "Could I come to visit you?"

Hotlin gave me a broad smile. "You are most welcome."

I scribbled down her directions on the back of my programme. "You can fly to Pontianak from Kuching or Jakarta," Hotlin said. "Then take a smaller plane to Ketapang and we will pick you up by car. It's about a two-hour drive to Sukadana, where the clinic is. Or else you can go by boat from Pontianak on the river all the way to Sukadana. That takes about six hours." She thought for a moment. "Maybe the best thing will be for you to take the plane to Ketapang when you first arrive, but make the return journey to Pontianak by boat."

Hotlin left London the following day, but she was remarkably efficient in responding to my emails. Less than six weeks after the RGS event, I found myself at Kuching International Airport in Sarawak waiting to board the Air Batavia plane to Pontianak, with an onward connection to Ketapang.

It wasn't my first trip to Indonesia. I had visited Java in the 1960s for the United Nations and had been back several times since including tours of Sumatra, Bali and Komodo on environmental business. Most pertinently, five years earlier I had visited Tanjung Puting National Park in south-central Kalimantan and had written about the devastating impact of the remorseless expansion of the palm oil industry on Kalimantan's remaining lowland forests. I had inveighed against the ever-growing demand for palm oil in consumer products and also against the EU's lunatic biofuel directive, which required us to put ever-increasing proportions of "biodiesel" in our tanks. As a result, the Indonesian government was allowing, and even encouraging, the destruction of the last remaining habitats of the orangutan and other threatened forest species.

In late 2005, when I was last there, the once-forested areas around Tanjung Puting National Park had already been totally devastated by palm oil plantations and it was quite clear that major encroachments were taking place within the boundaries of the National Park itself. One of my most vivid memories from that earlier visit was the sight of huge lines of tankers, laden with palm oil, which you could see each day heading to the coast against a backdrop of smouldering forests.

Would the situation I wondered be any better in West Kalimantan, one of the remotest regions of the country? Or would the chainsaws have already wreaked their havoc even there?

The airport at Ketapang is a small friendly place. Hotlin came onto the tarmac to greet me when the plane from Pontianak touched down. She had come out from Sukadana with a driver, which meant that in the car on the way back we had time to talk.

Now almost thirty-seven years old, she told me she had trained as a dentist in Medan in Sumatra. After she had graduated, she had worked first in community outreach programmes in rural Sumatra, then on a mobile boat clinic. When the tsunami hit Aceh, Sumatra's most northerly province, in December 2004, she had coordinated a medical and dental relief team. Even now, more than five years on, it was clear that this had been a traumatic experience.

"200,000 people were killed. Two weeks after the tsunami I still saw bodies of dead people in the street. In one village all the people were dead."

One of the reasons Hotlin speaks English so well is that, after her work on tsunami relief was over, she spent a year in England gaining a Certificate of Higher Education at Redcliffe College, Gloucester. Soon after she returned to Indonesia, a "friend of a friend" called her to ask whether she would like to come to work on a new programme in West Kalimantan. The idea was to combine human health with environmental health.

That telephone call – from an American woman, Kinari Webb, whom I would meet next day – obviously marked a turning-point in Hotlin's life.

As we drove through one village after another, overtaking motorcycles and scooters and dodging all varieties of livestock, Hotlin explained her point of view to me.

"Many people, including my family, my friends, and even the community that I am working with wonder what I am doing. They are very surprised that a dentist is also doing conservation work."

She turned round to face me, eyes glowing: "They are wrong. It's a beautiful life. Once we had a patient who had a burn all over her face. Yet she greeted me every morning with a smile. She was so happy."

We reached Sukadana in the early evening. Once, long before the Dutch discovered the "East Indies", Sukadana was one of the main trading ports on the west coast of Kalimantan. Though the glory days may have passed, the town's location at precisely the spot where the tropical rainforest meets the South China Sea still gives it an immense charm. As we sat on the terrace of my hotel, Hotlin explained that the location of the town at the very edge of Gunung Palung National Park was a factor in her decision to come here, rather than somewhere else, in Kalimantan.

Illegal logging, she explained, driven by global demand for timber and palm oil, was destroying vast areas of Indonesian forest each year. Bornean orangutan numbers had dwindled from hundreds of thousands to about 45,000 in the wild. Orangutan could be extinct in the wild within twenty years. Gunung Palung National Park – she gestured in the direction of the surrounding heavily forested hills – was haven to about 2,000 orangutan, one of the most dense and largest populations of the species, about 17 per cent of the estimated population in Borneo and close to 10 per cent of the world's population. Gunung Palung was also home to endangered species such as sun bears, proboscis monkeys and gibbons, plus hornbills among an estimated 178 types of birds. With the relentless expansion of palm oil plantations all around, there were more and more pressures on the National Park, not just from those who wished to chip away at the park boundaries to establish palm oil plantations, but from local people who now increasingly turned to the park to meet their needs for firewood and timber.

"That is why what the clinic does to help protect the forest is so important," Hotlin concluded.

I went to bed that night with the sound of the waves lapping against the beach below my window. I had come a long way to see these "front-line conservationists". I hoped that the clinic would live up to its billing.

The full name of the Hotlin Ompungsunggu's clinic is Alam Sehat Lestari which, literally, means Healthy Nature Everlasting. The name by which the place is usually known is the Asri clinic, Asri being an abbreviation of the full title. The driver came to pick me up in the morning and I arrived in time to hear Etty Rahmawati, a young woman responsible for "community outreach", explaining the basic principles on which the clinic worked to a roomful of outpatients – some fifteen or twenty so far. Each village and sub-village in the district, Etty said, had been classified according to the actions being taken there to prevent illegal logging.

She pointed to a chart on the wall. "If you come from a village which has protected the park, that's one of the green areas on the chart, you get the largest discount on the cost of the treatment. If you come from a blue area, you only get half the discount. And if you come from a red area, where illegal logging still continues, you have to pay the full price."

Etty went on to explain that there were many ways of paying the clinic's fees. "You can pay with seedlings, or with woven mats or baskets, or even with bags of manure."

After the briefing, the outpatients waited for their treatment. Hotlin had her own dental surgery. With the patient's permission, I was allowed to sit quietly and watch while Hotlin did some root-canal work on a middle-aged woman who had arrived an hour earlier on her little put-put motorcycle from one of Sudakana's outlying hamlets.

"Once I had a woman patient," Hotlin told me as she poked and probed, "who brought her baby with her and the baby fell asleep on her breast as I worked."

Dentistry is not exactly a spectator sport. It is a slow, painstaking business, even under the unusual circumstances that prevail in the Asri clinic. After a while, I went next door where Dr Nur, one of the clinic's doctors, was busy removing a foreign body from a young man's eye.

It was here that I encountered, for the first time, Kinari Webb, the American woman, the "friend of a friend" who five years earlier had made the crucial telephone call that had brought Hotlin Ompusunggu to Sudakana, sight unseen. Kinari is herself a fully qualified doctor. She explained that, as a foreigner, she is allowed to "assist and advise" in all aspects of the clinic's medical work.

And that is precisely what she does now, taking her turn to fish with a needle and fine tweezers in the man's eye and eventually extracting an irksome splinter from the eyeball. Later that morning Kinari has to deal with a real medical emergency when a woman with a hugely enlarged spleen arrives for treatment. Kinari shakes her head: "What makes it worse is that she's six months pregnant. Splenamegaly! That's what she has. She'll never go to term unless we can do something for her." In practice that may mean getting the poor woman to hospital and the nearest hospital is in Pontianak. In terms of accessibility, it might as well be on the other side of the moon. Kinari hopes one day soon to raise enough funds to build a proper hospital in Sudakana.

Dr Kinari Webb is President and Founder of an American NGO called Health in Harmony, whose main purpose is to support Hotlin's clinic, is married to Campbell Webb, PhD, an Englishman who works for the Arnold Arboretum of Harvard University. "You must meet Cam," she says. "Please come to dinner tonight."

I arrive early at the Webbs' house. Cam and Kinari actually met in Borneo, some fifteen years ago, when they were both working in the Gunung Palung Research Centre, deep in the forest. They have been here, on and off, ever since. Cam and I have a pre-prandial beer.

"When we first came to West Kalimantan," Cam tells me, "the forest was everywhere. Pontianak itself was a timber town. Now the timber companies have largely gone because 70 per cent of the lowland forests have gone. The palm oil companies go in for clear-cutting, selling the timber, then planting. Of course, there are still forests in the central and northern parts of Kalimantan – the montane forests. But they don't have the rich biodiversity of the lowland forests. The tallest trees here could reach a height of 85 metres!"

Kinari joins us as we wait for Hotlin. In her forties, she is a warm, good-looking humorous woman who decided long ago that working in the field, about as far from so-called "civilization" as you could possibly be, was what she wanted to do.

"I had this vision," she told me, "of combining human and environmental health. I spoke to my friend about it and she said 'you have to have Hotlin'. I said 'I don't know Hotlin'. But my friend said 'just call her anyway'. So I did. We spoke on the telephone. I was so impressed with her response to my request. Hotlin said: 'This is what I've been waiting for.' She just got on a plane and came. At the time we could only pay her $100 a month. She said: 'I don't care. I'm doing it because I believe in it.' When she got here, she slowly began to understand the conservation work as well as the medical side. This programme would never have made it without her. She has this passion, intensity and willingness. She is so scrupulously honest. She is one of the most moral people I have met."

I don't know whether Hotlin's ears were burning when she arrived. They certainly should have been.

At dinner, I raised an issue that had been bothering me. "I understand that you modulate the medical and dental charges in accordance with the status of the forest: green, blue or red or whatever. But how do you really know what is going on? How do you find out about the illegal logging, who is doing it and where?"

"We have our forest guardian programme," Hotlin replied. "We have thirty forest guardians spread around the different villages and sub-villages. They know what is going on."

Over the next days, I met several of these forest guardians. The £30,000 which Hotlin received from the Whitley Fund for Nature has helped to put the forest guardian programme on a sound financial basis, at least for the next year. These young men and women are truly at the sharp end of conservation.

What Hotlin and Kinari have realized of course is that it is not enough to try to persuade the villages to stop going into the forest with a chain-saw; you have to give them an alternative source of income. So Asri has had to expand its horizons. Yes, it is still a clinic with a mission to bring better health to the villagers of the area. But, willy-nilly, it has also had to become involved with farming and agriculture. Asri now runs a nursery for plants and saplings.

One afternoon, Hotlin takes me to a village to see some cows. There are twelve of them, tethered in an open-sided shed, munching on bundles of grass the villagers gather from the surrounding open areas. The grass goes in one end; the manure comes out the other.

"We have helped the villagers practise organic farming," Hotlin explains. "They are saving a lot of money because now they don't have to buy fertilizer."

Looking at the cows munching away, I can't help wondering whether Asri, in seeking to turn itself into an agricultural as well as a medical enterprise, may not have bitten off more than it can chew. But when I talk to Hotlin and those who work with her, absorbing their confidence and vitality, these doubts melt away. Alam, one of the forest guardians whose village we are visiting, tells me proudly: "I have convinced two illegal loggers to stop logging. There is still one man in the village illegally logging, but I hope to persuade him too."

Illegal logging is one thing. I am ready to believe that the Asri approach will deliver the goods and that within the boundaries of Gunung Palung National Park we will continue to see progress. But the relentless expansion of the palm oil plantations is quite another story.

On my last day in Kalimantan Hotlin and I visited the manager of a large palm oil company whose headquarters were about an hour's drive along the coast from Sukadana. The company had acquired 18,000 hectares of forest adjacent to Gunung Palung National Park. The manager told us proudly that more than a third, around 6,600 hectares, was going to be set aside for conservation.

He had prepared a snappy powerpoint presentation showing the areas where the trees would not be cut down. The company hoped to be compensated by the government or the international community for "avoiding deforestation and degradation".

My heart sank as I looked at the map. Of course, it was good that some forest areas were going to be reprieved. Even so, a huge expanse of rich lowland rainforest was about to be devastated and a vital wildlife corridor was about to be destroyed.

Following the suggestion Hotlin had made when I first met her at the RGS in Kensington, I left Sukadana by boat. The craft I travelled in is known as the Bresoul Express, Bresoul being a corruption of Brussels. Years ago, during the three and a half centuries of Dutch rule, Sukadana was known as New Brussels.

From time to time during the six-hour journey we were caught in vicious tropical downpours but the boat's tarpaulin roof kept off the worst of the rain. About halfway through the journey, we stopped for lunch at one of the little riverside villages that are a feature of West Kalimantan.

As food goes, the meal I had on that occasion was probably the best – and the cheapest (less than a US dollar) – of my whole Borneo trip. This is the somewhat succinct summary of my visit to Sudakana, as inscribed in my damp notebook at around 1pm on 12 July, 2011 while consuming a plateful of prawns and *nasi goreng*.

"Left Sukadana this am. Believe Hotlin has a good chance of success, at least in terms of keeping Gunung Palam free of illegal logging. Much bigger issue is continued spread of palm oil plantations."

To expand briefly on that last thought, now that I am safely back in England. One of the underlying problems, it seems to me, is the failure to curb the ever-increasing demand for palm oil. Until politicians and the public are ready to confront this issue head on, brilliant programmes such as those promoted by Hotlin Ompusunggu and Asri will at best be rearguard actions.

I can think of one measure which would have an amazing symbolic and practical effect: namely, a pledge by the UK government to withdraw unilaterally from the EU's mad and damaging biofuel directive unless that directive is drastically modified or, better still, totally repealed.

A shorter version of this article was published in the *Independent,* 30 August 2011

44

The Marquesas:
Take the Cargo Ship to Paradise

Travelling on a working vessel through Polynesia is the best way to see the beautiful Marquesas.

Every month a cargo ship called *Aranui 3* sails 800 miles from Tahiti to a remote archipelago called the Marquesas. On board are vital supplies, such as food and medicines. The *Aranui* is a lifeline to the 8,000 people who live on these islands. No wonder the locals give it such a warm welcome when it docks.

That's one of the reasons this cruise is so out of the ordinary. While the accommodation, food and service are excellent, this is a working ship, the main role of which is to deliver supplies. That means that at every moment of our journey we were in regular contact with the Marquesans.

Because the ship's monthly visit is the high point of their calendar, the locals usually came down en masse to greet us at the dock as we moved from island to island. The islanders set up stalls by the water's edge, selling *pareos* (sarongs), *tapa* (bark cloth) and wood and stone carvings. The money they earn from the passengers is hugely important to them. If France ever reduces the subsidies that it pays to its overseas territories, these commercial transactions will become even more significant.

The Marquesans are overwhelmingly friendly. Did any grudge, I wondered, the hours they must have put in making the shell necklaces or garlands of flowers that they hung about our necks? They didn't seem to.

On the last Sunday of the voyage, we put in at Tahuata, the Marquesan island "discovered" by the Spaniards in 1595. This was also the site of the first French settlement in 1842. Catholic missionaries followed a few years later.

Along with several other passengers, I attended mass that morning in the tiny village of Vaitahu. The church was built a few years ago with funds provided by the Vatican. Brilliantly designed, it is a light, airy structure. If your attention wanders, you can lift your eyes to the surrounding tree-covered hills. High above the altar there is a stained-glass window of surpassing beauty, depicting a Polynesian Madonna and Child. There was a wonderful cheerfulness about the service. Several of the Marquesans had brought drums and ukuleles, and the congregation broke into song, or so it seemed, on every possible occasion.

In spite of a population collapse (from 100,000 in 1774 to 1,500 in 1921) caused by the arrival of the Europeans and their diseases, the Marquesans have retained – or at least reinvented – a strong cultural presence. On the fifth day of the voyage the *Aranui* put in at Taiohae, a spectacular bay on Nuku Hiva, the largest and most populated of the islands. While cargo was loaded and unloaded, we rode in Jeeps up winding mountain roads to the Taipivai valley. With the possible exception of Easter Island, this must be one of the finest examples of Polynesian culture in the South Pacific. Though only a fraction of the site has been cleared, you are able to gain a clear impression of what must have been an immense archaeological complex.

For me, the high point came when a group of Marquesans stood on a vast *paepae* (stone platform) in front of the biggest banyan tree I have ever seen to perform a ceremony known as the Pig Dance. How much of that dance was genuinely traditional and how much newly invented wasn't quite clear. And I never found out precisely what the dance symbolized. But there was no doubting the enthusiasm with which it was performed.

On these islands the past merges with the present. In a dry spell recently one of the giant banyan trees caught fire, revealing the skulls and skeletons of Marquesans whose bodies, according to tradition, had been concealed among its roots.

When you are moving, as we did, from island to island almost every day, you tend to ask yourself, as Paul Gauguin did in one of his most famous paintings: "Where did we come from? What are we? Where are we going?" Well, on Hiva Oa, you can visit Gauguin's grave. Though his most productive period in the South Pacific was probably spent on Tahiti, he came back from Europe at the beginning of the 20th century and settled in the Marquesas. Talking to the Marquesans, you get the feeling that Gauguin was a rather suspect character. He seduced the local girls, argued with the church and didn't pay his bills.

Jacques Brel, the Belgian singer, also died and is buried on Hiva Oa. He is much more popular than Gauguin, at least among the Marquesans. He brought a plane with him when he came to live on the islands, a Beechcraft that has been restored and is on display in a specially constructed hangar in Atuona village.

Visiting the Marquesas provides the ideal excuse for a stopover in Tahiti, Moorea or Bora Bora on the way out or on the journey home. We spent three nights on Moorea. For me the high point was the morning spent on a small catamaran watching the humpback whales. Our guide warned us not to expect too much. Most of the humpbacks, he said, had already started on their long journey back to Antarctic waters.

We were lucky that day. In four hours we must have seen half a dozen humpbacks at close quarters. There was one unforgettable moment when my wife and I quickly put on our flippers and facemasks and slipped from the boat into the water to swim alongside a mother and her calf.

First published in *The Times*, Saturday 10 December 2011

45

Horse fighting in the Philippines

On the surface at least, it seemed like a good morning to be leaving Manila. Huge crowds were already gathering for the annual Black Nazarene festival. Philippines President, Benigno Aquino, had warned of a possible terrorist attack. Yet I couldn't help wondering, as I caught the mid-morning Philippines Airways flight to Cotabato City, in south-west Mindanao, the Philippines' most turbulent and violence-prone province, whether this might not be a case of "out of the frying pan and into the fire".

Why was I in the Philippines in the first place? The short answer is that a few months ago my old friend Brian Davies invited me to see the work the charity he had founded, Network for Animals, was doing there. "We are concentrating on the horse fighting," he told me. "In theory it's banned under the law. In practice, illegal horse fights still take place in Mindanao in the far south of the country. In terms of animal welfare, they are truly horrific. We want to see the law enforced."

I knew about bullfighting and cockfighting. But horse fighting! Of course, I said yes. Over the years, along with environmental issues, promoting animal welfare has been one of my abiding interests.

Brian Davies put me in touch with Andrew Plumbly, a forty-four-year-old Canadian, who is Network for Animals' day-to-day director. When we spoke on the telephone (he is currently based in Canada, though planning to move to London soon) Andrew didn't try to minimize the dangers. In some areas of Mindanao, kidnapping, he said, was an almost daily occurrence, part of normal money-making activity. Local businessmen were mostly at risk. But there was the political element too as the separatist groups, particularly the Moro Islamic Liberation Front, looked for high-value targets, particularly foreigners, asking huge sums by way of ransom. "Starting offers can be above US$20 million, so I've heard," he told me. "If they don't get what they want, you're liable to be beheaded."

As I listened, Kipling's famous poem came to mind. "If you can keep your head while others all about you are losing theirs ..."

I had already looked at the Foreign Office's website. While all travel to Mindanao was strongly discouraged, some areas were strictly off limits.

"Couldn't we find a horse fight in one of the less dangerous parts of Mindanao?" I suggested.

"Let's hope so," Andrew replied.

I have to admit that what I heard gave me pause for thought. I spoke to my wife and she told me that she certainly wasn't going to sell the house to get me out of trouble. I rang the bank to warn them, though I was not particularly optimistic. RBS has enough difficulties of its own nowadays.

I still hadn't made up my mind when Andrew telephoned. According to the information he had received, a horse fight was definitely going to be staged the following week in Mindanao. The bad news was that it would take place in one of the most high-risk areas: Maguindanao Province. That meant flying to Cotabato City first, another high-risk destination, and a long drive through disputed territory.

I could hear the PA announcements in the background. Andrew was clearly at an airport. "I'm going to Manila today anyway," he said. "I've got things to do there for the charity. But we'll go on to Mindanao if you're sure you're up for it."

Of course, I wasn't sure. "Can we at least get a bodyguard?" I asked.

Dino Yebron met us at Cotabato airport and whisked us to his car. A sixty-two-year-old veterinarian, and well-connected former university professor, Dino works as a volunteer for Network for Animals in Mindanao. He had, brilliantly, arranged for two bodyguards, not just one. Tem and Nilo were standing by the vehicle toting innocuous-looking travel-bags. As we set off, all five of us in the chunky Toyota, Dino told us the guards were both policemen. The reason they were not in uniform was simple. Uniformed police carrying guns are apparently themselves a target. "The separatists will attack you just to get the weapons," he said.

We didn't dawdle in Cotabato City. This is not a place to dawdle. It's not just a question of kidnapping. Violence, whether random or premeditated, is the norm and you don't want to stick around to find out which version you are dealing with.

In any case, we were in a hurry. By the time we left the town it was after 2pm. Dino's scouts had informed him precisely where the "illegal" horse fight was being held and it was well over an hour's drive away.

"They started this morning already," Dino said. "In one day there may be thirteen or fourteen fights. The maximum fight time is one hour. In the past, there was no such ruling. One fight lasted five hours!"

Dino puts his foot on the pedal. We don't want to miss the fight, not after coming all this way. But it is not easy to make rapid progress. The state of the road is bad, not to say atrocious, with numerous one-way sections where traffic comes to a complete standstill. And then there are the constant checkpoints.

"There was a time when the checkpoints were every 100 metres," Dino comments. "So you knew it was a high-risk time. Now they are a bit further apart, so you feel more confident."

In spite – or possibly because of – the dangers and difficulties of his job, Dino has a highly developed sense of humour. "They call them checkpoints. But there are times when they don't accept cheques, they want cash. So we call them cashpoints instead!"

We have been driving for nearly an hour, when Dino points to a turning. "That's where the bus was diverted. A few months back, fifty-seven people were killed in one attack. Thirty-six of them were journalists. The mass grave was already prepared. They pushed the bodies and even the vehicle into the hole, then back-hoed the earth over it."

I wouldn't say I picked up every nuance of the story, but I got the gist. Maguindanao's incumbent provincial governor apparently resented being challenged by a rival so he arranged for his rival's campaign bus, laden with journalists and supporters, to be "rerouted" into a deadly ambush.

Dino tells us the governor lost the election and the rival won, but the (former) governor's trial has not yet taken place. He shakes his head in wonder. "How did they think they could get away with it?"

I surreptitiously check my passport, hoping it doesn't reveal my new career as a "journalist". Phew! I'm glad to see that the EU-style passports, unlike the old British model, don't ask you to state your profession.

We are less than 5 miles from a town called Midsayup when, over to the right, off the road, we see flags flying and banners waving and hear a loud-speaker blaring with what is obviously a running commentary. A huge sign, depicting two rearing stallions engaged in mortal combat, waves over a makeshift arena. Two or three hundred spectators are pressed up against the railings. This is clearly a great family occasion. Young and old, men and women, all turn out.

Police are present in case of trouble. Horse fighting may be a proscribed activity in the Philippines in the sense that it is banned by law, but the spectacle we are about to witness, illegal though it may be, has actually been licensed by the Mayor of Midsayup. The local constabulary is present to see that things don't get out of hand.

We park the car. Nobody pays us much attention. They are too busy concentrating on what is going on in the arena. Someone offers me a chair to stand on so I can look over the heads of the crowd.

The scenes I witnessed that afternoon were almost surreal. Inside the ring, two stallions, already lathered in sweat and blood, tried to fight each other to a standstill. They reared, they gouged, they kicked, and they slashed, all the while competing for the tethered mare. At times they came to a trembling halt, and almost nuzzled each other, before launching once more into a horrific attack. At other times, they raced around the arena at full speed, causing the referee and officials to step smartly aside or even slip quickly under the railings and out of harm's way.

For the most part the stallions that are entered in these local derbies are not reared specifically as fighters. They are animals which, when they are not fighting, are being used as beasts of burden or as a means of transport.

As I looked around that afternoon, it was quite obvious that the spectators were deeply involved in the fight. They are "aficionados" of the sport. If they didn't themselves appreciate the finer points of the contest, the broadcast commentary put them straight. But there is far more to horse fighting than the horse fight itself. The real reason these fights continue to take place, even though they are banned under the law of the land, seems to lie in the money that changes hand.

Yes, the owner of a winning horse will earn a tidy sum. If he has several winners, claiming the "Derby-Champion" title, he will gain a small fortune. But even more important are the bets placed by the spectators. Markers – "cristos", as they are called – make a mental note of the wagers shouted out by the crowd as the fight runs its course. For a few minutes at the end, the exits are blocked so that bets can be collected and money paid out. Yes, the police are on hand to make sure there is no violence. But they are there too, perhaps more importantly, to see that no one slips out of the venue without paying up.

As it turned out, the horse fight we watched that afternoon in Midsayup was the last of the day. I don't know when the fight actually started but by my watch the two stallions in the ring fought each other for over forty minutes before one of them was declared a winner.

The rules, as I understood them, are quite precise. If a stallion fails to challenge another, he can lose a point. If he runs for the exit chute, he can also lose a point. Once he loses two points, the other horse wins. En route to the verdict, there are lashings of blood and gore. One horse may gouge the other's leg or testicles. It may bite the other's neck and sides. No, it is not a pretty sight.

Dino, with his long veterinary experience, is as much concerned for the welfare of the mare as for the stallions.

"That mare," he explained, pointing to the quivering animal roped in the middle of the arena, "has been out there in the sun all day. There may have been ten or twelve fights. She will have been mounted as many times. That's the winner's perk. You might say she's 'gang-raped'. And she will also be bitten and scratched and kicked as the stallions fight it out. For me," Dino concluded, "there is nothing noble or natural about the horse fight. This is a purely induced anger."

As Andrew and I stood there among the crowd, absorbing the spectacle, we encountered more than a few curious glances. There are few, if any, European or American faces to be seen in this part of Mindanao, and certainly not at these underground and "illegal" events.

But Dino had already prepared a cover story for us. After the last fight of the day was over, he took us around and introduced us to the referee and the other officials.

"Meet Mr Johnson," he urged them. "He is a big businessman from America. From Texas! Soon he will be introducing horse fighting in the rodeos over there!"

I did my best to look the part. "Y'all have a great day," I said, doffing my hat.

When it was all over, we went round the paddocks. We inspected the winning horses and the losing horses too. There was a time when Dino would use his veterinary skills to patch up any obvious wounds. He doesn't do that anymore.

"I don't want anyone to think I am here to keep them in business," he explained. "My job is to work with the local communities, with the mayors and the police departments, to persuade them to enforce the law. We have already succeeded in some provinces, but there is still a long way to go. Particularly here in Maguindanao. And in Cotabato too."

As he says this, he walked over to one of the stallions that has fought – and lost – that afternoon. The animal is lying down on the grass. There is blood on its flanks and its nostrils are badly torn. Dino looks at the beast with a practised eye. "He does not have a good disposition. There is an internal injury, I am sure of it. Within two weeks he will be dead. Or else the owner will have slit its throat."

Later that day, still accompanied by our police guards, we drive on into the town to check into our hotel. The streets are arrayed in festival bunting and the crowds are out in force.

Our hotel itself is a modest affair, costing us about £10 a night each. The two policemen join us for dinner. As we sit at the table, Tem opens his tote-bag and shows us his weapon, a Walther PPK. I am curious. "If your gun is in the bag," I ask, "how do you get it out quickly enough if someone stops us at a road-block and threatens to shoot us?"

Tem smiles but doesn't answer. He is obviously quite capable of shooting through the bag. Fortunately, at least while he was with us, he didn't have to put his skills to the test.

After dinner, we all turn in. It has been a long day. There is no window in my room. We have, perhaps unwisely, agreed that our escorts can go back to the police station for the night to get some sleep, so I wonder how I will escape if gunmen come banging at the door. I try to put a chair under the door-handle but it doesn't work. Either the chair is too small or the handle is set too high in the door.

Around 5am next morning, we pile into our vehicle to call on the local Congressman. He has been Dino's friend for over thirty years. Before he was a Congressman, he was Mayor of Cotabato City and then Governor of the North Cotabato province.

He has been here fifty years with a farm in the heart of the town (the town has, literally, grown up around him). We pass through the security gates and drive down the track to his house. Cocks are already crowing and the light is breaking through the coconut and durian trees.

The Congressman gives me his card. It reads "Rep. Jesus Jesus N Sacdalan, 1st District, North Cotabato".

"May I call you Jesus?" I ask.

"Please call me Susing. That's the name we use here. If people call me Jesus and hate me, they may hate Jesus too."

We spent more than two hours with the Congressman that morning. First, we had strong, sweet coffee on the terrace of his house. Then he took us on a tour of his farm. He has nurseries full of plants that he hands out to help local farmers. The whole system is organic. The grass under the fruit trees is cut to feed the cattle and the manure is returned to the soil in the orchard. Then we came back again to the house for a full-scale breakfast. Discussion resumed in earnest.

"Susing" Sacdalan is one of the key political personalities in the Philippines. He is chairman of the Congress's Special Committee on Peace, Reconciliation and Unity. Not long ago, he successfully appealed to the Supreme Court, arguing that former President Arroyo's government had acted unconstitutionally in its negotiations with the Mindanao rebels and separatists. He is definitely not in favour of a "sub-state" solution.

"I do not see this as being a fight between Christians and Muslims," he told us. "It is a question of poverty. The people of Mindanao need to feel they have been justly treated. Development will bring peace."

He is intrigued by the Good Friday Agreement between Britain and Ireland and wonders whether that model could be relevant to the Philippines' own problems in Mindanao.

As far as horse fighting is concerned, he is 100 per cent behind his friend Dino and the work he and Network for Animals is doing. Here too he sees the issue in developmental terms. If the political problems of Mindanao can be sorted out, there will be a brighter economic prospect ahead. The "extra income" earned by horse fighting and through the holding of the illegal derbies may become less important. And with a peaceful settlement between warring factions, the government may be in a much better position to enforce existing legislation.

We left the Congressman's house to drive north. Susing had organized another police escort. This time our guards came complete with uniforms, firearms and their own police vehicle. They tailed us to the Maguindanao-Bukidno border. After that we were on our own.

Our next destination, Cagayan de Oro, is one of the safer cities in Mindanao. Ironically, a few days before our arrival, it had been hit by a devastating flood, as the river, swollen by torrential rain, overflowed its banks. Over a thousand lives had been lost and as many were unaccounted for.

The Network for Animals local team had been active here, rescuing animals in the stricken regions of the city, trying to reunite animals with owners, as well as caring for stricken pets.

We are accompanied that morning by Dr Benue Resma, a local vet. He had experienced the force of the flood – an "inland tsunami" – at first hand. His own house was almost washed away but he and his family miraculously survived. "I prayed to God and God told me to take my family to the roof."

Then he himself contracted leptospirosis and he was hospitalized for several days.

"There have been fifteen deaths already from leptospirosis with more than 100 people hospitalized," Dino explained. "When there is flooding, rats swim in the water. They spread the disease through their urine. Leptospirosis bacteria can penetrate the skin even without an open wound."

There is anger as well as sadness here in Cagayan de Oro. Experts long ago warned that the area affected was vulnerable to flooding. But once again it boils down to economics. Where else are the poor people to go? They live on the flood-plain because they have nowhere else.

"I hope Network for Animals is bringing rice for the people as well as food for the dogs," I said to Andrew.

"We already have," he replied, "and we will be bringing more."

The Network for Animals team is, of course, not the only relief agency at work. We walked round the temporary settlement, where tents donated by the European Union had been set up for the survivors.

"Will the government resettle these people?" I asked. "Or will they try to rebuild their homes in the flood-plain in spite of the danger?"

"Many will try to come back," Dino said, "this is where they work. This is where the jobs are."

On the plane to Manila later that day, I read a headline in the *Philippine Daily Enquirer*. The vice-mayor of Cotabato City, Muslimin Sema, had, the paper reported, been gunned down by political opponents, suffering multiple bullet wounds. President Aquino had ordered the police to hunt down the perpetrators of the attack. As far as I could understand, the shooting had occurred about an hour after we had left Cotabato en route to the horse fight.

I couldn't help wondering whether Mr Sema's bodyguards were in mufti or in uniform. It would have been interesting to find out. But the paper didn't go into details on that particular point.

To be published in the *Sunday Times*

46

Tanzania's Serengeti

My return visit to the Serengeti, thirty-six years after I was first there, was almost aborted on take-off. I got to Heathrow Terminal 4 in plenty of time for the 10.20am Kenya Airways flight to Nairobi. I had booked in online and printed out my boarding-card but anyway had to drop off my bags. Actually, I didn't have much luggage. There was a 15kg limit on the flight from Arusha to Kogatende, the airstrip in the heart of the Lamai Wedge, the relatively unfrequented part of the northern Serengeti where I was heading.

To my surprise, I had been given an upgrade so I found the business lounge near Gate 10, poured myself a coffee and sat down with my laptop to clear some last emails. I put a smug out-of-office notice on my Hotmail Account. "I will be in the Serengeti, in Tanzania, for the next few days and may not be able to reply immediately to your message."

For some reason, when the time came to board the plane, I failed to check which boarding gate I should be heading for, but instead homed in on Gate 10 where the flight was already boarding. The man at the door gave my boarding card a cursory look.

"Seat 1A," I said firmly.

The man took a closer look. He seemed puzzled. "This is the Continental flight to Houston, Texas. You're going to Nairobi on Kenya Airways."

When finally I arrived, panting, at the right gate, I was greeted by the kindly Kenya Airways airport manager. She was tremendously sympathetic but there was nothing she could do. I had missed my plane and my bag had been off-loaded.

In the end, I was rebooked on the evening flight. I caught up with *Condé Nast Traveller* photographer, Hugo Burnand, and his assistant Radu Brebene, in Nairobi next morning as we waited to board the plane for Kilimanjaro in Tanzania.

"Sorry, chaps," I said. "I know I almost blew it."

Things could only get better. After we landed at Kilimanjaro International airport, we were transferred by car to the smaller, local airport at Arusha. Then we boarded a twelve-seater Cessna Caravan.

"First stop will be Lake Manyara," the pilot announced. "Flying time will be twenty-two minutes. It may be a bit bumpy. In an emergency always exit by the back, away from the propellers."

For me, that flight across Tanzania was indeed a trip down memory lane. That night, at dinner in the newly opened Lamai Camp, so cunningly built around a *kopje* that from a distance you barely know it is there, I explained to my colleagues that, yes, I had been to the Serengeti before, in 1976 actually, and that trip too had not been incident-free.

By then night had fallen and a chill was in the air. The camp staff put some more wood on the fire. We had a good bottle of South African red wine in front of us.

"In those days," I explained, "you could drive from Kenya into Tanzania through Kenya's Masai Mara Game Reserve into the heart of the Serengeti. I hired a Land Rover in Nairobi to take three of my children on their first safari. Somewhere along the road between Seronera and Ngorongoro, I managed to lose a briefcase containing our money, passports, cameras and air-tickets – the lot! It must have bounced out of the vehicle."

Hugo rolled his eyes. "Why does this sound familiar? What happened next?"

"I went back to look for it. I had driven about 20 miles back when, amazingly, I saw a notice pinned to a signpost. It said: "FOUND ONE BRIEFCASE. APPLY DR MARY LEAKEY, OLDUVAI GORGE". So I drove down to the bottom of the gorge to find an old lady standing outside the *boma*, holding my briefcase in her hand.

She had obviously looked inside and found our documents because she greeted me warmly. 'Stanley, I presume!' she said."

That first trip through the Serengeti in the mid-'70s had been in June. As I drove my Land Rover and its cargo of children south and east through the grassy plains I had my first glimpse of that extraordinary abundance of wildlife which makes the annual migration of the wildebeest, zebra and assorted antelopes one of the greatest spectacles on earth. Of course, at the time of year I was first in the Serengeti the animals were all heading north. Since time immemorial, the great migration has followed a circular clockwise pattern. In January the migration is in the south-eastern Serengeti on the short-grass plains. February is the main month for wildebeest calving. By March the short-grass plains' pastures are nearing exhaustion and the newborn can keep up with the herds. By May good forage may still be available but water begins to be a limiting factor. The herds begin to head for the Western Corridor. By August the various branches of the migration begin to meet up and by September the migration has entered Kenya's Masai Mara Game Reserve. October/November sees the beginning of the great trek home with the Mara River being crossed once again, but this time – of course – in the reverse direction.

Actually, there is nothing automatic and predictable about the migration, except that it happens. The precise timing of the movement of the herds seems to be dictated by the animals' own sense of the pattern of rainfall and the prospect of nutritious grazing. It is hard to be precise about the numbers. As we drove out from camp that evening on our first game-drive, Chedi, the guide who looked after us while we were staying at Lamai Camp, told us there might be 1.5 million migrating wildebeest, along with 150,000 zebra and perhaps half a million eland and gazelle.

"Of course not all of them will go all the way. Not all of them will make the crossing."

The crossing! Let's be frank about this. However amazing the sheer spectacle of several thousand wildebeest and zebra and their accompanying outriders churning up the dust on the plains may be, the "money-shot", as Hugo put it, has to be that extraordinary moment when the animals gather by the banks of the Mara River and, after waiting for hours or even days, finally decide to cross.

As far as actually seeing the river-crossings, we were – I believe – extraordinarily lucky. On our first full day at Lamai we had set out early in our Toyota Land Cruiser. Around noon we were driving along the south bank of the Mara River when we saw a herd of wildebeest gathering on the other side. It was not a large herd, maybe two or three hundred animals. But through the binoculars we could see a mass of other animals in the distance, which also seemed to be heading for the river. In the end a kind of irresistible pressure seems to build up as the newcomers add their weight to the scrum.

Chedi parked several hundred yards away from the river. "We have to be careful not to put them off. They may be getting ready to cross and we mustn't block them."

Experienced hands like our guide Chedi are well aware that it is impossible to predict just when a crossing will take place. As we sat there, our eyes glued on the distant scene, he told us: "It's just luck if you're there when they start crossing. The first ones across may make it, but the crocodiles hear the noise and will gather in no time. As a matter of fact, the crocodiles are there already."

We looked where he pointed to see a line of brown reptiles looking like large logs half-submerged in the muddy but fast-flowing water.

On that particular occasion, after an hour or so waiting, we decided to head back to camp. But we returned in the afternoon to take up our position once again. By then, the herds on the bank opposite had grown considerably in size. There seemed to be a lot of tension in the air as the animals pranced around the steep banks and the crumbling surfaces that led down to the river.

"Even when they are actually in the river," Chedi said, "you can never be sure they are going to cross. I've seen them get halfway across and then turn back."

In the event we saw not one but two crossings that afternoon. Once the crossings have actually started, your driver gets to river's edge as fast as he can since, if the herd on the far bank is small, the crossing may be over in minutes.

Of course, we didn't – and couldn't – make a precise count but I would say that on both occasions that afternoon the number of animals which took the plunge, as it were, was in the hundreds, not thousands. During the first crossing we saw a young wildebeest taken by a crocodile. The crocodile lunged to grab the animal's leg before pulling it under. On the second crossing, a bit further downstream, the same thing happened but this time the crocodile, having drowned the wildebeest, simply let the carcass float away downstream.

"Basically, the crocodiles are not very hungry at the moment," Chedi explained. "There is a lot of water in the river and a lot of animal carcasses around."

Whereas at the Mara River crossings in Kenya's Masai Mara, you can get forty or fifty vehicles on the riverbank, jostling for a view, in the Lamai Wedge you can find yourself virtually alone. There may be one or two other vehicles but seldom more than a handful. You really do feel privileged.

When we left Lamai Camp, having seen two river crossings and a host of other wildlife – elephants, giraffes, hippopotamuses, lions, baboons, eagles, vultures etc. – we already felt that we had more than our fair share of good luck. We shook hands with Titus, our guide, and the other camp-staff and when we said "*Asante-sana!*" we really meant it.

We moved on to the second of the two permanent camps in the Wedge, Sayari Camp. Whereas the Lamai Camp is built on an elevation, Sayari – by contrast – has been set up on the plain, less than half a mile from the river. Hippos have been found in the camp's swimming pool. At night, you can hear the wildebeest moving around, not to speak of leopards and lions. If you want to move from your tent to the communal dining-area, you have to use the walky-talky to call for an askari to escort you.

Because the camp is so close to the river, we decided – on our first day at Sayari – to go back to base for lunch. The plates were just being cleared when word came that a crossing had just started. At Sayari we had a new guide called Titus who also doubled up as a driver. Though we had already seen two crossings, we certainly were ready to see another. Titus drove like a maniac down to the river, and then followed the track bank.

"They're at crossing number eight!" he shouted to us. The most-used river-crossing points are numbered from one to eight, going upstream from west to east. (The Mara flows through Kenya into Tanzania and then into Lake Victoria.)

I felt sure it would be all over before we got there, but it wasn't. That afternoon the herd that had gathered on the other side was truly enormous. Titus reckoned it must have contained four or five thousand animals. The riverbanks opposite were, literally, heaving with wildlife as the wildebeest jostled each other before leaping into the foaming tide. Oddly enough, the crocodiles seemed to have taken the afternoon off. Or maybe even they were daunted by the sheer size of the cloven-hoofed army that confronted them.

The herd was still crossing a full twenty minutes after we arrived at the river. Later, determined not to lose sight of them, we followed the animals as they headed south. Once we even got ahead of them. I shall never forget the sight of thousand upon thousand of wildebeest and zebra heading at the gallop towards our parked Land Cruiser, and then veering aside at the last moment, to pass us less than a hundred yards away.

We had one full day left at Sayari Camp and we made the most of it. If Chedi had been brilliant, Titus excelled him because on our last day we saw not one, but four cheetahs. Bear in mind the sheer improbability of this. There are fewer than 10,000 cheetahs left in the whole world and a quarter of these are in Namibia. Yet that day in the Serengeti we saw four of them. And it wasn't a case, as it so often is on safari, a trying to see the animals through a dense surrounding wall of other people's vehicles. On the contrary, we were once again the only people around. The cheetahs lay there quietly in the morning sun. They looked as though they were enjoying our presence as much as we enjoyed theirs.

Next day, as we flew back to Arusha in another small low-flying Cessna, I found myself gazing down at the plains below. I took out my binoculars and was rewarded by the sight of a great herd of animals moving south. Was it, I wondered, the same herd that we had seen the previous day? There was no way of telling. Thank God, I thought, the Tanzanian government had at last scrubbed the idea of building a tarmac highway across the Serengeti. At least that was one less hazard for the wildebeest to contend with on their long journey home.

First published in *Condé Nast Traveller*, May 2012

47

South African Safari and
Boer War Battlefields

We left Johannesburg's Tambo airport in a Cessna Caravan, heading for Madikwe, one of the largest of South Africa's national parks, occupying 75,000 hectares in the North-West Province, hard up against the border with Botswana. An hour later, my wife and I were the only passengers to disembark at the little airstrip in the bush. Makanyane Lodge, where we were staying, had sent a young black African driver to meet us with an open-topped Toyota Land Cruiser.

He smiled broadly as he told us his name was Justice. "Did you see the wild dogs?" he asked.

It was a wonderful beginning. It had been raining heavily over the previous few days and the wild dogs – five of them altogether – had found a large puddle of water at the edge of the runway and were lying next to it, stretched out in the sun.

"You can see from their full bellies that they must have killed recently," Justice said. "This is a small pack. You could get as many as seventeen wild dogs in a big pack."

We couldn't believe our luck. Within minutes of arriving in Madikwe we had seen one of the most endangered mammals in Africa. Not more than 2,000 African wild dogs are thought to survive in the wild. I'm not much of a mathematician but I worked out that we were looking at 0.25 per cent of the total world population.

On the way to the lodge, Justice recalled the excitement that had surrounded the recent visit of Michelle Obama, President Obama's wife, to Makanyane.

"She came with her mother and her two kids. They drove in across the border from Gaborone in Botswana in a great convoy. The US Secret Service people wanted Dillon, who was going to act as her guide on safari, to surrender his gun. But Dillon said 'no way'. He took a look at the American M16s and told them you needed a proper gun to stop a charging elephant!"

It turned out that my wife and I were booked not just into the same safari lodge that the wife of the US President had recently visited but into the very same suite! A huge plate glass window in the bedroom gave out onto the river. The bathroom was designed so that on three sides you could gaze out into the bush and its myriad wildlife while taking a bath. We were told that just minutes before we arrived no fewer than nine hippopotamuses had been performing their own ablutions in the pool just below our rooms.

In my view, Michelle Obama and her family could not have made a better choice. Makanyane has its own 1,800-hectare reserve with access to the full 75,000 hectares of the greater Madikwe Game Reserve. In terms of the wildlife to be seen, I would say that Madikwe must certainly be in the top rank of South Africa's national parks and game reserves. If you are a "birder", a stay in Madikwe is especially rewarding.

Our guide during our stay was a young South African called Eugene Bothma. Though he had grown up in Johannesburg, he was now a fully qualified safari guide and he clearly loved his job. No bird was too small, or too quick, to engage his attention.

"None of our vehicles have roofs," he explained on our first game drive, late in the afternoon of the day we arrived. "You need to be able to look up as well as all around. That's particularly important as far as the birds are concerned."

When I look at my notes from that first afternoon's drive, I see I have jotted down the following: crested francolin, fork-tailed drongo, Swanson's francolin, crimson-skirted shrike, black-shouldered shrike, pale-shouldered goshawk, yellow-billed hornbill, pied kingfisher, woodland kingfisher and the lilac-breasted roller.

The lilac-breasted roller, Eugene pointed out, was a universal favourite. When we spotted one perched on a branch at the side of the track, he explained: "If you get engaged to a girl in these parts, you have to make an engagement ring out of the tail feathers of the lilac-breasted roller. If the ring breaks before the date of the wedding, that's a sign to call the marriage off!"

Most people, I suppose, want to be sure of bagging Africa's Famous Five: lion, leopard, elephant, buffalo and rhino. If you come to Madikwe, you will not be disappointed.

Madikwe is unusual among South African parks and reserves in that it is the creation of the post-apartheid era, having been carved out of the former homeland of Bophuthatswana. As a result, many wild animals (including the Big Five) had to be imported from other parts of South Africa or even from other countries in southern Africa such as Zimbabwe and Namibia.

On the whole, the immigrants have thrived. "We have trouble with the elephants sometimes," Eugene explained. "Some of them have bad memories."

His gun, a 375mm rifle manufactured in the Czech Republic, is kept handy on the dashboard of the Land Cruiser. "The bullet is 500 grains. It leaves the weapon at 3,600 feet per second."

No wonder the US Secret Service was impressed!

The real tragedy of course is not the damage that wild animals can do to human beings but the impact of human beings on wild animals. We arrived in South Africa at the height of the rhino crisis. The staggering total of 411 rhinos was poached in South Africa in 2011. With rhino horn fetching $60,000/kg and the average horn weighing in at around 2.5kg, the financial incentives provided by consumer demand in Asia, particularly China and Vietnam, have proved irresistible.

"Twenty-eight rhino have been killed in January this year already, twenty of those in the Kruger. I'm sorry to say we've lost four in Madikwe."

Eugene told us he had been too young for national service (now suspended) but, having spent a year on anti-poaching work, he recognized the need for a tough approach. "You need people patrolling out there in the bush. Living in the bush. Sleeping in the bush. That's the only way."

Officially, Madikwe has fifty-eight white rhinos and thirty-two black. Given the tragic circumstances then prevailing, we imagined that we would be lucky to catch even a distant glimpse of these iconic beasts. How wrong we were! Over our three days in the park, we saw – at close quarters – seventeen white rhinos and (distantly) one black one. That astonishing statistic alone would have made our journey to Madikwe totally and utterly memorable.

How long will the rhinos last in South Africa? Nobody is taking any bets. As we flew back in our little plane to Johannesburg, I found myself hoping that the powers that be would listen to knowledgeable men like our guide Eugene Bothma. Given the surge in demand in Asia for rhino horn (apart from the so-called aphrodisiac properties, some even believe it can cure cancer!) it seems to me that the only solution is to double and redouble the defences against poachers. And the key to this may well be gaining the support of the local populations as they realize that a live rhino in a huge wildlife haven such as Madikwe is worth much more than a dead one.

Our visit to South Africa coincided exactly with the anniversary of the famous battle of Spion Kop, one of the most famous events of the Boer War, the bloody contest between the British and Afrikaaners, which took place at the beginning of the last century. We were immensely fortunate in that our hosts in Kwa-Zulu Natal Province, Raymond and Lynette Heron, not only run the splendid Spion Kop Lodge, where we were staying; Raymond Heron is also one of the world experts on the battle, lecturing both at home and abroad on the subject.

The events that took place at Spion Kop in January 1900 resonate even now. Many people alive today, both in Britain and South Africa, will have grandparents or great-grandparents or even great-great-grandparents who fought in the Boer War, on one side or the other. But what Raymond Heron does so well is to place that war in the context of South African history. And he presents the battle of Spion Kop itself in such an authoritative, yet dramatic, way that you feel you have grasped on an hour-by-hour, or even a minute-by-minute, basis precisely what went on.

"The Voortrekkers' Great Trek," he told us, "began in 1834. It was one of the most amazing journeys undertaken by modern man. The Boers had to carry their wagons piece by piece over the Cape Mountains and then reassemble them. It took them four years to get to Natal where we are now."

The English, Heron continued, had told the Boers that they would be left alone to get on with their own lives if they could get themselves beyond the Orange and Vaal Rivers. Yet when diamonds were discovered at Kimberley and gold in the Rand, it was clear that Britain was ready to tear up earlier agreements in order to grab back territory they had once ceded to the Boers.

Soon after breakfast, the day after our arrival at Spion Kop Lodge, Heron drives us up to a hill just behind his property. We sit down in the shade of a battlefield memorial while he sets the scene.

"We are actually at the very site of General Redvers Buller's battlefield headquarters. If you look over there," he points to the hill directly ahead of us, "you will see Spion Kop and to the right the twin peaks which played such a crucial part in the battle. Remember, Ladysmith has been under siege since the beginning of the war. Spion Kop's location is crucial if you want to relieve the town. But to capture Spion Kop you first have to cross the Tugela River."

As we sit there, listening to Raymond Heron, we can appreciate that crossing the Tugela in the face of Boer guns is going to be no easy matter. Buller points into the middle distance. "You can't see the place now because it is under water since they dammed the Tugela upstream, but basically Buller decided to cross the river at Trichardt's Drift. At 10pm on the night of 23 January, 1,700 British soldiers began to climb. The aim was to get a force to the top of Spion Kop under cover of night and for that force to be well dug in before daybreak."

Of course, things go wrong. They always do. British troops pause and start digging in before they have actually reached the top. Only as day dawns do they realize their mistake. They barely have time to reposition themselves before they face a barrage of fire.

Later that day, we make our way to the summit of Spion Kop. Raymond Heron tells us: "This acre of ground where we are standing remains the smallest area where the greatest number of people lost their lives. That's anywhere in the world and at any time in history."

Standing among the graves, we relive the battle. Buller, from his HQ, can barely see what is going on. Warren, the general who has launched the attack, is unsighted owing to the lie of the land. As the sun rises, total carnage ensues. Heron tells us: "Over seventy men were shot in the right temple, turning their heads away from the sun. Major-General Woodgate, up here on the hill, is mortally wounded. He signals Warren: 'Send reinforcements. All is lost.'"

We spend two or three hours at the battlefield. The British suffered 243 fatalities during the battle, with a further 1,250 men being either wounded or captured. The Boers suffered 335 casualties of which sixty-eight were dead. By some extraordinary coincidence, three men who would later become world leaders were all present that afternoon at Spion Kop: Louis Botha, the Boers' leader, would in 1910 become the first Prime Minister of the newly established Union of South Africa; Mahatma Gandhi, one of several Indians who served as stretcher bearer in the battles (being paid three shillings a day), would lead India to independence and Winston Churchill, having famously escaped from confinement in Pretoria as a war correspondent, returned to Natal as a cavalry officer and found himself in the thick of the action as the British fought desperately to retain the heights.

As the sun set, Raymond Heron walked us round the graves of British dead. "When these young men dug themselves in that morning in their trenches," Heron said, "they were in a very real sense digging their own graves."

We stood in silence in front of one of these graves. I read the inscription. "HS McCorquodale, Lieutenant, Throneycroft's Mounted Infantry. Killed in Action, Spion Kop, January 24, 1900."

Raymond Heron told us: "They had no dog tags in those days. Identity details were sewn into the jacket but this officer, McCorquodale, had somehow lost his jacket in the heat of the battle. He would have been buried in an unmarked grave but Winston Churchill happened to be passing and recognized the body. 'That's Hugh McCorquodale,' Churchill said, 'I knew him at Harrow.'"

As I stood there, the sun began to set over the endless plains. I could hear the sound of gunfire, the shouts of officers and men, and the cries of the wounded. I am sure I am not the first person to have bitten back the tears at Spion Kop.

To be published in the *Sunday Times*

48

Pride of Etosha

We heard the lion roaring soon after dawn. From the balcony of our chalet in the amazing newly built Dolomite Camp in the recently opened western section of Etosha, Namibia's largest and probably most famous national park, we scanned the waterhole on the plains below. Where was he – or she – we wondered? As we watched, the lion roared again, not once but a dozen times. According to the scientists who have studied them, the average full-throated roar of an Etosha lion lasts for 36.6 seconds, and is repeated between four and eighteen times. Apparently the roar of a Kenyan lion lasts a few seconds longer, but as we stood there that morning my wife and I were in no mood to quibble.

"The lion's obviously had its breakfast," I said to Jenny, "let's go and get ours."

An hour later, we found not one but eleven lions. Unlike some of the national parks and game reserves in some other parts of Africa, the authorities in Etosha request visitors to stick to the gravel or dirt roads which, on the whole, run east to west across the park. Unless the kill is made close to the road, you won't necessarily be able to view a lion at close range as he feasts on the carcass of a zebra, gemsbok, impala, springbok or whatever. This may be a disappointment to some. But I am sure the authorities are right. I am not sure what the lions feel, but I definitely prefer the less-intrusive approach.

As it happened, we were lucky that morning. The lion we had heard roaring earlier that morning had killed about three hundred yards into the bush. Though we could not get a clear view of the carcass, even with binoculars, we were able to count at least eleven lions in the pride: one big male, three females and six or seven gambolling cubs.

We must have spent an hour there that morning, standing up in the back of our Toyota Land Cruiser, with the telephoto lenses balanced on the roof of the vehicle.

As far as I was concerned, this particular moment was one of the high points of an amazing trip to Namibia. Like many other conservationists, I have been horrified at the dramatic decline in lion populations in many parts of Africa. Taking the African continent as a whole it has been estimated that there has been a 30–50 per cent population drop in the last twenty years. In 1975 the number of free-ranging lions in sub-Saharan Africa was roughly estimated at 200,000. At the end of the 20th century, numbers had dwindled to below 100,000. By 2005, population counts concluded that numbers could have plummeted to as few as 16,500.

On our first full day in the country, Kathryn, our brilliant driver and guide – she was highly competent and knowledgeable besides being the greatest fun – drove us over 500km from Windhoek to Etosha. En route, we had a welcome break when we were able to call in on Tammy Hoth, a director of the AfriCat Foundation, an organization dedicated – *inter alia* – to protecting Namibia's large carnivores and to demonstrating that even outside the protected areas it is possible to minimize human-lion conflict.

Tammy and her husband run a sanctuary for wild animals, including half a dozen lions that are able to roam over several hundred hectares. Perhaps more importantly, AfriCat works with the local farming community to demonstrate that it is possible for farmers and carnivores to coexist. Tammy grew up as one of four siblings on the Hanssen family farm. But more than twenty years ago, the Hanssens changed from being farmers to becoming major conservationists.

"The Hanssen family proved," Tammy told us, "that the only way to manage livestock farming in prime carnivore country was to adopt methods of keeping young calves out of the wild at night and protecting small stock, such as sheep and goats, with herdsmen and guard dogs."

The point Tammy and AfriCat insists on is that both sides benefit. Half of Namibia's population of lions (around 500 out of the 1,000 total) actually lives outside the protected areas. The benefits to both wildlife and tourism from peaceful coexistence are immense. With the growth of communal conservation areas, as well as freehold conservancy areas, the areas under conservation management in Namibia have grown from 13 per cent of the country in 1990 to 42 per cent today, equivalent to the total area of the United Kingdom.

When we left the Dolomite Camp, we drove east through Etosha visiting the vast Etosha Pans and spending the night at Okaujuejo Camp with its famous waterhole. Thousands of animals may visit Okaujuejo and other waterholes in the dry season. Separated from the waterhole by a low stone wall, you can observe at close quarters what must be one of the most extraordinary wildlife spectacles in the whole of Africa. Competition for drinking space is fierce. Springbok and other smaller animals often wait patiently for hours for their chance to drink after dominant species like elephant and gemsbok have moved off. If for some reason you aren't able to visit Etosha to coincide with the dry-season, then book a return trip for another time.

On our penultimate day in Namibia, we drove down from Etosha to Okonjima, the Hanssen family home, where Tammy's sister, Donna, and brother Wayne still live. I shall never forget the thrill of being driven round the 16,000-hectare private estate, now wholly dedicated to the rescue and rehabilitation of endangered wildlife.

There are around 2,500 cheetahs in Namibia, about a quarter of the world's population. When we consider that 95 per cent of these actually live on farmland, not in national parks, the importance of resolving human-animal conflicts, and of finding a way for farmers and wildlife to coexist, becomes blindingly obvious.

In global terms, Namibia's population of 3,500 leopards is almost as important as its population of cheetahs. In 2008, the IUCN classified the African leopard as "near threatened", stating that the subspecies might soon qualify for "vulnerable" status due to habitat loss and fragmentation and that they were becoming increasingly rare outside protected areas.

So what happens to the leopard in Namibia is truly vital for the African leopard's future survival.

I shall never forget the sheer passion and enthusiasm of Rohan, the AfriCat guide who took us out into the bush on our very last morning in Namibia to look for leopards. We had started late because it had been raining hard all night. Leopards, he said, like human beings were not so keen on the rain. But he had a hunch they were up there on the hill somewhere and he kept on forcing the vehicle through the bush.

We were extraordinarily lucky that day. We saw not one but two leopards at close quarters, as well as a pair of cheetahs perched high on a termite mound, looking around to see what the morning might bring forth.

To be published in *Express Newspapers*

49

Stanley Johnson's Top Five Places

BAMIYAN

A few weeks after my twenty-first birthday, I drove a BSA 500cc twin-cylinder Shooting Star motorcycle about 130 miles north from Kabul, Afghanistan's capital, to visit the Bamiyan Valley, the site of two gigantic statues of Buddha, built in the 2nd century AD. I climbed up a winding narrow staircase inside the tallest of the two Buddhas (165ft high!). When I reached the top, I was able to sit cross-legged in the space that was left between the top of the Buddha's head and the roof of the cave where the statue had been carved.

Forty years later the Taliban blew up the statues, finding them "idolatrous". Thankfully, the new Afghan government has plans to rebuild them.

THE PANTANAL

I first went to the Pantanal, the world's largest wetland, in my gap year in 1959. I caught a train that chuntered on a single-track line across Mato Grosso towards the Bolivian border, the engine's boiler fed on wood. Some distance after Campo Grande, the track had been washed away and we had to finish our journey by boat up the Paraguay River.

Seven years ago, with my son Max, I visited Brazil again. We spent a week at the Fazenda Rio Negro, a 7,000-hectare ranch. Most days, we paddled a canoe on the Rio Negro, watching the giant river otters. But the high point was the hyacinth macaws. You could lie in your hammock and watch these gorgeous creatures.

With their brilliant blue plumage, they are possibly the most beautiful birds in the world, and one of the most endangered.

ANTARCTICA

In the summer of 1984, I joined the British Antarctic Survey's research vessel, the *John Biscoe*, on one of its journeys to supply British bases in Antarctica.

I shall never forget that first Antarctic landfall. I was up on the bridge. On the port bow, I could see my first proper iceberg, gleaming white and majestic. Two or three whales blew to starboard, spouts of water shooting in the air, deep calling to deep.

Soon we were near enough for the barrier of ice ahead to be clearly distinguished. It grew and grew until it seemed that we were approaching great towering cliffs of ice, dwarfing the *Biscoe*. Then there was a sudden rush of sound as a glacier "calved", sending a shockwave of water to rock our solid, ice-strengthened vessel.

KAHUZI-BEIGA NATIONAL PARK

In 2005 I tracked gorillas in Kahuzi-Biega, a national park in the eastern part of the Democratic Republic of the Congo. We set off from the headquarters at Tsivanga and spent the next two hours following a gushing watercourse.

After a strenuous uphill stretch, we heard a sudden stentorian roar as a fully grown male gorilla burst out of the undergrowth.

I knew what I was meant to do – stand still and lower my head. But when Chimanuka sprang from the bush, I jumped behind our Pygmy tracker and held my breath. This was a huge and magnificent animal.

Chimanuka must have charged us half a dozen times. He seemed to enjoy it. A charge would be followed by a period of chewing the cud. After ten minutes, he would rise, turn away from us to show off his magnificent coat, before crashing off again. Shock and awe.

EXMOOR

I grew up on Exmoor; my parents bought a farm there in 1951 and we still have it. Our valley is magical. We have buzzards and barn owls, red deer and kingfishers. We even have one of the few sites in the region where the high brown fritillary, one of the rarest of Britain's butterflies, still survives.

My wife and I live in the house my parents used to live in, my daughter Rachel and her family live in the "middle" house and my sister Birdie lives in the "cottage".

It would be nice to think that Exmoor hasn't changed over the fifty-six years I have lived there, but I know it has. For example, for the last decade we have had mains electricity, so we can make toast for breakfast.

First published in the *ES Magazine*, 25 January 2008

Organizations and Websites

If you would like to know more about some of the organizations featured in this book, please find the details below.

ACAP (The Agreement on the Conservation of Albatrosses and Petrels): www.acap.aq
Asri (Alam Sehat Lestari): www.alamsehatlestari.org
Charles Darwin Foundation: www.darwinfoundation.org
CMS (The Convention on Migratory Species): www.cms.int
Earthwatch Institute: www.earthwatch.org
Friends of the Earth: www.foe.co.uk
Friends of the Galápagos: www.gct.org
Galápagos Conservation Trust: www.savegalapagos.org
Global Tiger Patrol: www.globaltigerpatrol.org
Gorilla Organization (previously The Dian Fossey Gorilla Fund): www.gorillas.org
International Polar Year: www.ipy.org
Jane Goodall Institute: www.janegoodall.org.uk
Kid for Kids: www.kidsforkids.org.uk
Network for Animals: www.networkforanimals.org
Orangutan Foundation: www.orangutan.org.uk
Piero Ravá: www.spazidavventura.com
Rainforest Concern: www.rainforestconcern.org
Roundtable on Sustainable Palm Oil: www.sustainable-palmoil.org
Sahara Conservation Fund: www.saharaconservation.org
Sahelo-Saharan Antelopes Project: www.naturalsciences.be
SPANA: www.spana.org
UK Antarctic Heritage Trust: www.ukaht.org
Whitley Fund for Nature: www.whitleyaward.org
WWF: www.wwf.org.uk

Index